THE COST OF THE WAR TO RUSSIA

ECONOMIC AND SOCIAL HISTORY OF THE WORLD WAR

James T. Shotwell, LL.D., *General Editor.*

RUSSIAN SERIES

Sir Paul Vinogradoff, F.B.A., *Editor.*
(Died, December 19, 1925.)

Michael T. Florinsky, Ph.D., *Associate Editor.*

THE
COST OF THE WAR
TO RUSSIA

THE VITAL STATISTICS OF EUROPEAN RUSSIA DURING THE WORLD WAR
1914–1917

By STANISLAS KOHN

ASSISTANT PROFESSOR OF STATISTICS
RUSSIAN SCHOOL OF LAWS, PRAGUE
FORMERLY ASSISTANT DIRECTOR, RUSSIAN AGRICULTURAL CENSUS

SOCIAL COST OF THE WAR

By BARON ALEXANDER F. MEYENDORFF, D.C.L.

FORMERLY VICE-PRESIDENT OF THE DUMA
READER IN RUSSIAN INSTITUTIONS AND ECONOMICS
UNIVERSITY OF LONDON

NEW HAVEN : YALE UNIVERSITY PRESS
LONDON : HUMPHREY MILFORD : OXFORD UNIVERSITY PRESS
FOR THE CARNEGIE ENDOWMENT FOR INTERNATIONAL
PEACE : DIVISION OF ECONOMICS AND HISTORY
1932

EDITOR'S PREFACE
40–1858

In the autumn of 1914, when the scientific study of the effects of war upon modern life passed suddenly from theory to history, the Division of Economics and History of the Carnegie Endowment for International Peace proposed to adjust the program of its researches to the new and altered problems which the War presented. The existing program, which had been prepared as the result of a conference of economists held at Berne in 1911, and which dealt with the facts then at hand, had just begun to show the quality of its contributions; but for many reasons it could no longer be followed out. A plan was therefore drawn up at the request of the Director of the Division, in which it was proposed, by means of an historical survey, to attempt to measure the economic cost of the War and the displacement which it was causing in the processes of civilization. Such an "Economic and Social History of the World War," it was felt, if undertaken by men of judicial temper and adequate training, might ultimately, by reason of its scientific obligations to truth, furnish data for the forming of sound public opinion, and thus contribute fundamentally toward the aims of an institution dedicated to the cause of international peace.

The need for such an analysis, conceived and executed in the spirit of historical research, was increasingly obvious as the War developed, releasing complex forces of national life not only for the vast process of destruction, but also for the stimulation of new capacities for production. This new economic activity, which under normal conditions of peace might have been a gain to society, and the surprising capacity exhibited by the belligerent nations for enduring long and increasing loss—often while presenting the outward semblance of new prosperity—made necessary a reconsideration of the whole field of war economics. A double obligation was therefore placed upon the Division of Economics and History. It was obliged to concentrate its work upon the problem thus presented, and to study it as a whole; in other words, to apply to it the tests and disciplines of history. Just as the War itself was a single event, though penetrating by seemingly unconnected ways to the remotest parts of the world, so the analysis of it must be developed according to a plan at once all embracing and yet adjustable to the practical limits of the available data.

During the actual progress of the War, however, the execution of this plan for a scientific and objective study of war economics proved impossible in any large and authoritative way. Incidental studies and surveys of portions of the field could be made and were made under the direction of the Division, but it was impossible to undertake a general history for obvious reasons. In the first place, an authoritative statement of the resources of belligerents bore directly on the conduct of armies in the field. The result was to remove as far as possible from scrutiny those data of the economic life of the countries at war which would ordinarily, in time of peace, be readily available for investigation. In addition to this difficulty of consulting documents, collaborators competent to deal with them were for the most part called into national service in the belligerent countries and so were unavailable for research. The plan for a war history was therefore postponed until conditions should arise which would make possible not only access to essential documents, but also the coöperation of economists, historians, and men of affairs in the nations chiefly concerned, whose joint work would not be misunderstood either in purpose or in content.

Upon the termination of the War, the Endowment once more took up the original plan, and it was found with but slight modification to be applicable to the situation. Work was begun in the summer and autumn of 1918. In the first place a final conference of the Advisory Board of Economists of the Division of Economics and History was held in Paris, which limited itself to planning a series of short preliminary surveys of special fields. Since, however, the purely preliminary character of such studies was further emphasized by the fact that they were directed more especially toward those problems which were then fronting Europe as questions of urgency, it was considered best not to treat them as part of the general survey, but rather as of contemporary value in the period of war settlement. It was clear that not only could no general program be laid down *a priori* by this conference as a whole, but that a new and more highly specialized research organization than that already existing would be needed to undertake the Economic and Social History of the World War, one based more upon national grounds in the first instance, and less upon purely international coöperation. Until the

facts of national history could be ascertained, it would be impossible
to proceed with comparative analysis; and the different national
histories were themselves of almost baffling intricacy and variety.
Consequently the former European Committee of Research was dis-
solved, and in its place it was decided to erect an Editorial Board
in each of the larger countries and to nominate special editors in
the smaller ones, who should concentrate, for the present at least,
upon their own economic and social war history.

The nomination of these boards by the General Editor was the
first step taken in every country where the work has begun. And if
any justification were needed for the plan of the Endowment, it at
once may be found in the lists of those, distinguished in scholarship
or in public affairs, who have accepted the responsibility of editor-
ship. This responsibility is by no means light, involving as it does
the adaptation of the general editorial plan to the varying demands
of national circumstances or methods of work; and the measure of
success attained is due to the generous and earnest coöperation of
those in charge in each country.

Once the editorial organization was established, there could be
little doubt as to the first step which should be taken in each instance
toward the actual preparation of the History. Without documents
there can be no history. The essential records of the War, local as
well as central, have therefore to be preserved and to be made available for research in so far as is compatible with public interest. But
this archival task is a very great one, belonging of right to the Governments and other owners of historical sources and not to the historian or economist who proposes to use them. It is an obligation of
ownership; for all such documents are public trust. The collaborators on this section of the War History, therefore, working within
their own field as researchers, could only survey the situation as they
found it and report their findings in the forms of guides or manuals;
and perhaps, by stimulating a comparison of methods, help to further the adoption of those found to be most practical. In every country, therefore, this was the point of departure for actual work; although special monographs have not been written in every instance.

The first stage of the work upon the War History, dealing with
little more than the externals of archives, seemed for a while to
exhaust the possibilities of research, and had the plan of the History
been limited to research based upon official documents, little more

could have been done, for once documents have been labeled "secret" few government officials can be found with sufficient courage or initiative to break open the seal. Thus vast masses of source material essential for the historian were effectively placed beyond his reach, although much of it was quite harmless from any point of view. While war conditions thus continued to hamper research, and were likely to do so for many years to come, some alternative had to be found.

Fortunately such an alternative was at hand in the narrative, amply supported by documentary evidence, of those who had played some part in the conduct of affairs during the War, or who, as close observers in privileged positions, were able to record from first- or at least second-hand knowledge the economic history of different phases of the Great War, and of its effect upon society. Thus a series of monographs was planned consisting for the most part of unofficial yet authoritative statements, descriptive or historical, which may best be described as about halfway between memoirs and blue-books. These monographs make up the main body of the work assigned so far. They are not limited to contemporary war-time studies; for the economic history of the War must deal with a longer period than that of the actual fighting. It must cover the years of "deflation" as well, at least sufficiently to secure some fairer measure of the economic displacement than is possible in purely contemporary judgments.

With this phase of the work, the editorial problems assumed a new aspect. The series of monographs had to be planned primarily with regard to the availability of contributors, rather than of source material as in the case of most histories; for the contributors themselves controlled the sources. This in turn involved a new attitude toward those two ideals which historians have sought to emphasize, consistency and objectivity. In order to bring out the chief contribution of each writer it was impossible to keep within narrowly logical outlines; facts would have to be repeated in different settings and seen from different angles, and sections included which do not lie within the strict limits of history; and absolute objectivity could not be obtained in every part. Under the stress of controversy or apology, partial views would here and there find their expression. But these views are in some instances an intrinsic part of the history itself, contemporary measurements of facts as significant as the facts with which they deal. Moreover, the work as a whole is planned to furnish its own corrective; and where it does not, others will.

In addition to the monographic treatment of source material, a number of studies by specialists are already in preparation, dealing with technical or limited subjects, historical or statistical. These monographs also partake to some extent of the nature of first-hand material, registering as they do the data of history close enough to the source to permit verification in ways impossible later. But they also belong to that constructive process by which history passes from analysis to synthesis. The process is a long and difficult one, however, and work upon it has only just begun. To quote an apt characterization; in the first stages of a history like this, one is only "picking cotton." The tangled threads of events have still to be woven into the pattern of history; and for this creative and constructive work different plans and organizations may be needed.

In a work which is the product of so complex and varied coöperation as this, it is impossible to indicate in any but a most general way the apportionment of responsibility of editors and authors for the contents of the different monographs. For the plan of the History as a whole and its effective execution the General Editor is responsible; but the arrangement of the detailed programs of study has been largely the work of the different Editorial Boards and divisional Editors, who have also read the manuscripts prepared under their direction. The acceptance of a monograph in this series, however, does not commit the editors to the opinions or conclusions of the authors. Like other editors, they are asked to vouch for the scientific merit, the appropriateness, and usefulness of the volumes admitted to the series; but the authors are naturally free to make their individual contributions in their own way. In like manner the publication of the monographs does not commit the Endowment to agreement with any specific conclusions which may be expressed therein. The responsibility of the Endowment is to History itself— an obligation not to avoid but to secure and preserve variant narratives and points of view, in so far as they are essential for the understanding of the War as a whole.

*   *   *   *   *

In the case of Russia, civil war and revolution followed so closely upon the World War that it is almost impossible for history to measure with any degree of accuracy the effects of the World War itself upon the economic and social life of the country. Those effects were so distorted by the forces let loose in the post-war years and so confused with the disturbances of the revolutionary era that the attempt to isolate the phenomena of the War from the data of civil war and to analyze the former according to the plan followed in the other national series of this collection has been a task of unparalleled difficulty. Over and above the intricacies of the problem and its illusive character, the authors of the Russian monographs have had to work under the most discouraging circumstances and with inadequate implements of research. For those who know the scarcity of the documentary material available, it will be a matter of no little surprise to find, in the pages of this Russian Series, narratives and substantiating data which measure up so well in comparison with those prepared by the collaborators in other countries. The achievement of the Russian Division of the History is, all things considered, the most remarkable section of the entire collection. This is due, in the first place, to the fact that the authors, all of them exiles who live in foreign lands, have not only brought to this task the scientific disciplines of their own special fields but also an expert knowledge drawn from personal experience which in several instances reached to the highest offices of State.

While these volumes in the Russian History constitute so very considerable an achievement, they cannot in the very nature of the case cover with adequate statistical or other specific data many of the problems with which they deal. No one is more conscious of their shortcomings in this regard than the authors themselves. Nevertheless, with inadequate material and under hampering circumstances they have prepared a body of text and a record which, if admittedly incomplete as history, contains at least one element that would otherwise be lost for the future understanding of this great crisis in human affairs, an element which no other generation working from Russian archives could ever supply. We have here the mature comment upon events by contemporaries capable of passing judgment and appraising values, so that over and above the survey of phenomena there is presented a perspective and an organization of material which will be a contribution to history hardly less important than the substance of the monographs.

The Russian Series was in the first instance planned by one of the

most distinguished of Russian scholars who had long been a resident
of England, Sir Paul Vinogradoff, Corpus Professor of Jurispru-
dence at the University of Oxford. To the planning of the Series Sir
Paul gave much time and thought. His untimely death in December,
1925, prevented him from seeing its fruition or from assuming the
editorial responsibility for the texts. Nevertheless, the Series as a
whole remains substantially as he had planned it.

The monograph of Professor Stanislas Kohn offers a careful and
objective analysis of the demographic changes which took place in
Russia during the War, a subject which has received so far no attention in scientific literature. It provides the Russian Series with the
necessary sociological background and brings to light some interesting facts relating to the changes in the population due to the War.

Baron Alexander F. Meyendorff, formerly vice-president of the
Duma and now reader in Russian institutions and economics in the
University of London, has brought to the discussion of the social cost
of the War to Russia the high competence of his former experience
combined with the application of the academic disciplines. His account of the effects of the War upon the peasants, industrial workers,
and foreign investors will offer new and suggestive material for a
page of history otherwise obscure.

J. T. S.

CONTENTS

I

THE VITAL STATISTICS OF EUROPEAN RUSSIA DURING THE WORLD WAR, 1914–1917

PART I

DIRECT INFLUENCE OF THE WAR ON THE NUMBER AND DISTRIBUTION OF THE POPULATION

CHAPTER I

CHAPTER II

PART II

THE NATURAL GROWTH OF THE POPULATION DURING THE YEARS OF THE WAR

CHAPTER I

CHAPTER II

CHAPTER III

CONTENTS

I

THE VITAL STATISTICS OF EUROPEAN RUSSIA DURING THE WORLD WAR
1914–1917

By STANISLAS KOHN

AUTHOR'S ACKNOWLEDGMENT

THE author considers it his duty to point out that the plan of this present work was drawn up (conjointly with the author) by the deceased Professor A. A. Chuprov, who primarily took upon himself the treatment of this subject for the Russian Series of "The History of the World War." Subsequently Professor Chuprov gave up the work, which was then offered to the undersigned. Professor Chuprov also received from Russia some printed matter, which was afterward used by the author himself. The author proffers his sincere gratitude to all those persons who primarily helped Professor A. A. Chuprov and afterward the author himself by supplying them with the required information. He considers it also his pleasant duty to express his thanks to Professor S. N. Prokopovich and Gen. V. V. Chernavin for reading the manuscript work and communicating a series of valuable observations, as well as to Dr. Michael T. Florinsky of the Carnegie Endowment for International Peace, and American editorial assistants for the editing of the English text of the monograph.

S. K.

INTRODUCTION

DESCRIPTION OF THE MATERIAL, METHOD, AND PLAN OF THE WORK

ANY exhaustive inquiry into the vital statistics of Russia during the years of the War is greatly impeded by the unsatisfactory condition of the available material. Vital statistics in Russia have never been accurately collected or regularly published. The detailed analysis of the figures setting forth the natural changes in the population used to be published, after a delay of several years, by the Central Statistical Committee.[1] The last volume, which appeared in 1916, relates to the year 1910. The same Committee used also to publish the *Statistical Yearbook of Russia*[2] which contained general preliminary figures of the number of marriages, births, and deaths for the several provinces, and their respective rates. The last *Yearbook* was for the year 1914. A similar compilation, except for data on marriages, was published in the reports of the Chief Medical Inspector of the Ministry of the Interior.

These publications were based on information furnished to both the Central Statistical Committee and the Office of the Chief Medical Inspector by provincial statistical committees. The latter in their turn received from the clergy, in the form of abstracts for every parish, the material on which they based their summaries. One will remember that the only registration of births, deaths, and marriages carried on in Russia was in the hands of the clergy. The card registration of such data and their further arrangement in the statistical bureau of the province was, however, by no means common. The original material, revealing the natural fluctuations in the population, was confined, therefore, to the summaries prepared by the clergy which offered little guaranty of accuracy.

The preliminary information as given in the statistical yearbooks and in the reports of the Chief Medical Inspector was not always the same and often varied considerably from the final figures given in the *Numerical Changes in the Population* published by the Central Sta-

[1] *Dvizenie Naselenya Evropeiskoi Rossii za . . . God (Numerical Changes in the Population of European Russia for the Year . . .).*
[2] *Statisticheski Ezhegodnik Rossii.*

tistical Committee. The rates per thousand population were especially unreliable, as the total population was inaccurately estimated.

Even this fragmentary information respecting the changes in the
numbers of the population is lacking for the years of the War, from
1915 onward. The Central Statistical Committee, as stated above,
was able to publish in the *Yearbook* of 1916 only the preliminary
abstract for the year 1914. The Revolution of 1917 abolished the
former Central Statistical Office, and the institutions that it called
into being did not begin their regular work on vital statistics until
several years later. The War and still more the Revolution disor-
ganized the activities of the statistical and registration bodies of the
parishes and provinces. Owing to the fact that the publication of the
summaries was subjected to a delay of several years, the effect of the
Revolution was necessarily retroactive and affected the years 1915
and 1916. We lack, as a consequence, all information concerning the
natural increase or decrease of the population for a group of provinces, and possess, in respect to the nation as a whole, a knowledge of
the subject that diminishes with every year of the War.

In 1920, a Commission was organized by the Soviet People's Commissariat of Public Health, "to investigate the Effect upon Public
Health of the War of 1914–1920," and included a number of experts
on demography and vital statistics.[3] This commission, which undertook among other things the collection of materials relating to natural increase or decrease of the population during the War, assembled
information from the office of the Medical Inspector, the local medical offices, and the local statistical committees, concerning the number of marriages, births, and deaths for the following number of
provinces in European Russia:

Number of Provinces for Which Information is Available.

Year	Marriages	Births	Deaths
1915	27	41	41
1916	10	18	15
1917	6	7	6

A brief summary of the information thus obtained was published
by the Commission in the first volume of its *Proceedings*[4] and the

[3] Among its original members were Messrs. M. M. Gran, P. I. Kurkin,
A. N. Sysin, V. I. Binshtok, and S. A. Novoselsky.

[4] *Narodni Kommissaryat Zdravookhranenya, Trudi Kommissii po Obsled*

figures therein contained constitute the principal source consulted by the author of the present work.

Though this material is neither complete nor accurate, it is more satisfactory than could be expected under the circumstances. In any case, it is the only existing material of a national character on the vital statistics of Russia for the years of the War. There is no great hope that the future will disclose to the public more comprehensive and trustworthy information. On the other hand, it should be observed that the official sources decline in fulness and reliability from 1915 onward and are especially unreliable and incomplete for 1917.[5]

In addition to this material of a national character, some help can be derived from two agricultural censuses, which were taken during the years 1916 and 1917. These censuses, which exhibit principally the agricultural situation and the conditions of land tenure, contain also a certain amount of general information regarding the population. The census of 1916, however, is less detailed than that of 1917. Such figures as have hitherto been made public are only summarily compiled, and indicate merely the number of the population, divided according to sex. The fact that both censuses are geographically incomplete and that they embrace a different territory dimin-

ovanyu Sanitarnikh Posledstvi Voini 1914–1920 Godov (People's Commissariat of Public Health, Proceedings of the Commission to Investigate the Effects upon Public Health of the War of 1914–1920), edited by M. M. Gran, P. I. Kurkin, and P. A. Kuvshinnikov, Vol. I [Moscow and Petrograd, 1923]. The figures referring to the changes in the population resulting from natural causes consist of data of marriages, births, and deaths in each province without distinction of sex or between urban and rural population. In the text, however, the Commission gives for certain provinces general data regarding the number of births and deaths for the urban and rural population separately.

The Proceedings of the Commission were briefly summarized by Dr. Bagotzky in an article "Les pertes de la Russie pendant la guerre, 1914–1917," in Revue Internationale de la Croix-Rouge [Geneve, 1914]. They were also used by Dr. Sysin for his article Sanitarnoe Sostoyanie Rossii Prezhde i Teper (The Sanitary Conditions of Russia Now and Before) in the Russian review Sotsialnaya Gigiena (Social Hygiene) Vol. I–III. We are acquainted with this last article only by its summary in the Monitor of the Czechoslovak Ministry of Public Hygiene and Physical Education, edited by Dr. Govseev.

[5] Of course, by this fact the general impression of the destructive effects of the War becomes too mild, because these effects grew from one year to the other.

ishes their utility for statistical comparison and for determining the total population. Some information pertinent to this subject, however, can be derived from an examination of the census reports. The census of 1917 is particularly important, for it contains the figures of the refugee households that had settled in the provinces included in the census. These figures are supplementary to those supplied by the "Committee of the Grand Duchess Tatiana for the Aid of the Victims of the War" which, unfortunately, we have been unable to obtain in their original form. The census of 1916 embraces only the rural areas, whereas that of 1917 includes also the urban districts. But the figures hitherto published in reference to the 1917 urban areas are fragmentary and incapable of comparison with other data.[6]

There are certain territorial units in regard to which information concerning vital statistics is more complete. For Petrograd, for example, it is found in the publications of the statistical bureau of the Petrograd municipality as well as in the subsequent publications of of the statistical bureau of the city and province of Petrograd.[7] Statistics for Moscow, which are even more comprehensive, are found in the publication of the Moscow Soviet of Workmen's and Soldiers' Deputies, entitled *Red Moscow*.[8] Some interesting facts concerning the province of Moscow have also been accumulated in the *Proceedings*, quoted above, of the Commission appointed to investigate the effects of the War upon public health.

As regards the Ukrainian provinces, we possess, in addition to the information in the *Proceedings* of the above-mentioned commission, the data contained in the publications of the Ukrainian Academy of Science.[9] The figures relating to the war period are arranged according to sex and distinguish between urban and rural population. The sources of this information are partly the same as those of the Commission appointed to investigate the effects of the War upon

---

[6] O. Kvitkin, *Naselenie Gorodov Evropeiskoi Chasti R.S.F.S.R. po Perepisyam 1897, 1917, 1920 i 1923 Gorodov* (*The Urban Population of the European Part of the U.S.S.R., according to the Census of 1897, 1917, 1920 and 1923*), in the Bulletin of the Central Statistical Office, No. 77, 1923.

[7] *Materyali po Statistike Petrograda i Petrogradskoi Gubernii* (*Statistical Returns for the City and Province of Petrograd*), especially Vol. V, 1921.

[8] *Krasnaya Moskwa* [Moscow, 1920].

[9] *Materyali shcho do Prirodnago Rukhu Naselenya Ukraini* (*Statistics Relating to the Natural Growth of the Population of Ukraine*) [Kharkov, 1924].

public health, which for the sake of brevity, we shall hereafter designate the *Narkomzdrav Commission*.[10] They consist of the reports of the local statistical committees, and partly of an independent compilation of the records prepared by the clergy especially for the years 1916 and 1917. Unfortunately, these records, as indicated by the authors themselves, are both inaccurate and incomplete; as they comprise only the orthodox population, no comparison is possible with the data of preceding years.

We have also a number of monographs[11] dealing with the provinces of Kiev and Kharkov, in addition to the information contained in the publications of the Ukrainian Academy of Science, but the contradictory character of the information contained in these sources greatly impairs their usefulness. There are also several monographs relating to other territorial divisions,[12] but they add little to the above-mentioned fundamental material.[13]

[10] *Narkomzdrav* is the abbreviated name of the Soviet Commissariat of Public Health (*Narodni Kommissariat Zdravookhranenya*).

[11] N. Gvozdev, *Estestvennoe Dvizhenie i Prirost Naselenya (Numerical Changes in the Population)* in the *Bulletin* of the Statistical Bureau of the Province of Kharkov, 1922, No. 3–4; M. R. Khodos, *Predvaritelnya Dannya o Estestvennom Dvizhennii Naselenya Kievskoi Gubernii za Vremya 1915–1920 (Preliminary Returns Dealing with the Numerical Changes in the Population of the Province of Kiev, 1915–1920)*, in the *Bulletin* of the Statistical Bureau of the Province of Kiev, 1922, No. 4–5; same author, *Rozhdenya, Smerti, Braki, i Razvodi Kievskoi Gubernii za 1923 (Births, Deaths, Marriages and Divorces in the Province of Kiev in 1923)* in the *Bulletin* of the Statistical Bureau of the Province of Kiev, 1925, No. 4–5; M. V. Ptukha, *Naselenie Kievskoi Gubernii (The Population of the Province of Kiev)*, in the *Bulletin* of the Statistical Bureau of the Province of Kiev, 1925, No. 4–5.

[12] K. Bukhman, *K Voprosu o Monograficheskom Izuchenii Estestvennago Dvizhenya Naselenya za Poslednie Godi (The Problem of Studying the Natural Changes in the Population in the Last Years by the Monographic Method)*, in *Vestnik Statistiki (Statistical Messenger)*, Vol. XII, 1922; J. Pobedonostsev, *Dvizhenie Naselenya v Kazani s 1863 po 1921 God (Natural Changes in the Population of Kazan from 1863 to 1921)*, in *Vestnik Statistiki*, Vol. XI, 1922.

[13] L. I. Lubny-Hertsik's monograph, *Dvizenie Naselenya na Territorii RSFSR za Vremya Mirovoi Voini i Revolutsii (Natural Changes in the Population of the USSR During the World War and the Revolution)* [Moscow, 1926], has been published after the present was completed. The author, however, deals chiefly with the revolutionary period, after 1917; he devotes relatively little space to the war period which alone interests us here. The

Very important information concerning war casualties and conscription in Russia—that is to say war statistics as distinguished from the natural changes in the population—is contained in the 1925 publication of the Central Statistical Office under the title *Rossya v Mirovoi Voine (Russia in the World War)*. The *Proceedings* of the Narkomzdrav Commission contain also much information on the subject.

It should be remembered that this material can claim even less authority, in point of accuracy, than the data referring to the natural increase or decrease of the population. In fact, most of the figures are merely based on probable calculations; they remain, however, the only existing material for ascertaining the Russian war losses. The limited extent and unsatisfactory condition of the statistical data not only reduce both the volume and the scope of a monograph[14] concerning the influence of the War on the population of Russia, but also call for special methods of treatment. Great care must be taken in the first place to control the accuracy of the data. Attention should chiefly be directed to the examination of what may be called the self-consistency of the figures. The presence of this self-consistency justifies to a certain degree confidence in our data. We have insisted, therefore, perhaps more than is necessary, upon the certain facts of obvious knowledge. Thus testing the accuracy of the data enables us, in spite of the above-mentioned defects, to consider the material as not without value in estimating the general tendencies of the phenomena with which we are concerned.

The absence of trustworthy figures of the population in the period under review frequently deprives the author of the possibility of computing the usual marriage, birth, and death rates. This omission is not, however, very important because, owing to the far-reaching changes in the age and sex distributions of the population produced

data that he furnishes give no reason for making any important corrections or additions to the present work. But we have made use of them in some of our calculations.

[14] We must also note the peculiar difficulties that confront an author living at present outside Russia. We have succeeded in obtaining almost the entire published material referring to the war period but much useful information, especially that concerning the pre-war period, has had to be taken at second-hand. Some comparisons with this period we have even been forced to abandon altogether.

by the War, any crude ratios to the population taken as a whole are of little value. In order to obtain a clearer idea of the changes in the studied phenomena, and to gain a better understanding of the factors to which they were due, we have had to proceed in a manner somewhat unusual in demographical research. We have compared the indexes showing the changes in the number of marriages, births, and deaths, with the indexes showing in some rough form the numerical changes in the factors influencing these phenomena (among others the changes in the number and composition of the population). In order to ascertain, for example, even approximately, whether the decrease in fertility was due solely to the withdrawal of the men to the front (i.e. the direct cause), or equally to a restriction of the birth rate by the remainder of the population, we have compared the indexes showing the changes in the number of births with the approximate indexes summarizing the average changes in the number of men of the different age-groups and weighted in accordance with the part played by each age-group in reproduction. We have attempted also to confirm our conclusions by computation of certain correlations between series of provincial figures. These computations, approximate as they are, allow us to corroborate our statements about the relations between the demographical changes and the factors that caused them.

As regards the geographical boundaries of the present work, we have had to confine ourselves to European Russia, since there is no information whatever with regard to Asiatic Russia. We have also left beyond the scope of our work those parts of the present Polish State which formerly belonged to the Russian Empire, and also Finland, limiting our investigation to the remaining fifty provinces of European Russia.[15] As regards chronological limits, in conformity with the general plan of the Russian Series of the "Economic and Social History of the World War," we have confined ourselves to the period 1914–1917, that is, to the years of Russia's participation in the World War. The question of the durability of the effects of the War, as well as that of the so-called compensational changes which usually occur after a war, in the growth of the population, have not been treated here. They would be certainly interesting for an investigator, but 1918 and the following years were a period of upheaval in

[15] Always, on further pages where we are speaking simply of "European Russia," we are meaning these fifty provinces.

the social and economic life of the country, as well as years of extreme economic depression, which had a catastrophic repercussion upon the natural progress of the population. To identify among these causes the part played by the World War is impossible. Inquiry into the influence of the World War on the population of Russia after the year 1917 can therefore hardly yield any useful results.[16]

Partly owing to lack of space, and partly to the consideration that a comparative view of the influence of the War on the social and especially the demographical life of various countries should be given from the standpoint of the History of the World War as a whole, we have refrained from international comparisons. There seems to be no reason for anticipating this general picture in a series dealing with a particular country.

As regards the plan of our exposition, we have in Part I treated the direct (physical) influence of the War on the number, composition, and territorial distribution of the population—that is the influence exerted by conscription, and by the movements of the masses of refugees and war prisoners. The physical influence of the War on the population is the fundamental factor modifying the natural changes of the population during the War; it is therefore logical to place the section devoted to its analysis prior to the chapter dealing with natural changes. Part II is devoted to natural changes and is divided into the usual four chapters: marriages, births, deaths, and natural increase (or decrease). It is followed by a third short section dealing with the war casualties. These casualties, added to the effect of the modification of the natural growth, represent the total loss caused by the War to the population of Russia.

[16] Of course, it can be considered that the whole revolution is an "effect of the war" and that the demographical effects of the revolution should be included in the investigation. But that would be a too wide interpretation of the problem. We must remember that our subject is not "the demographical effects of the war," but "the vital statistics during the war."

PART I

DIRECT INFLUENCE OF THE WAR ON THE NUMBER AND DISTRIBUTION OF THE POPULATION

INTRODUCTORY

THE principal factors exerting a direct influence on the number, constitution, and territorial distribution of the population during the years of the War were conscription, the withdrawal of refugees from the area of military operations, and lastly the settlement within the boundaries of the country of foreign prisoners of war.

The movements of the so-called "civil prisoners," or enemy aliens who were forced to move into some distant provinces had also their share in this process. A certain importance must be attached also to the removal of many industrial enterprises from the borderland to the interior, but unfortunately we do not possess any numerical information on this subject.

The data we have elucidate principally the question of conscription, which is obviously the most important.

CHAPTER I

MILITARY SERVICE

THE publication, *Russia in the World War*, referred to above,[1] gives
a complete list of classes called to the colors during the War down to
April 1, 1917. It indicates the age limit within each class, the territory embraced by each separate mobilization order, and the number
of men actually called. This list is based on the figures of the former
War Office. We reproduce it in Appendix I. In Appendix II we give
the results of our approximate estimate of the number of mobilized
men according to categories and age-groups for the fifty provinces of
European Russia, which, for the reasons mentioned above, constitute
the principal subject of our work. Our estimate is computed on the
basis of the number of allowances granted to the families of conscripts in these provinces,[2] which data are reproduced in Appendix
III. Our computation leads us to estimate that the fifty provinces of
European Russia yielded approximately 83 per cent of the total
number of mobilized men, notwithstanding the fact that the population of this territory did not exceed 72 per cent of the entire population.[3] By such a great percentage we may assume that the run of
subsequent annual numbers of men mobilized in European Russia
corresponds approximately to a similar run for the whole Empire.

Table 1 gives the number of mobilized men for the whole Empire,
distributed in quarterly periods.[4]

During the World War, down to April 1, 1917, Russia had thus
mobilized 13.7 million men, in addition to the peace-time army. The
latter numbered at the beginning of the War 1,423,000 men. We do
not possess the figures of the Ministry of War for the period subsequent to April 1, 1917; but from the above-mentioned publication of
the Central Statistical Office, *Russia in the World War*, especially

[1] *See* p. 8.

[2] Data from *Russia in the World War,* Tables 40 and 41 (*see* reference,
pp. 18–19, this text, and Appendix III, n. 18).

[3] *See* footnote to Appendix II for data on the population of the whole
Empire and of European Russia, and *see* below, pp. 16 *sqq.*

[4] Data from Appendix I; total is exclusive of peace-time army, numbering
1,423,000 on July 18, 1914.

TABLE 1

Number of Men Mobilized in Whole Russian Empire.

Period	Number of men mobilized (in thousands)
To September 31, 1914	4,215
October 1, 1914 to December 31, 1914	900
January 1, 1915 to March 31, 1915	1,180
April 1, 1915 to June 30, 1915	1,150
July 1, 1915 to September 30, 1915	2,250
October 1, 1915 to December 31, 1915	430
January 1, 1916 to March 31, 1916	775
April 1, 1916 to June 30, 1916	700
July 1, 1916 to September 30, 1916	920
October 1, 1916 to December 31, 1916	350
January 1, 1917 to March 31, 1917	630
Total	13,500
Holders of "white certificates"[5]	200
Total	13,700

from Table 5 thereof, compiled on the basis of the data of the General Headquarters, we learn that the number of men called to the colors during the War is reported to have been 14,375,000 (exclusive of the peace-time army). It would follow then that after April 1, 1917, about 675,000 men had been mobilized. The figure is very questionable. The unofficial information which we have from different sources tells us that the number of men called after April 1, 1917, could hardly be over 300,000, from which would follow (if our table is correct) that the total number of men called—without the peace-time army—did not exceed 14 millions and including the peace-time army was about 15.5 millions. But let us admit the figure of 14,375,000 men (without peace-time army) because emanating from an official source. That gives for the total number of men mobilized, together with the army on the peace footing, approximately 15,800,000 men.

As can be seen from the above figures the number of men called to the colors in the successive periods follows, upon the whole, a

[5] "White certificates" were issued to men who were exempted from military service in time of peace; in time of war their status was subject to revision.

strongly accentuated curve, the principal mobilizations occurring in the earlier period of the War. During the first year of the War (from July 1, 1914 to June 30, 1915) there were mobilized 7,445,-000 men; during the second year 4,155,000, and during the third 2,575,000 (exclusive of the holders of "white certificates" and of the peace-time army). Expressed in percentages, these numbers give the following distribution: first year 52.5 per cent, second year 29.3 per cent, third year 18.2 per cent. If we distribute these figures in calendar years we obtain Table 2.

TABLE 2

Percentage of Men Mobilized[6] Annually from 1914 to 1917.

	Number (in thousands)	Percentage
1914	5,115	36.1
1915	5,010	35.3
1916	2,745	19.4
1917	1,305	9.2
Total	14,175	100.0

The decrease in the number of men mobilized from year to year (shown in Table 2) is obviously due to the gradual exhaustion of the reserves of man power.

In regard to the distribution of the mobilized men according to age, precise information is lacking. We can only ascertain them by approximations based on the classification of men liable to military service and on their ages, at the time when they were originally called. These ages, however, are in most cases known only within certain very wide limits. The total number of men mobilized to April 1, 1917, may be divided into the groups shown in Table 3.

It is impossible to make an accurate distribution according to smaller age-groups for the reserves and territorials in the above classes. A certain idea of their age distribution can be approximated, however, from a calculation on the basis of Appendix I, supplemented by certain figures contained in the publications of the Narkomzdrav Commission. It follows from this computation that of the entire mass of men mobilized to April 1, 1917 (all groups) approxi-

[6] Exclusive of the "white certificates."

TABLE 3

Age-Groups Included in Various Mobilization Classes.

	Limits of age-groups[7]	Number (in thousands)
Peace-time army	24–26 years	1,400
Classes of 1914–1919	18–24 years	4,200
Reserves	27–40 years	3,100
Territorials and holders of "white certificates"	20–43 years	6,400
Total		15,100

mately 55 per cent were men from 18 to 26 years of age; 30 per cent from 27 to 35 years, and 15 per cent from 36 to 43 years.

The problem of establishing the ratio of the mobilized men to the total population, especially to the male population, is rendered difficult by the absence of accurate figures for the population of the Russian Empire and particularly of European Russia at the beginning of the War.

That the official figures published by the Central Statistical Committee are to be considered as highly exaggerated, has been established by competent critics.[8] These figures were merely the result obtained by adding to the data of the census of 1897 (the only census that had been taken) the figures of the natural increase, supplemented to some extent by figures representing movements of the population. These latter corrections were not accurate owing to the fact that the Committee frequently added the immigrating population to the centers of immigration without making the corresponding deduction from the areas of emigration. The Central Committee estimates the total population of the Empire on January 1, 1914 as 178.4 millions and that of the fifty provinces of European Russia at 127.8 millions. In addition to the computations of the Central Statistical Committee, we possess the calculations contained in the reports of the Chief Medical Inspector's Office of the Ministry of the Interior. Though these figures approach nearer the truth, they must

[7] The age is given at the date when the class was called and for the standing army at the date of the beginning of the War.

[8] *See* especially Professor A. A. Chuprov, *Plan Preobrazovanya Statisticheskoi Chasti Imperii* (*A Plan for the Reorganization of the Department of Statistics*), in *Statisticheski Vestnik* (*Statistical Bulletin*), Vol. I–II [Moscow, 1916–1917].

likewise be regarded as exaggerated, as can be shown by comparing them with the data of the agricultural censuses of 1916 and 1917.

Comparing the figures of the census of 1916 (which is more trustworthy than that of 1917) for the provinces in which the census was general with the corresponding figures of the Central Statistical Committee and making allowance for the number of men mobilized previous to the taking of the census of 1916, on the one hand, and for the natural increase of the population, on the other, we arrive at the conclusion that the figures of the Central Statistical Committee should be reduced by some 5 or 6 per cent. Reducing the total figure for the fifty provinces of European Russia as given by the Statistical Committee (127.8 millions) by 6 per cent, we obtain the figure 120.1 millions. A similar correction for the whole Empire will give a population of 167.7 millions instead of 178.4 millions. The well-known Russian specialist on economic geography, Professor Den, gives[9] for the year 1914 figures very nearly approaching the foregoing. He estimates the population of the Empire at 166,997,000, which figure corresponds with that given for the year 1914 in the *Yearbook* of the Soviet Central Statistical Office for 1918–1920. For the sixty provinces of European Russia (including the ten provinces of Russian Poland) the figure given by Den is 131,872,000, which, if the population of Russian Poland is deducted, leaves for the remaining provinces of European Russia approximately 120 millions. The last crude figure and also the approximate figure of 167 millions for the whole Empire we will take as the starting point of our future calculations. We must remember, however, that these figures are, like the others, merely general approximations.[10]

[9] V. E. Den, *Kurs Ekonomicheskoi Geographii* (*Textbook on Economic Geography*) [Moscow, 1925], p. 9.

[10] Among others who have attempted to introduce corrections in the calculations of the Central Statistical Committee we should mention the authors of a collective publication entitled *Opit Ischislenya Narodnaho Dokhoda 50 Gubernii Evropeiskoi Rossii v 1900–1913 Godakh* (*An Attempt to Calculate the National Income in 50 Provinces of European Russia in the Years 1900–1913*) edited by S. N. Prokopovich [Moscow, 1918], pp. 64–65. These authors estimate the population of the fifty provinces of European Russia in the middle of 1913 at 116,484,000 persons. In the collective publication entitled *Vlyanie Neurozhaev na Narodnoe Khozyaistvo Rossii* (*Influence of Bad Crops on the National Economy of Russia*) edited by V. G. Groman in the *Proceedings of the Institute of Economics* [Moscow, 1927], pp. 60, 65, Zaitsev estimates

The ratio of the men mobilized during the entire period of the War (15,800,000), to the entire population reckoned at 167 millions is 9.5 per cent. If we estimate the number of mobilized men in the fifty provinces of European Russia roughly at 12.9 to 13 millions (Appendix II), this figure will give the ratio to the population of 120 millions as 10.7 to 10.8 per cent.

But the more important ratio is that of the total number of conscripts to the male population. In the absence of other data, we must compute this population from the ratio of the male population to the total population in 1914, as it results from the figures of the Statistical Committee; this for European Russia is 49.47 per cent. Multiplying by this ratio the admitted (by us) total population of fifty provinces of European Russia—that is, 120 millions—we state that the total male population in these provinces was 59.4 millions.[11] The 13 million mobilized men thus would represent 21.9 per cent of the male population of European Russia. The ratio of mobilized men to the men of laboring age (assuming this group to include, in conformity with the local government practice, men of ages ranging from 18 to 59, i.e., under 60 years) reaches 45.6 per cent. In this calculation the proportion of this age-group to the total male population of European Russia is estimated, according to the census of 1897, at 48 per cent.[12]

It is interesting to follow the same computation for the rural and urban population separately. Here again only approximate estimates can be made, but as regards the rural population these can be checked by a comparison with the data of the censuses of 1916 and 1917.

On the basis of the figures of the Central Statistical Committee, the ratio of the rural to the total population of the fifty provinces of

the population of the fifty provinces of European Russia at the beginning of 1914 at 120,848,000 persons. L. I. Lubny-Hertsik, *op. cit.*, supplies estimates of the population in a series of provinces but does not give a comprehensive estimate for the fifty provinces as a whole for 1914.

[11] This procedure is of course identical with reducing the number of males given by the Central Statistical Committee by the same percentage, by which we have reduced the total number of population given by the Committee, that is by 6.1 per cent (120 millions instead of 127,800,000).

[12] This is the most recent information we possess as to the age distribution of the population; the age distribution, however, is fairly stable, therefore these figures can be used without greatly altering the facts.

European Russia in 1914 was 85.5 per cent; the total rural count would thus amount to 120 million times 0.855 or 102.6 millions.[18] The number of mobilized men in the rural areas of European Russia is calculated[14] at approximately 90 per cent of the total number of men mobilized in the European Russia.

The number of mobilized men from rural areas can thus be estimated at 11.7 millions, or 11.4 per cent of the total rural population, and 23.2 per cent of all rural males (these being estimated as 50.5 million males, because according to the data of the Central Statistical Committee they made 49.2 per cent of the rural population). The proportion of the rural mobilized men to the rural men of laboring age—i.e., of 18 to 60 years—would accordingly be 50.7 per cent.[15] (The number mobilized from urban districts of European Russia would be 1.3 millions.)

The foregoing estimate can be checked by using data from the 1917 census as regards the number of mobilized men and their ratio to the rural population in thirty-seven provinces of European Russia.[16] According to these 1917 census data the ratio of mobilized men

[18] Although the yearbooks of the Statistical Committee fail to make a definite statement, it seems probable that this ratio refers to the "normal" population of towns and villages, that is it includes soldiers of the peacetime army in the population of the localities from which they are drawn. If this were not so and soldiers were counted as belonging to the population of towns where their regiments are stationed, the proportion of men in the "normal" population would be higher in the rural villages than in the towns, which seems extremely improbable. We must yet observe that it is not fully correct to use the ratio of the rural population, following from the figures of the Central Statistical Committee, that is to reduce by the same proportion the figures given by the Committee for rural and urban population. The Committee probably exaggerated both figures in different proportions, rural districts being as a rule the place of emigration and the towns the place of immigration. We have no data for necessary corrections. But for our crude computations the resulting inaccuracy has not a great importance.

[14] *Russia in the World War,* Tables 40 and 41. Our computation is based on information concerning the number of allowances granted to the families of mobilized men in the towns of European Russia and on the average number of allowances for the whole of Russia per mobilized town dweller.

[15] We assume the rural able-bodied men to be 45.8 per cent of the rural male population. This is in accordance with the only available published proportion, namely that given in the 1897 census.

[16] Cf. *Pogubernskie Itogi Vserossiskoi Selsko-Khozyaistvennoi i Pozemelnoi Perepisi 1917 Goda (Provincial Returns of All-Russian Agricultural and*

to the total population is 12 per cent, and to the male population is 24.2 per cent. These figures come very near to those which we have just given for the whole fifty provinces, a fact that can be taken as an indication that our estimates, approximate as they are, are not based on incorrect premises.

As to the towns, the above-mentioned approximate estimate of the number of men called to the colors from the urban and rural districts separately gives 1.3 millions for the urban districts. From the total population of European Russia (120 millions) after the deduction of the rural population (102.6 millions) 17.4 millions remain for the urban population. Thus the mobilized urban males constitute 7.5 per cent of the total urban population. The number of males in the urban population can be stated by an analogous deduction to be 8.9 millions (59.4 million males in the total population less 50.5 million males stated above for the rural districts). The mobilized town dwellers represent thus 14.6 per cent of the total number of urban males. Finally compared with the number of men of laboring age (18 to 60 years) the mobilized constitute 24.0 per cent (we use again the age distribution according to the census of 1897, which gives for the age limits 18–60 years 60.8 per cent of the total population). We thus see that the urban population was much less affected by the mobilizations than the rural population. This is due to the fact that temporary exemptions from military service were granted to men employed in institutions and industrial concerns working for national defense.

Let us now consider the question of the effect of the mobilizations on the composition of the population according to sex. We do not, of course, mean the "final" post-war distribution of the population according to sex, which is the result both of the war losses sustained, and of the natural changes. What we mean is merely the composition of the civil population according to sex after the withdrawal of men called to the colors. The estimates which can be made concern only the rural areas, as the composition of the urban population was to a great extent determined by the influx of refugees, as well as by the influx of wounded and disabled soldiers. Data concerning these are almost completely lacking. An estimate can be computed only for

Land Census of 1917), Proceedings of the Central Statistical Office, Vol. V, Part I [Moscow, 1921], pp. 42–43.

1916, since reliable information on the natural increase of the population in 1917 exists for a very limited number of provinces. But the estimate for 1916 presents special interest, since its results can be checked with the figures of the Agricultural Census of 1916, which embraces almost the entire territory of the fifty provinces of European Russia (except the provinces of Kovno, Grodno, and Courland).[17] We assume, as before,[18] the figure 102.6 millions as representing the total number of the rural population at the beginning of 1914. As can be inferred from Appendix II, the total number of mobilized men drawn from the rural areas down to the middle of 1916, when the census took place, is roughly 9.6 million men.[19] The remaining (civil) population of both sexes will accordingly number 93 millions. The natural growth of the population for two and a half years (1914, 1915, and half of 1916) should be added to this figure. According to the information on the natural increase of population during these years, a detailed analysis of which will be given later, this increase should be reckoned at roughly 3 per cent[20] or approximately 3.1 millions. Adding this figure to 93 millions, we obtain 96.1 millions as the presumable total of the agricultural civil population (both sexes) at the middle of 1916 (93.7 per cent of what the full population was at the beginning of 1914). The change which oc-

[17] In addition to these, several omissions were made in the provinces in the neighborhood of the front. Only relatives not members can accordingly be used for computations.

[18] *See* above, p. 19.

[19] We compute this as 90 per cent of the total number of mobilized men in fifty provinces of European Russia, including those serving in the army before the mobilization of 1914. *See* above, p. 19, and n. 14.

[20] This percentage could be assumed as representing the natural increase of the total population (urban and rural), if the natural changes in the population in the provinces for which we possess information could be considered as representative for the whole of European Russia. These provinces however (especially in 1916) were in a more favorable condition than normally as regards the growth of their population. On the other hand this percentage is given for the total population, whereas we are here concerned with the rural population alone. The conditions favoring rural growth were more pronounced than those affecting urban population growth. These two considerations compensate each other to a certain extent. Of course this computation is recognizedly inexact, but it cannot greatly affect the inferences we have made since the natural increase was so small in proportion to the total population count.

curred in the number of males can be estimated as follows. At the beginning of 1914, the number of rural males as computed on page 19 above, was 50.5 millions. Deducting from this the number of men called to the colors (9.6 millions by the middle of 1916) we arrive at the figure of 40.9 million "civilian" males. Taking the natural increase of males to equal approximately half the total increase, that is about 1.5 millions[21] and adding this to the total just established, we obtain an estimate of 42.4 millions, representing the aggregate number of civilian males at the middle of 1916, or 44.1 per cent of the rural civil population already estimated for the middle of 1916 as 96.1 millions.

Now, the ratio of males in the total rural population in forty-eight provinces according to the census of 1916 is 43.9 per cent.[22] This figure, which approaches very nearly to the one we have just computed, proves that in spite of the lack of scientific accuracy our estimate is based on figures which correspond pretty closely to the truth and also that the census of 1916 may be considered fairly reliable as a source of information concerning the population. This conclusion is important in view of several other calculations which we shall have to make.

The proportion of males in the civil population of the rural areas had thus diminished by the middle of 1916 to about 44 per cent. The census of 1917 shows a further decrease to 42.8 per cent. There were in the middle of 1916, for every 100 men 127.7 women, and in the middle of 1917 there were 133.7 women per 100 men. The normal pre-war ratio was 103.2 women per 100 men, according to the data

[21] Information on the distribution of births and deaths according to sex during the years of the War is available only for certain provinces of the Ukraine. The average proportion of males in the natural increase of the population during the period 1914 to 1916 in these provinces is 47.7 per cent.

[22] Cf. *Predvaritelnie Itogi Vserossiskoi Selso-Khozyaistvennoi Perepisi 1916 Goda (Preliminary Returns of the All-Russian Agricultural Census of 1916)* [Petrograd, 1916], I, 624–625. Our computation is based entirely on figures dealing with peasant households, and does not include non-peasant households at all. This method has been adopted, on the one hand, in order to make a comparison with the 1917 census which gives but incomplete data concerning non-peasant owners, and on the other, because even the 1916 census contains trustworthy information chiefly in reference to peasant households. According to the census of 1916, the peasant population represents 97.2 per cent of the total rural population of European Russia.

ARCHANGEL

OLONETS

VOLOGDA

ESTHONIA

LIVONIA

PETROGRAD

NOVGOROD

COURLAND

PSKOV

VITEBSK

KOVNO

VILNA

TVER

YAROSLAV

KOSTROMA

VYATKA

PERM

VLADIMIR

MOGILEV

SMOLENSK

MOSCOW

NIZHNI-NOVGOROD

KAZAN

GRODNO

MINSK

KALUGA

RYAZAN

SIMBIRSK

UFA

TULA

PENZA

VOLHYNIA

CHERNIGOV

OREL

TAMBOV

SARATOV

SAMARA

ORENBURG

KURSK

KIEV

POLTAVA

VORONEZH

PODOLIA

KHARKOV

BESSARABIA

KHERSON

EKATERINOSLAV

DON
TERRITORY

TAURIDA

ASTRAKHAN

BLACK
SEA

CAUCASUS

CASPIAN
SEA

CHART I

*Showing Location of the Fifty Provinces of European
Russia. To Be Used as a Key in Reading all of the Graphic
Charts that Follow.*

of the Central Statistical Committee for January 1, 1914. The ratio of women to men thus by the middle of 1916 had increased 23.7 per cent over the 1914 ratio and by the middle of 1917 had increased 29.6 per cent.

It is interesting, both for its own sake and for purposes of future reference, to establish the territorial distribution of proportions of men mobilized. Table 4, computed on the basis of the census of 1917, gives the percentage of mobilized men to the total rural population, to the total male population, and to the number of able-bodied men, in the various provinces. The calculation is based on the peasant population in thirty-seven provinces of European Russia.[23]

TABLE 4

Ratio of Mobilized Men in Thirty-seven provinces of European Russia to Total Population, Total Males, and to the Able-bodied Males According to the Census of 1917.[24]

	Ratio of mobilized men		
Province or territory	To total population	To total male population	To able-bodied males[25]
Archangel	10.8	22.4	45.9
Astrakhan	10.7	17.2	45.7
Chernigov	12.4	24.7	50.6
Don territory	10.4	20.7	43.4
Ekaterinoslav	8.4	17.7	34.2
Kharkov	11.7	23.0	49.1
Kaluga	11.5	24.0	48.1
Kazan	10.7	21.4	44.8
Kiev	12.2	24.7	51.8
Kostroma	11.5	24.2	49.0
Kursk	12.6	25.1	53.3
Mogilev	12.6	25.2	50.7
Moscow	10.6	22.4	45.1
Nizhni-Novgorod	10.9	22.6	46.9
Novgorod	12.2	25.1	49.0
Olonets	12.8	26.3	51.8

[23] *Russia in the World War,* Table 6.
[24] *Ibid.*
[25] The source does not give the exact meaning of this category of men; but there is reason to believe that the census includes in this category all the *de facto* able-bodied men of full and semilaboring age; i.e., from fourteen to sixty years.

| | Ratio of mobilized men | | |
Province or territory	To total population	To total male population	To able-bodied males[25]
Orel	11.4	23.0	47.4
Orenburg	11.7	23.1	49.6
Penza	10.6	21.4	46.7
Perm	9.0	18.2	36.8
Petrograd	9.8	20.1	39.7
Poltava	12.0	23.8	49.4
Ryazan	11.2	22.8	48.1
Samara	11.4	22.8	49.1
Saratov	11.2	22.4	47.3
Simbirk	11.4	23.1	49.4
Smolensk	10.4	21.4	43.9
Tambov	11.1	22.4	47.6
Tula	11.3	23.0	48.5
Tver	10.1	21.3	42.5
Ufa	10.6	20.9	44.6
Vyatka	11.8	24.2	49.1
Vitebsk	13.0	25.8	52.2
Vladimir	10.7	22.4	46.3
Vologda	12.7	26.2	52.3
Volhynia	12.1	24.1	49.9
Yaroslav	11.9	25.5	50.0

The ratio of mobilized men to the total male population (it moves almost parallel, diagrammatically, with the ratio of mobilized men to the number of able-bodied men) is given in Chart II.[26] The territorial distribution of this ratio, as can be judged from the chart, has a characteristic aspect: the dividing line runs roughly from northeast to southwest, the ratio of mobilized men in the eastern and southeastern provinces being on the whole lower than that in the western and northwestern provinces. The absence of information concerning a number of provinces (especially those situated in the neighborhood

[26] Note to Charts: The *four grades* of shading in Chart II and those following correspond roughly with the quartile grouping of the provinces, for which we have information. The same principle we applied also in the majority of the other charts. We renounce it only in the cases where the quartile grouping is not convenient—for instance, because it gives too wide divisions in a part of the scale, in which a greater detailization is desirable (*see* Charts IV and XVII); in Charts VI, X, XIV, XV, XVI the quartile principle is corrected in order to discern the cases, where the percentage studied is more than 100 per cent.

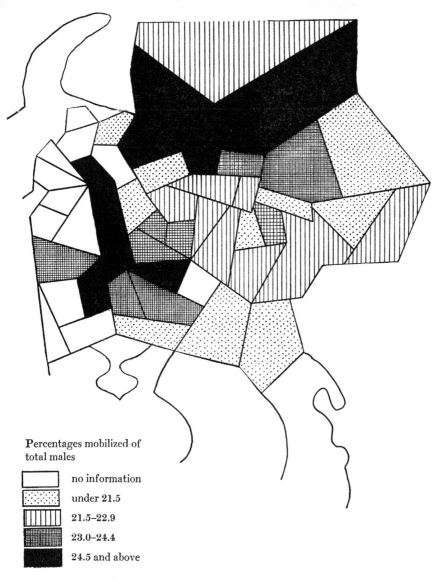

Percentages mobilized of
total males

☐	no information
▦	under 21.5
▥	21.5–22.9
▨	23.0–24.4
■	24.5 and above

CHART II

*The Proportion of Mobilized Men to the Total Male Popula-
tion According to the Agricultural Census of 1917,* by
Provinces of European Russia.*

* See n. 22, p. 22; data from Russia in the World War, Table 6; see Table
4, opus hic.

of the front) unfortunately detracts from the completeness of the picture.

We are able to draw for the year 1916 the territorial picture of the effects of the calling of new classes in most of the provinces on the basis of the census of that year. This calculation, however, is not direct, as that particular question was not dealt with in the questionnaire. We can obtain it indirectly by comparing the ratio of women to men in each province in 1916 with the similar ratio in 1914. By assuming for each province that the proportion of women to men in 1914 equals a base number of 100, and computing the similar ratio of women to men in 1916 as a proportion of the 1914 ratio we can construct an index series (a variable) which is in self-evident direct correlation with the provincial ratios of men mobilized.

In Table 5 we give for each separate province the number of women per hundred men as shown in the agricultural census of 1916 (in peasant households),[27] and the same kind of data for January 1, 1914, taken from the data of the Central Statistical Committee.[28] The third column gives the ratio of items in column 1 to those in column 2; this series of ratios we shall designate as "the indexes of the changes in the provincial ratios of women to men."

The computed index series (column 3) shows throughout a consistent increase in the 1916 proportions of women to men as over the 1914 proportions. These variations in amount of increase are shown in Chart III. A comparison of this chart with Chart II shows a considerable similitude in the territorial distribution of the indexes for proportion of women (1916) and for proportion of mobilized men (1917). There are of course deviations from this similarity, but it is clear that these proportions show definite likeness.

How is this characteristic distribution of both indexes to be explained, especially the increase in the indexes in the eastern and southeastern over the northern and northwestern provinces?

The ratio of mobilized men depends to a certain extent on the difference in the age-groups of the population in each province—i.e., on the greater or smaller proportion of men liable to military service

[27] Except the provinces of Kovno, Grodno, and Courland, for which no information is given in the census of 1916. We also exclude the figures of the province of Vilna since only an insignificant part of it was subject to the census.

[28] *See* prior references to these data.

TABLE 5

Relative Changes in the Proportion of Females to Males in 1916 as Compared with 1914, European Russia.[29]

Provinces	Females per 100 males		Index of changes in this ratio (column 1 as percentage of column 2)
	Middle of 1916 (1)	Beginning of 1914 (2)	(3)
Archangel	131.0	108.2	121.1
Astrakhan	104.5	95.3	109.6
Bessarabia	121.4	96.3	126.1
Chernigov	127.6	101.5	125.7
Don territory	117.9	98.3	120.0
Ekaterinoslav	111.9	96.1	116.4
Esthonia	135.6	103.5	131.0
Kharkov	122.4	98.7	124.0
Kherson	124.8	98.0	127.4
Yaroslav	164.8	126.8	130.0
Kaluga	152.8	119.4	128.0
Kazan	125.3	101.5	123.4
Kiev	130.0	100.8	129.0
Kostroma	142.1	116.3	122.2
Kursk	127.2	100.8	125.7
Livonia	132.2	106.5	124.1
Minsk	124.8	99.9	124.8
Mogilev	129.9	101.8	127.6
Moscow	141.9	115.8	122.6
Nizhni-Novgorod	137.7	109.0	126.3
Novgorod	134.8	108.5	124.2
Olonets	134.0	108.7	123.3
Orel	132.8	104.1	127.6
Orenburg	117.1	98.9	118.4
Penza	129.9	107.1	121.3
Perm	123.7	104.7	118.1
Petrograd	132.1	108.3	122.0
Podolia	123.4	99.5	124.0
Poltava	126.7	99.8	127.0
Pskov	130.3	106.5	122.3
Ryazan	136.3	105.7	128.0
Samara	123.3	101.5	121.5

[29] Data are for forty-six provinces; for 1916 (col. 1) from 1916 Agricultural Census (*see* above, p. 23, n. 25); for 1914 (col. 2) from *Yearbook* of Central Statistical Committee. In column 3 the relatives are computed from the data in columns 1 and 2.

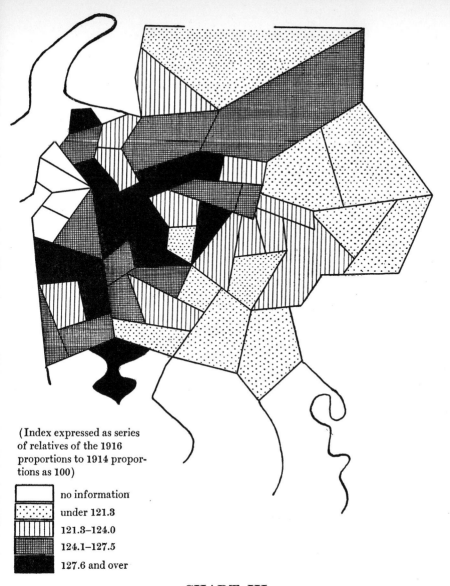

(Index expressed as series
of relatives of the 1916
proportions to 1914 proportions as 100)

- no information
- under 121.3
- 121.3–124.0
- 124.1–127.5
- 127.6 and over

CHART III

*Relative Proportion of Females per Hundred Males, in Ru-
ral Population of the Provinces of European Russia, in 1916
as Compared with the Proportion on January 1, 1914 (Index
Numbers as a Series of Provincial Relatives for the 1916
Proportions as Base or 100).**

** Data from Agricultural Census for 1916 and from report of Central
Statistical Office for 1914; relatives computed by the author are the basis of
this chart, see Table 5, column 3.*

Provinces	*Females per 100 males*		*Index of changes in this ratio (column 1 as percentage of column 2)*
	Middle of 1916	*Beginning of 1914*	
Saratov	121.8	102.5	118.8
Simbirsk	129.6	105.5	122.8
Smolensk	141.1	105.8	133.4
Tambov	126.2	103.6	121.8
Taurida	123.1	95.0	129.5
Tula	133.3	112.1	118.9
Tver	154.9	114.0	135.9
Ufa	118.5	100.0	118.5
Vyatka	130.5	109.5	119.2
Vitebsk	130.5	100.6	129.7
Vladimir	139.9	112.7	124.1
Vologda	134.1	107.7	124.5
Volhynia	130.4	99.6	130.9
Voronezh	121.3	100.3	120.9

(that is, between the ages of 18 and 43). This liability proportion is, however, but one of several factors determining the ratio of mobilized men, as may be seen from the fact that the ratio of able-bodied

TABLE 6

Number of Provinces Having Given Proportions of Able-bodied Men.

Ratio of able-bodied men to total males	Number of provinces
45.5 to 45.9	1
46.0 to 46.4	2
46.5 to 46.9	4
47.0 to 47.4	4
47.5 to 47.9	4
48.0 to 48.4	4
48.5 to 48.9	4
49.0 to 49.4	4
49.5 to 49.9	2
50.0 to 50.4	4
50.5 to 50.9	1
51.0 to 51.4	2
51.5 to 51.9 (incl.)	1
	37

men to the total number of males, according to the census of 1917, varies from province to province, much less than does the ratio of mobilized men. This ratio of able-bodied to the total male population in the thirty-seven provinces (mobilization figures for which were given in Table 4) varied as may be seen in Table 6.

For the total population the standard deviation of the provinces in percentage of able-bodied men is 1.54 and the coefficient of variation[30] is 3.2 per cent. Table 7 shows that the relative variation of the

TABLE 7

Number of Provinces Having Given Proportions of the Total Male Population Mobilized.

Ratio of mobilized to total male population	Number of provinces
17.0 to 17.4	1
17.5 to 17.9	1
18.0 to 18.4	1
18.5 to 18.9	..
19.0 to 19.4	..
19.5 to 19.9	..
20.0 to 20.4	1
20.5 to 20.9	2
21.0 to 21.4	4
21.5 to 21.9	..
22.0 to 22.4	5
22.5 to 22.9	3
23.0 to 23.4	5
23.5 to 23.9	1
24.0 to 24.4	4
24.5 to 24.9	2
25.0 to 25.4	3
25.5 to 25.9	2
26.0 to 26.4	2
	37

[30] The coefficient here used is Pearson's "V," representing the percentage relation of σ (standard deviation) to the arithmetic average; that is, $\frac{100\sigma}{M}$. The difference between this coefficient and the standard deviation lies in the fact that the latter measures the *absolute* size of the variations around

ratio of mobilized men to the total male population in the same thirty-seven provinces is much greater. Calculated from Table 7, the standard deviation of provinces in percentage of total males mobilized is 2.21 and the coefficient of variation is 9.7 per cent. Thus the relative variability, measured by the coefficient of variation, is in this case over three times the relative variability in the ratio of the able-bodied men.

A factor exercising a great influence on the ratio of men mobilized in the different provinces seems to have been *morbidity*, which conditions the percentage of men unfit for military service. If we admit that the provincial differences in the death rate in pre-war time corresponds to a certain extent[31] to the differences in the morbidity of the population[32] and compare it to the variations in the ratio of the mobilized men, we shall discover whether these figures appear to any extent related. In order to increase the field of this comparison we shall substitute for the ratio of mobilized men, known only for thirty-seven provinces, the index showing the changes in relative proportions of females to males, which we possess for forty-six provinces.[33] The correlation data to enable us indirectly to analyze any possible relationship between morbidity and mobilization will be found in Table A (*table omitted*).[34]

The general appearance of this table suffices to show a definite inverse (negative) correlation between the two sets of figures; the higher the mortality (or thus according to our assumption, the morbidity) of the population, the lower is the index of the relative proportion of women, that is, the lower the amount of increase in proportion shown (1916 as compared with 1914 female proportions), which

the mean while the coefficient of variation measures their *relative* size in terms of the size of the mean itself.

[31] We say to a certain extent only, since the general death rate depends largely on infant mortality which has no influence on the actual morbidity of the adult population of the age-groups liable to military service.

[32] A further implied assumption is that the geographical distribution of the war-time sickness rate does not differ very much from the distribution of pre-war rate.

[33] *Cf.* Table 5, column 3, based on 1916 agricultural census as compared with 1914 data from Central Statistical Committee.

[34] All correlation tables are omitted for reasons of economy in printing. For reference, however, they are on file with the original manuscript at the Carnegie Endowment.

we have used as indicating by inference the ratio of mobilized men. The coefficient of correlation[35] here is —0.52.

We shall see further that mortality like many other demographical phenomena in European Russia presents in its geographic distribution a picture of ratios differing characteristically in the east and southeast from ratios in the west and northwest, the line of partition running roughly southwest to northeast.[36]

This territorial distribution for mortality thus indirectly to a certain extent explains the analogous distribution for the ratios of mobilized men, as already shown in Chart II.

Another cause must probably have had its share in the general influence, namely, the degree of facility with which the conscription could be evaded in different parts of Russia. In this respect the area of military districts may have been of importance; in the eastern part of European Russia, where the population was more scattered, these districts extended over a much larger territory than in the west; the possibility of escape was accordingly greater. On the other hand, there may have existed also a difference in the severity of the medical examinations when determining the fitness of men for mili-

[35] Ordinarily correlation coefficients are considered with regard to their *probable errors,* which teach us to what extent we can consider the coefficient as significant and not fortuitous. The generally used formulas for this probable error assume (although it is not always remembered) an *independence of individual cases,* for which we have our data—in our instance, the individual provinces. But in the case of such provincial data we can not assert this independence since, as we have seen, the territorial distribution of our figures shows certain "regional" factors influencing alike the provinces situated in a given neighborhood. Though this problem is not yet sufficiently elucidated by the theory for the case of territorial series (it has been more elaborated in the case of time series), it is evident that in the first case also the mentioned doubts must arise. This is the reason why we do not give here probable errors of the correlation coefficients (though we have calculated them); the meaning of these probable errors is not sufficiently clear in this instance. We have observed nevertheless that almost all the coefficients used here and below equal more than three to five times their probable errors. On the other hand, it must be remembered, that the correlation coefficients used by us have in our inferences only a *subsidiary* rôle, they will only corroborate the statements made at the base of other arguments. Then the question of their "significance" is here not so important as ordinarily. (For the problem of the probable errors of correlation coefficients in the time series *see* the *Proceedings* of the American Statistical Association, March, 1929.)

[36] *See* below, Chart XIII.

tary service. In the western provinces, nearer the front, the severity
may have been greater owing to psychological reasons. This statement is to some extent supported by the fact that if the relationship
between mortality and the index of the proportionate increase of
women is calculated for thirty-five provinces[37] instead of forty-six—
that is, if the provinces contiguous to the front are excluded from
the calculation, together with some unreliable data—the coefficient
rises from −0.52 to −0.63. This would seem to suggest that in the
provinces contiguous to the front the influence of morbidity on the
ratio of mobilized men is more disturbed by other influences, among
which we should include first, the influence of the facility with which
the military service could be evaded.

Finally, other causes may have exerted an influence on the origin
of the territorial picture under review. Among these, we may refer,
for instance, to the exemption from military service of certain non-
Russian inhabitants, who were settled mostly in the western part of
Russia. Another factor is the complex system of exemptions granted
according to family conditions, combined with the differences in the
distribution of the population, according to age and family. The
full investigation of these problems is, however, the task of specialists. It lies outside the scope of the present work; it is principally
important here to grasp the general picture of the territorial distribution of the levies and of the factors influencing this distribution,
since this distribution of levies was an essential factor affecting the
natural changes in the population in the years of the War, which is
the proper subject of our study.

[37] In the chapters that follow we shall often have to use this smaller group
of thirty-five provinces instead of forty-six, when calculating the correlation
between various demographical factors.

CHAPTER II

REFUGEES, CIVIL PRISONERS, AND WAR PRISONERS

THE movement of war refugees presents to the historian of the demographical phenomena during the War a great intrinsic interest, since it is the principal aspect of the migrations of the population during that period. It is also important as a factor influencing the natural changes in the population, especially mortality. The refugees were not only dying at an incredible rate, owing to the extremely insanitary and unfavorable conditions in which they lived, but they also spread diseases and increased mortality among the natives of the regions where they settled.

As indicated in our introduction, the material concerning this all-important demographical phenomenon of the war period exists unfortunately only in crude form—chiefly in the shape of cards in the Statistical Department of the People's Commissariat of the Interior. Even the work of analyzing the partial material concerning the refugees which has been intrusted by the Narkomzdrav Commission to Professor Ustinov and completed by him in a report to the Commission, so far as we know, has not yet been published. The *Proceedings* of the Commission contain merely general statements and figures based principally on this report.[1] The fundamental material already published on this subject is contained in the information supplied by the Committee of the Grand Duchess Tatiana for the Aid to the Victims of the War (Tatiana Committee). It is unfortunate that we have not been able to procure this material in its original form.

The number of refugee cards in the possession of the Statistical Department of the People's Commissariat of the Interior is approximately two and a half millions. According to the data of the Tatiana Committee[2] there were 2,706,309 refugees registered in the territory of the Empire (excluding the Trans-Caucasia) up to December 20, 1915. This figure represents 1.83 per cent of the permanent population of the Empire, and of this total 2,496,640 refugees were settled in the fifty provinces of European Russia. The information of the

[1] Cf. *Proceedings* of the Commission, pp. 37–38.
[2] L. I. Lubny-Hertsik, *op. cit.*, p. 23.

Tatiana Committee for May 29, 1916, gives 3,306,051 as representing the total number of refugees (or 3,150,126 if the Trans-Caucasia is excluded). This figure is to be considered as minimal; it means that during five months the number of refugees increased by nearly 450,000. Distributed in very rough territorial units the figures for the latter date are shown in Table 8.

TABLE 8

Regional Distribution of Refugees in Whole Russian Empire (Tatiana Committee Data).[3]

| | Refugees | |
Regions	Number	Percentage
Area adjacent to the front	855,312	25.9
Central area (except the province of Smolensk) .	1,342,724	40.6
Southern area	408,275	12.3
Eastern area	324,299	9.8
Northern area	27,458	0.8
Siberia	78,021	2.4
Central Asia	114,037	3.5
Trans-Caucasia	155,925	4.7
Total	3,306,051	100.0

According to other data of the Tatiana Committee, the refugees may be classified with reference to their nationality as in Table 9.

Table 9 shows among other things that while a great proportion of the refugees consisted of people originating from portions of Russian territory which now form independent states, the fundamental of the mass of refugees consisted of Russian natives.

The above figures comprise not only refugees proper, but also compulsory refugees. These were enemy aliens expelled from territories adjacent to the front, as well as from certain other areas—the so-called "civil prisoners," and also Jews—who at the beginning of the War were expelled in great numbers from the area of military operations. These two official groups do not, however, embrace the entire group of compulsory refugees. In fact a certain number of ordinary refugees consisted also of persons obliged to quit their homes in pursuance of orders emanating from the military authorities.

[3] *Ibid.*

TABLE 9

Number and Percentage of Russia's Refugees, According to Nationality (Tatiana Committee Data).[4]

Nationality	Refugees Number	Percentage
Russians	1,726,068	53.9
Poles	513,434	16.0
Letts	285,814	8.9
Jews	199,895	6.3
Armenians	120,167	3.8
Lithuanians	85,552	2.7
Others (principally Germans compulsorily removed)	192,596	6.0
Not classified	76,986	2.4
Total	3,200,512	100.0

Another source of information regarding the refugees is the agricultural census of 1917. This gives for separate provinces the number of refugee households and the civil prisoners who settled in the rural districts of the province. Table 10 reproduces the data for thirty-eight provinces where they exist (the figures refer to peasant households).

TABLE 10

Number of Peasant Households, and Number and Percentage of Refugees and of Civil Prisoners, in Thirty-eight Provinces of European Russia, 1917.

Provinces	Total number of peasant households[5]	Refugees Number	Percentage of peasant households[6]	Civil prisoners Number	Percentage of peasant households[6]	Percentage refugees and civil prisoners of peasant households[6]
Archangel	68,882	2	*	8	0.01	0.01
Astrakhan	104,977	1,726	1.64	323	0.31	1.95
Chernigov	378,583	1,841	0.49	....	..	0.49

[4] *Proceedings* of Narkomzdrav, p. 38 (according to *Izvestia* of the Tatiana Committee, No. 19).

[5] Including those absent. The average ratio of absent householders, in the thirty-nine provinces where the census was taken is 5.4 per cent.

[6] Percentage of peasant households in column one.

| Provinces | Total number of peasant households[5] | Refugees | | Civil prisoners | | Percentage refugees and civil prisoners of peasant households[6] |
		Number	Percentage of peasant households[6]	Number	Percentage of peasant households[6]	
Don Terr'y[7]	431,741	....	..	....	..	..
Ekaterinoslav	450,447	22,941	5.09	310	0.07	5.16
Kharkov	461,644	12,094	2.62	142	0.03	2.65
Yaroslav	231,549	738	0.32	4	*	0.32
Kaluga	214,720	3,914	1.82	....	..	1.82
Kazan	483,137	7,932	1.64	385	0.08	1.72
Kiev	587,678	931	0.15	50	0.01	0.16
Kostroma	304,752	520	0.17	267	0.09	0.26
Kursk	421,326	5,446	1.29	52	0.01	1.30
Mogilev	255,441	3,442	1.35	5	*	1.35
Moscow	291,315	1,337	0.46	4	*	0.46
Nizhni-Novgorod	320,981	2,303	0.72	17	0.01	0.73
Novgorod	272,996	344	0.13	7	*	0.13
Olonets	72,603	7	0.01	76	0.08	0.09
Orel	355,301	2,339	0.66	73	0.02	0.68
Orenburg	243,318	6,996	2.88	3,789	1.56	4.44
Penza	310,707	....	..	....	..	..
Perm	385,292	801	0.21	792	0.02	0.23
Petrograd	153,043	275	0.18	5	*	0.18
Poltava[8]	462,668	....	..	....	..	..
Ryazan	360,189	5,336	1.48	6	*	1.48
Samara	534,914	21,263	3.98	564	0.11	4.09
Saratov	465,299	16,302	3.50	468	0.10	3.60
Simbirsk	331,760	5,449	1.64	26	0.01	1.65
Smolensk	291,225	1,317	0.45	2	*	0.45
Tambov	571,601	16,525	2.89	10	*	2.89
Tula	282,041	2,742	0.97	....	..	0.97
Tver	368,130	905	0.25	9	*	0.25
Ufa	537,502	8,310	1.55	1,937	0.36	1.91
Vyatka	540,807	241	0.04	1,781	0.33	0.37
Vitebsk	127,733	220	1.72	2	*	1.72
Vladimir	279,665	912	0.33	....	..	0.33
Vologda	294,725	26	0.01	1,003	0.34	0.35
Volhynia	225,077	5,191	2.31	200	0.09	2.40
Voronezh	506,221	3,068	0.61	59	0.01	0.62

* Less than 0.005 per cent.

[7] With reference to the Don Territory it is not quite clear in the original table whether the dashes mean an absence of refugee households (as in other provinces) or the absence of information.

[8] In this province the refugees numbered 1,287 families, but they were not settled among the peasants.

The total number of households (families) of refugees and of civil prisoners in thirty-eight provinces was approximately 176,000 (1.36 per cent of all the households of these provinces). The ratio of the households of civil prisoners is only 7 per cent of the total count of refugee families. Reckoning each family as comprising four members,[9] the total number of refugees and civil prisoners with their families would be something over 700,000 persons—obviously only an inconsiderable part of the total mass of refugees, which is estimated at 3,300,000 persons. The smallness of the number of refugees registered by the 1917 census may be explained as follows: In the first place, the census does not embrace all the provinces. The area adjacent to the front, in which many refugees were concentrated, is omitted. Secondly, the bulk of the refugees congregated in towns and not in the country. This fact can explain also the contradiction between the data of the census, giving for the central provinces very low figures, and the data of our Table 8 which estimates the part of refugees concentrated in the central area to be 40 per cent of the total mass of refugees. But, in spite of their numerical insignificance, and possible inaccuracy, the data of the census are valuable in so far as they allow one to identify in greater detail the areas of concentration of refugees in those rural districts *other than* the area adjacent to the front.

Chart IV illustrates the proportion of refugee households to the total number of peasant households in the separate provinces. The chart gives only slight indications as regards the area adjacent to, or in the neighborhood of, the front, where, however, we find a relatively high percentage of refugees in the provinces of Vitebsk, Volhynia, and to some extent, in Mogilev. The migration in the provinces adjacent to the front had a character different from that which it assumed in the provinces more remote, for here it was less stable; adjacent provinces served often merely as halting places in the migration. The more remote area where refugees settled was composed chiefly of the Volga and Trans-Volga regions as well as of certain provinces in central and southern Russia, the proportions being

[9] This average composition of a refugee family is based on the special census of Jewish refugees taken in the provinces of Poltava, Nizhni-Novgorod, Saratov, and Ekaterinoslav by the Jewish War Relief Committee. The use of this average number for the entire mass of refugees involves, evidently, a certain inaccuracy.

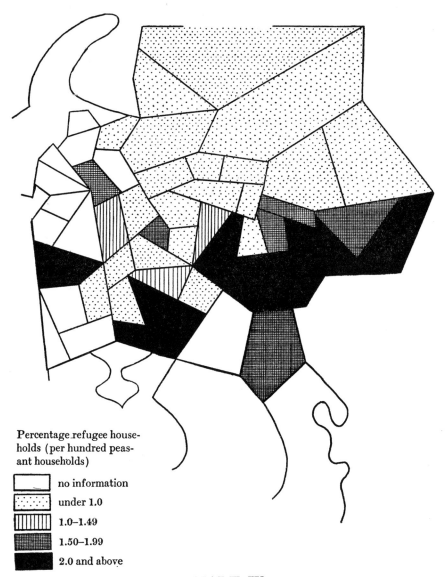

Percentage refugee house-
holds (per hundred peas-
ant households)

☐	no information
⋯	under 1.0
‖‖‖	1.0–1.49
▨	1.50–1.99
■	2.0 and above

CHART IV

*Number of Refugee Households per Hundred Peasant
Households in the Rural Districts of European Russia, According to the Agricultural Census of 1917.*

most notable in the provinces of Orenburg, Samara, Saratov, Tambov, Ekaterinoslav, and Kharkov.

It is difficult to say what determined the direction taken by the stream of refugees while settling in the more remote areas. It can be explained, to a certain extent, by the fact that the refugees were guided by the harvest. If we look at Chart XVII which represents the proportions of the mean harvest in 1914 and 1915 to that for the years 1909–1913 (the first years of the War being the years of most intensive movement of refugees) we shall see that excepting the area of the western provinces the harvest increased principally in the Volga and Trans-Volga provinces. The Orenburg and Astrakhan provinces held first place in the harvests of all European Russia. This is only one of several possible factors determining the direction of the movement of the refugees, but the limits of this discussion do not admit of our going into such further aspects of the question.

The areas or compulsory settlement of civil prisoners do not entirely agree with those of the concentration of refugees; the highest percentage of the former are to be found in the four following provinces: Astrakhan, Vologda, Orenburg, and Vyatka. Only the first and third of these have large settlements of refugees; in the provinces of Vyatka and Vologda the proportion of refugees is relatively insignificant.

Another factor that has some bearing on the war-time demography is the *prisoners of war* who were partly concentrated in camps and partly disseminated in relatively large numbers among the civil population of various regions, where they were employed as laborers. Table 11 gives some idea of the number of prisoners of war and of their distribution.

The number of prisoners down to September 1, 1917, thus amounted to approximately 2 million men, of whom 60,000 were sent abroad or escaped.

We have no information in respect of the distribution of prisoners of war among separate provinces. The schedule of the census of 1916 contained, it is true, a question as to the presence of prisoners of war among the laborers engaged in household work, but the replies were not analyzed in the preliminary returns that have been published. We possess only the data of the General Staff relating to the distribution of prisoners of war in large territorial units—the military districts adjacent to the front and districts removed from it. (See Table 12.)

TABLE 11

Number and Distribution of Prisoners of War,[10] from the Beginning of the War to September 1, 1917.

Distribution	Number of prisoners of war
In camps, hospitals, and employed as laborers	1,813,458
Enrolled in newly formed regiments[11] and sent to allied countries	39,278
Repatriated invalids	19,780
Interned in neutral countries	1,484
Died[12]	51,608
Escaped	35,725
Total	1,961,333

According to the data in Table 12, 836,437 or slightly less than half of the total number of prisoners are found in the districts removed from the front; and of this half approximately two-thirds (537,457) are reported in the districts of European Russia (the Moscow and Kazan military districts). However, it must be remembered that the area adjacent to the front in its administrative sense embraces a large territory not actually contiguous to the front and comprises provinces situated at a considerable distance from the fighting line.

We possess also the data of the distribution of prisoners settled

[10] *Russia in the World War,* Table 33.

[11] Special regiments were organized in Russia during the War from the prisoners of war who expressed a desire to fight against the Central Powers. Men who enlisted in these regiments were the subjects of the Central Powers, mostly of Austria-Hungary, belonging to the Slavonic race, especially Czechs and later on (and to a much smaller extent), Poles.

[12] The number of deaths among the prisoners given as 51,608 is obviously incomplete. A rough calculation on the basis that each war prisoner spent in Russia, down to September, 1917, a year and a half (their influx was constant during the three years of the War but obviously the rate varied) would give the total result of 3 million "full years" spent in captivity. The rate would thus constitute 17 per thousand which is impossibly low, even for the civil population in Russia. This death rate is still less probable for war prisoners who often, though not always, lived under unfavorable conditions.

TABLE 12

Distribution of Prisoners of War According to Military Districts.

Districts	Districts removed from the front area	Districts adjoining the front area		Total
		Various employments	*Employed in the army*	
Moscow	252,081	....	....	252,081
Kazan	285,376	....	....	285,376
Omsk	207,001	....	....	207,001
Irkutsk	36,388	....	....	36,388
Amur	14,306	....	....	14,306
Turkestan	41,285	....	....	41,285
Petrograd	....	39,795	22,000	61,795
Dvinsk	....	41,447	15,500	56,947
Minsk	....	59,170	19,077	78,247
Kiev	....	156,078	250,000	406,078
Caucasus	....	50,091	30,000	80,091
Odessa	....	114,481	103,085	217,566
Don Territory	....	76,297	....	76,297
Totals	836,437	537,359	439,662	1,813,458

in remote military districts, classified according to whether they were at the direct disposal of the military authorities or were distributed among the civil population for agricultural labor.

Out of the total number of prisoners of war in the districts remote from the front some 12.3 per cent were in concentration camps; some 1.7 per cent were in hospitals, and the bulk (719,091 or 86 per cent) were engaged as agricultural laborers. As regards commissioned officers, who represent only 3.4 per cent of the total number of prisoners of war, the distribution was entirely different: the greater part, 96.4 per cent, were in concentration camps; only 2.7 per cent being in nursing homes and less than half as many were found employed in farming.

Thus, more than 700,000 prisoners of war were disseminated as agricultural laborers throughout the military districts removed from the front. Of this number 475,000 were employed in European Russia, in the Moscow and Kazan districts. In order to compare the number of prisoners of war who found employment in agriculture with the number of refugees and civilian prisoners settled down in the thirty-eight provinces of European Russia (most of which are remote from the front) for which figures have just been cited, we

TABLE 13

*Number of Prisoners of War in the Military Districts
Remote from the Front.*[13]

Districts	Rank	In camps	In hospitals	As agricul- tural laborers	Total
Moscow	officers	3,593	271	. . . .	3,864
	men	26,514	5,435	216,268	248,217
Kazan	officers	5,544	85	. . . .	5,629
	men	17,564	3,021	259,162	279,747
Omsk	officers	4,308	77	76	4,461
	men	4,875	983	196,682	202,540
Irkutsk	officers	7,963	141	23	8,127
	men	8,365	1,271	18,625	28,261
Amur	officers	4,369	120	1	4,490
	men	4,834	519	4,463	9,816
Turkestan	officers	1,476	84	204	1,764
	men	13,598	2,336	23,587	39,521
Total	officers	27,253	778	304	28,335
	men	75,750	13,565	718,787	808,102
Grand total		103,003	14,343	719,091	836,437

ought to know how many of the 997,000 prisoners of war located on
the territory of the military districts adjoining the front were employed as agricultural laborers within these thirty-eight provinces.
This, unfortunately, cannot be done. One thing, however, is certain:
the 440,000 prisoners employed by the army should not be included
in our computation. But what part of the remaining 557,000 men
(engaged in "various employments") shall be added to those employed in farming in the military districts removed from the front
we cannot say with any accuracy. We cannot be far wrong, however,
in estimating the total number of prisoners of war employed in agriculture in the thirty-eight provinces at 600,000 to 800,000 men.
This rough computation shows that the influx of prisoners of war
among the rural population of European Russia was probably almost equivalent to that of refugees and civil prisoners whose number
amounted in the thirty-eight provinces to about 700,000 persons.

The prisoners of war disseminated in towns for various work constituted an insignificant element in the urban population, while the

[13] *Russia in the World War,* Table 31.

refugees played there an important part. But with reference to the general sanitary conditions of the towns (as well as of rural areas), the prisoners-of-war camps, which were often located in the neighborhood of towns, possessed great importance, and in many cases acted as *foci* of epidemic diseases.[14]

[14] *Cf.* N. Zhdanov, *Russkie Voennoplennie v Mirovoi Voine 1914–1918 Godov* (*Russian Prisoners of War in the World War of 1914–1918*) [Moscow, 1921], Chapter XIV.

PART II

THE NATURAL GROWTH OF THE POPULATION DURING THE YEARS OF THE WAR

CHAPTER I

MARRIAGES

PRE-WAR RUSSIA was marked, as is well known, by a comparatively high marriage rate. During the last five years preceding the War (1909–1913), the general marriage rate (number of marriages per annum per thousand of population) was 8.1. For the last two decades preceding the War, the marriage rate, however, had shown a tendency to decline, though this fall was not numerically important and varied greatly from year to year. (This fluctuation corresponded chiefly with the alternation of years of good and bad harvests.) We give in Table 14 the marriage rates per thousand population for fifty provinces of European Russia, for the twenty years preceding the War, by five-year periods.[1]

TABLE 14

Marriage Rates Per Thousand Population in Fifty Provinces of European Russia for Twenty Years Prior to the World War, Averaged by Five-Year Periods.

Periods	Rates per 1,000 population
1894–1897	9.1
1899–1903	8.8
1904–1908	8.7
1909–1913	8.1

The territorial distribution of the pre-war marriage rates in European Russia is shown in Chart V. In general the marriage rates are seen to diminish from east to west. There are, however, two cen-

[1] Based on the figures of the Central Statistical Committee. As indicated above, the figures of the population given by this Committee and used by it for the calculation of marriage rates, birth rates, and death rates are somewhat exaggerated. Slightly more precise are the figures of the population given in the reports of the Chief Medical Inspector who used them for calculating the birth rates and death rates. As, however, the Chief Medical Inspector's reports calculate the population at the middle of the year and the Central Statistical Committee at the beginning of the year, the difference in the rates caused by the difference in the bases is insignificant.

ters of especially low marriage rates; these are the group of provinces situated to the extreme west and northwest and a smaller group of central provinces (Moscow, Ryasan, and Tula).

It is interesting to compare this Chart V with the territorial distribution of indexes of the pre-war changes in marriage rates, that are shown in Chart VI, which is based on the ratio of the provincial marriage rates averaged for 1909–1913[2] to the provincial marriage rates averaged for the years 1897 and 1899. It would have been better to base the comparison on the average marriage rates for the period 1895–1899 (especially as the annual fluctuations of the marriage rate are considerable) but unfortunately we do not possess data for the years 1895, 1896, and 1898.[3] A comparison of the two charts shows that the territorial distribution of the fall in marriage rates for a decade and a half before the War has some resemblance to the distribution of the average marriage rates for the five years immediately before the War. A series of western provinces as well as some provinces of the central area, where the marriage rate was especially low in the years immediately preceding the War, were also areas of an accentuated fall in the marriage rate. The principal contrast between the two charts appears in the fact that the central region of strong decrease in marriage rates as compared with the earlier period is larger and extends further to the east than the central area of the low pre-war marriage rates. It included some provinces of the central industrial and central agricultural regions (the provinces of Tver, Vladimir, Nizhni-Novgorod, Penza, Tula, and others) in which the marriage rate decreased rapidly, but had not reached such a low level as in the more western neighboring provinces.[4] As an offset to the tendency in the foregoing area, we may point out the three provinces situated in the extreme northwest (Esthonia, Livonia, and Petrograd) in which rather low marriage

[2] Data omitted for 1912; see Appendix IX.

[3] The figures on which Charts V and VI are based will be found in Appendix IV. For the years 1909–1913 they are borrowed from the yearbooks of the Central Statistical Committee, while those for the years 1897 and 1899 are taken from *Statistika Rossiskoi Imperii* (*Statistics of the Russian Empire*), a publication issued by the same Central Statistical Committee.

[4] A high marriage rate and its very slight decline may be noticed in the province of Tambov of this central area. It is difficult to say whether this is a permanent tendency, or a casual contrast shown merely by these two periods, or a result of the inadequacy of our information.

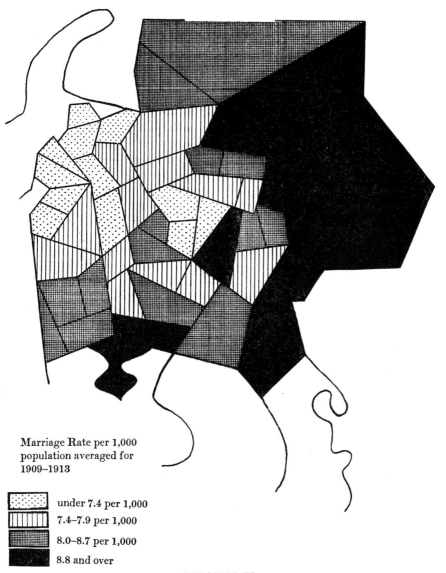

Marriage Rate per 1,000
population averaged for
1909–1913

under 7.4 per 1,000
7.4–7.9 per 1,000
8.0–8.7 per 1,000
8.8 and over

CHART V

Marriage Rates per Thousand Population, for Fifty Provinces of European Russia, Averaged for the Period, 1909–1913,* by Provinces.

* *The year 1912 is omitted. Data are from Appendix IV (see n. 3, p. 46).*

rates existed but whose later rates were nearly as high as those of the
fifteen years earlier.

As regards the influence exerted by the World War on the
changes in the marriage rate, we must in the first place point out,
with regret, that we have but little information concerning the
monthly number of marriages during the war period. This fact renders it impossible to calculate to what extent the characteristic wave
of "war-marriages" affected Russia during the first months of the
War, as it did other belligerent countries (the war-marriages are
chiefly legalization of earlier liaisons). We possess monthly data
with reference only to Petrograd and Moscow. "War-marriages," if
they took place at all, should have affected the largest cities to a
greater extent than any other part of Russia, since the patriarchal
morals were more relaxed and the number of irregular liaisons
greater in these than in other places.[5]

TABLE 15

*Number of Marriages in Petrograd and Moscow (cities) During
the Years 1913 and 1914, by Months.*[6]

	Petrograd		Moscow	
	1913	1914	1913	1914
January	1,571	2,020	1,936	1,950
February	2,380	1,688	32	1,244
March	70	65	251	31
April	1,096	1,670	1,727	1,462
May	1,038	1,351	905	972
June	1,011	399	233	462
July	814	1,097	1,046	1,282
August	399	470	637	365

[5] In the countries of Western Europe, the increase in the number of "war-
marriages" was chiefly notable in towns, and was especially large in large
cities.

[6] The figures refer to the city without the suburbs. Cf. *Kratki Svod Dan-
nikh po Gorodu Petrogradu za 1913–1914 God (Summary of Statistical Data
Referring to the City of Petrograd for the Year 1913–1914)*, published by
the Statistical Department of the Municipality of Petrograd [Petrograd,
1916]; also A. A. Chuprov, *Voina i Dvizhenie Naselenya (The War and the
Changes in the Population)* in a symposium published in honor of A. A. Post-
nikov. M. Chuprov seems to use preliminary figures for Petrograd for he
shows fewer marriages than the total figures that are given in the present
work, in Appendix V; but his Moscow totals agree.

	Petrograd		Moscow	
	1913	*1914*	*1913*	*1914*
September	971	595	998	540
October	934	836	1,047	673
November	845	839	1,029	672
December	73	54	81	26
For the year:	11,202	11,084	9,922	9,679

The numerical data at our disposal, however, show that in Petrograd and Moscow the increase in the number of marriages during the first months of the War scarcely exceeded the usual monthly fluctuations (which as a rule were considerable in Russia). Table 15 gives the monthly figures of marriages in Petrograd and Moscow during the years 1913 and 1914.

The number of marriages in Petrograd and Moscow, it is true, is two and one-half to three times as great in July, as in June, 1914, but a still greater increase can be observed in Moscow between the months of June and July, in 1913.[7] Thus, if "war-marriages" took place at all, they did so certainly on a much smaller scale than in many large cities of the western countries. The total number of marriages in Petrograd and Moscow in 1914 shows a slight decrease as compared with 1913.

However, as the variations in the number of marriages in the capitals will be dealt with in greater detail in a later section of this monograph we shall now proceed to study the change in the number of marriages on the basis of the annual data in all provinces of European Russia for which such data are available.

The information collected by the "Commission for investigating the effect of the War upon Public Health" and published in its *Proceedings* gives, as regards the period of the War, the following data as to marriages:

Data for:

50 provinces of European Russia	1914
27 provinces (including the province of Moscow and cities of Moscow and Petrograd)	1914, 1915
10 provinces (including the province of Moscow and cities of Moscow and Petrograd) . . .	1914, 1915, 1916
6 provinces (including the cities of Moscow and Petrograd)	1914, 1915, 1916, 1917

[7] A. A. Chuprov, *op. cit.*, p. 121.

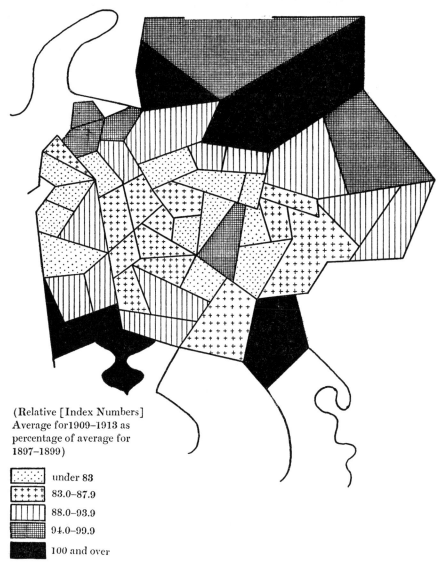

(Relative [Index Numbers]
Average for 1909–1913 as
percentage of average for
1897–1899)

under 83
83.0–87.9
88.0–93.9
94.0–99.9
100 and over

CHART VI

*Relative Changes in the Marriage Rates for Fifty Provinces
of European Russia, Averaged for the Years 1909–1913, as
Compared with the Marriage Rates Averaged for the Years
1897–1899.*

* Data from Appendix IV.

The provinces included in these groups for which information is available, can be seen in Appendix V, where the total number of marriages is given for each province, as well as the ratio of each number to the corresponding data for 1913 (i.e., the index number for each province). The distribution of the twenty-seven provinces for which information exists for the years 1914 and 1915, and that of the ten provinces for which we possess data for the year 1916 also, will be seen from Charts VII and VIII. We have no information for 1915 (Chart VII) for a whole series of western provinces, as well as for the provinces of Ryazan, Simbirsk, and Penza in the central region, and those of Orenburg, Ufa, Astrakhan, and the Don Territory, in the eastern and southeastern regions. The information available for 1916 (Chart VIII) extends to Petrograd (city) and Moscow (city and province), and to five provinces of the central region, also to the provinces of Vitebsk, Voronezh, Samara, and Saratov. For 1917, the available data refer to Petrograd and Moscow cities, to four central provinces (Vladimir, Kaluga, Tver, and Yaroslav) and to those of Vitebsk, in the west, and Saratov, in the southeast.

Table 16 shows the number of marriages in each of these groups of provinces for the years for which information is available. The figures for 1913 are included in this table for purposes of comparison.[8]

TABLE 16

Number of Marriages in Specified Groups of Provinces for 1913 and the War Years.[9]

	Number of Marriages			
Year	In 50 provinces of European Russia	In 27 provinces*	In 10 provinces*	In 6 provinces†
1913	1,015,642	591,587	220,041	118,406
1914	843,704	466,509	179,151	100,986
1915	. . . .	245,360	92,060	54,000
1916	. . . .	. . . .	93,503	51,591
1917	. . . .	. . . .	. . . .	76,687

* Including the province of Moscow and the cities of Moscow and Petrograd.

† Including the cities of Moscow and Petrograd.

[8] Cf. *Proceedings* of the Narkomzdrav Commission, p. 104.

[9] *See* Appendix V, for basic data by provinces.

Reckoning with the number of marriages for the year 1913 as 100, we obtain the indexes of the changes in the number of marriages during the years of the War.[10] (See Table 17.)

TABLE 17

Index Numbers for the Number of Marriages in Groups of Provinces, 1913 and the War Years[11] (1913 = 100).

Year	In 50 provinces of European Russia	In 27 provinces*	In 10 provinces*	In 6 provinces†
1913	100	100	100	100
1914	83	79	81	85
1915	..	42	42	46
1916	..	..	43	44
1917	..	..	..	65

* Including the province of Moscow and the cities of Moscow and Petrograd.

† Including the cities of Moscow and Petrograd.

The author of the article in the *Proceedings* of the Narkomzdrav Commission makes the following comment regarding these figures: "The evolution of the number of marriages during the years of the War shows on the whole considerable uniformity. Compared with the numbers for 1913, the number of marriages in 1914 in the whole of European Russia decreased by 17 per cent; in twenty-seven provinces by 21 per cent; in ten provinces by 19 per cent; and in six provinces by 15 per cent. In 1915 the decrease below the numbers for 1913 in twenty-seven provinces reached 58 per cent; in ten provinces, 58 per cent; and in six provinces, 54 per cent. In 1916 the decrease in ten provinces reached 57 per cent, and in six provinces, 56 per cent. The sharpest decrease, thus, took place in 1915 when it reached 58 per cent of the number of marriages in the last pre-war year (1913)."

This latter statement is based merely on the information possessed

[10] In the year 1913 the number of marriages was a little above the normal trend line, and then this year is not a very convenient base for comparison. But an average for a series of pre-war years would be a still less convenient base, since the pre-war marriage rate showed a general tendency to decline and an average for a series of years cannot be considered as representative for the moment immediately preceding the War.

[11] *See* Appendix V for basic data.

Index Numbers as Propor-
tion; 1915 marriages relative to 1913 marriages as
base, 100

no information

under 32.5

32.5–36.6

36.7–48.2

48.3 and over

CHART VII

*Showing the Provincial Indexes for Number of Marriages in
1915 as Compared with the Number in 1913.**

* Data available for twenty-seven provinces, see Appendix V.

for the groups of ten and six provinces, including in each case the cities of Petrograd and Moscow. The author seems thus to consider them as representative of the entire territory of European Russia, and bases his opinion on the fact that the evolution of the ratios for the different groups of provinces was in the preceding years more or less uniform. There is certainly some foundation for this statement, but it is insufficient to warrant an accurate conclusion. In the first place, attention should be drawn to the composition of the group comprising six provinces and the cities of Petrograd and Moscow, which is artificial and highly different in character from the generality of European Russia. It gives a marked preponderance to the urban population, as a result of the inclusion of the large population of the two capitals, numbering millions, in the total for only six provinces. The change in number of marriages is, however, widely different in towns from that among the rural population, and especially different in large cities: the decrease in the number of marriages is definitely smaller in the towns than in the country, for the proportion of men drawn into the army was much smaller in the towns, owing to the liberal grant of exemptions from military service to persons working for national defense. If we eliminate Petrograd and Moscow from the groups of twenty-seven, ten, and six provinces, and compute the indexes for the number of marriages in these provinces and separately in Petrograd and in Moscow, we obtain the results shown in Table 18.

TABLE 18

Indexes for Changes in the Numbers of Marriages in Provinces and Capital Cities Separately for Years 1913 to 1917, Inclusive (1913 = 100).[12]

Years	27 provinces	10 provinces	6 provinces	Petrograd	Moscow
1913	100	100	100	100	100
1914	78	80	82	98	96
1915	40	38	37	86	74
1916	..	38	34	84	76
1917	..	..	49	153	99

We immediately notice in Table 18 that the group of six provinces including the capitals (column 4) comprised a small rural

[12] *See* Appendix V for basic data.

territory where the decrease in the number of marriages was greater than the average decrease in the whole group, and that the decrease in the two capital cities themselves was notably less than when rural areas were included. It is clear that a fortuitously chosen group of six provinces cannot be taken as representative of the whole of European Russia, especially a group so abnormally composed. The fact that the index of marriages in this group for 1915 was more or less close to that of 1915 for a much larger territory of European Russia could be a mere coincidence and does not allow us to judge concerning changing numbers of marriages throughout the following years in the whole country. Though to a less extent, it is also true of the group of ten provinces with capital cities. Especially the conclusion that the maximum decrease falls in 1915 is not applicable either to the territory of the six or ten provinces, if the influence of the capitals be eliminated. The decline in the number of marriages was accentuated in 1916 in the six provinces and remained stationary in the ten provinces.

However, any estimate based on the six or ten provinces *without* the capital cities would constitute an error of overestimating the average decline in the number of marriages in European Russia. As can be seen from the 1915 data these provinces without the capital cities showed a decline somewhat exceeding that for the greater territory of twenty-seven provinces. On the other hand, the conditions prevailing in Petrograd and Moscow must to a certain measure affect the figures for the whole European Russia, though they did so to a much smaller extent than they did for the territory of the six-province group. We may, therefore, with great probability assert that the index of marriages in the six provinces excluding the capitals, and on the other hand, that same index including the capitals, constitute some rough *limits* between which the average index of the number of marriages in European Russia must be sought.

Thus we are led to suppose that the number of marriages in European Russia in 1916 probably bore to the number of 1913 in proportion somewhere between 34 and 44 per cent, and in 1917, in proportion between 49 and 65 per cent.[13]

For 1915 the index of twenty-seven provinces (42 per cent) may

[13] Properly these figures can be considered as limits only for European Russia without provinces adjacent to the front, because these last provinces were in a peculiar situation owing to the accumulation there of great masses

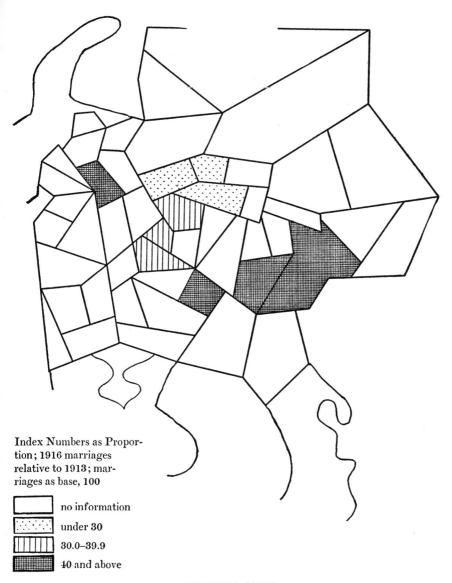

Index Numbers as Proportion; 1916 marriages relative to 1913; marriages as base, 100

- no information
- under 30
- 30.0–39.9
- 40 and above

CHART VIII

Showing the Provincial Indexes for the Relative Number of Marriages in 1916 as Compared with the Number in 1913.

* Data available for 1916 for only ten provinces, see Appendix V.

be accepted as approximately expressing the average decline of the number of marriages in European Russia (without the provinces adjacent to the front), providing the necessary reservations are remembered as to the fact that we have to do with a sample.

It is interesting to consider the question to the extent to which this enormous decline in the number of marriages during the years of the War, on the one hand, is the direct result of the withdrawal of a considerable number of men of 18–43 years, and on the other hand the result of abstinence from marriage by the home-staying population, because of unfortunate economic or other conditions due to the War. In order to answer this question it is not sufficient to compare the indexes showing decline in the number of marriages in each year with the proportion of men of military age drawn into the army at about the middle of any given year. In view of the irregularity with which the callings are distributed in the course of each year the computation needs greater accuracy. We must estimate for each calendar

of mobilized men who were only partially isolated from the civil population. In these provinces the decline of the number of marriages could be, of course, less than in capital cities. It is just the territory of European Russia without the provinces near to the front that is interesting for us in our further investigations. The territory adjacent to the front, with its specific conditions, should be an interesting independent object of study, but, unfortunately, the data relative to that territory are too faulty.

The territory of European Russia without provinces adjacent to the front, on which territory, perforce, we will concentrate our attention, is pretty well represented by the group of twenty-seven provinces with capitals for which we have the data on marriages till 1915. In this group is only one province adjacent to the front (Vitebsk), but the exclusion of this province leaves the average index of marriages for 1915 (that is forty-two) almost without change.

In this connection it is to be noted that from fifty provinces of European Russia the following were theaters of hostilities: Livonia, Courland, Kovno, Vilna, Grodno, Vitebsk, Minsk, Volhynia. In the autumn of 1915, after the occupation of Poland by the Central Powers, the middle part of the front passed through the provinces of Kovno, Vilna, and Grodno; up till the beginning of 1916 it had advanced to the province of Minsk. Besides the mentioned provinces, some unimportant operations took place in the province of Bessarabia, but also independently of this fact we must consider this province (as well as the provinces of Podolia, Kiev, and Mogilev, near to the front) as being to some extent in an analogous situation as to the accumulation of great masses of mobilized men (in Mogilev especially, General Headquarters was situated).

year the approximate number of "full twelve-months-at-home" before mobilization, spent by the male population of military age in each year. We must further calculate the proportion that the number of these units—which we shall designate as man-years—bear to the initial number of men of military age in 1913, that is, the effective relative decrease. This ratio or index for the decrease in the number of men of military age should then be compared with the index for the declining number of marriages. Such calculation should be easily made if based on the actual data showing the number of men called to the colors at different dates in European Russia. (See Appendix II.)

A supplementary question arises, however, as to the influence exerted by the peace-time army. If we assume that soldiers married in peace-time at the same rate as the rest of the population, and that it was war alone which created for them the same isolation as affected other categories of mobilized men, then the number of soldiers in the peace-time army should be added to the initial figure of the male population in 1913, and also included in the figure for men called to the colors since the outbreak of the War. If, on the contrary, we assume that even in peace-time soldiers were isolated and that marriages of soldiers occurred only rarely, then the number of men of the peace-time army should be excluded both from the number of men called to the colors during the War, and from the initial figure of the male population in 1913. In reality, neither of these assumptions is correct; the truth lies between them—the actual marriage rate among soldiers was less than that of the civil population, but never zero. It is desirable therefore to make both calculations, the results obtained representing the two extremes of estimate; we shall see that these two figures differ only slightly.

Another difficulty arises from the fact that we do not know what part of the peace-time army (approximately 1,400,000 men) falls according to their origin to European Russia. If we assume, on the basis of the population, that this part was one million men, we may commit an error of 100,000 to 200,000 men, but in view of the rough character of our calculation, this error is of negligible importance.

As we are comparing the number of marriages in the years of the War with that in 1913, we should choose as an initial figure for the male population, that for the middle of 1913. We have estimated, above, the total population of European Russia at 120 millions (at the beginning of 1914). As the natural increase of the population in 1913 was approximately 2 millions,[14] we may assume the population at the *middle* of 1913 as roughly 119 millions. The number of males will thus be 58,900,000 (according to the ratio of 49.5 per cent resulting from the figures of the Central Statistical Committee for January 1, 1914).[15] Assuming for 1913 the proportion of men 18 to 43 years old as the proportion cited in the 1897 census (i.e.— 36.2 per cent of the total number of males) then males of 18–43, in the middle of 1913 would number approximately 21.3 millions.

A calculation by our first suggested method (based on the assumption of a *normal* marriage rate among the soldiers in peace-time) would give the following result:[16]

Calculation for 1914: On the basis of the figures (reproduced in Appendix II) showing the estimated number of men actually mobilized and assuming that the first mobilization withdrew the entire peace-time army also from communication with the population, we shall find that out of the total of 21,300,000 of men of ages ranging from 18 to 43 years, the effective civilian man power may be calculated by means of the data in Table 19.

TABLE 19

Approximate Time Spent at Home as Civilians during 1914 by the Men of Military Age in European Russia.

Number of months spent at home[17]	Number of men
6⅗ months (January 1 to July 18)*	21,300,000
The next ⅛ of a month	17,810,000
The next 2 months	17,170,000
The next ¼ of a month	16,930,000
The next 1½ months	16,370,000
The next 1½ months	16,200,000

* All dates in this monograph are given in accordance with the Russian calendar.

[14] More precisely 1,930,000.   [15] *Cf.* above, p. 18.

[16] In all our further calculations, we shall depend on the age of the mobilized men *at the date of their mobilization* and shall not take into account the change in the age during the three years of the War. If we were to allow for this factor, our calculation would become extremely complicated without appreciably affecting the results.

[17] The calculation in *parts of months* makes a somewhat strange impres-

If we multiply by the number of men the corresponding number of months during which they were free from military service, sum the results, and divide the sum by 12, we shall obtain the figure of 19,180,000, representing the number of full man-years of freedom from military duty during 1914. The decrease, as compared with 1913, is thus 21,300,000 minus 19,180,000, or 2,120,000 man-years and is not fully explained by deaths.[18]

This result would be sufficiently correct, if we did not have to allow for the natural increase of men of the age in question, owing to the growing up of the younger generation. The natural increase of the population declined during the years of the War (though not in 1914), but this fall was principally due to the fall in the birth rate; the average mortality, in European Russia, evidently increased, but increased to an insignificant extent. The fall of the natural increase of the population therefore affected mainly the infantile part thereof. In regard to the natural increase of the age-group, 18 to 43, we may assume its progress to have been normal, not only in 1914, but also in the following years. Its normal increase can be crudely estimated at about 17.5 per cent of the total normal increase on the basis of the proportion of men of that group in the total population.

sion, but we use it in order to emphasize the crude character of our computations; the calculation in days gives essentially the same results.

We must also observe, that in our computations we can take into account only the *moment of mobilization,* after which the mobilized still remained some months in the reserve battalions, situated in diverse localities in the country; during this period of preparation (which in certain periods of the War was reduced to some weeks) the situation of the mobilized as demographical factor was more or less analogous to that of the peace-time army. Perhaps their isolation from their families and from the population generally was somewhat stronger than for the peace-time army. Although we cannot take into account the mentioned circumstance, it hardly can be of great importance for our crude computations. But in any case we must remember that a certain little exaggeration of the decline of man-years at home could result from this moment.

[18] We may reach an essential similar conclusion by departing from the numbers of men called to the colors at each mobilization and by multiplying them by the numbers of months spent by those men in the army. But we believe that the logic of the computation will be more forcibly brought out if the decrease in the number of men is determined as the difference between their pre-war number and the number of full years spent at home by men of military age during the War.

The normal pre-war annual increase should be estimated at 2 million persons and that of the men of the age-group 18 to 43 years, at 350,000 per annum. When computing, therefore, the decrease of full years, spent by the men among the population in 1914, compared to that in 1913, we should add to the figure of full years of 1914, as calculated above on the basis of the numbers mobilized, both the natural increase from the middle of 1913 to the beginning of 1914—that is, 175,000—and half the annual increase of 1914 (assuming this increase to be uniformly distributed over the whole year)—or another 175,000—which gives a total of 350,000.[19] The total number of full years spent at home in 1914 will then amount to 19,530,000, or roughly 19.5 millions, which represents 91.5 per cent of the number of men of that same group in 1913. The effective loss will thus be 1,800,000, or 8.5 per cent.

Calculation for 1915: The number of months spent at home by the men of the 18–43 age-group during 1915 is shown in Table 20.

TABLE 20

Approximate Time Spent as Civilians during 1915 by the Men of Military Age.

Number of months spent at home	Number of men
First ⅔ of a month	15,815,000
The next 2⅓ months	15,255,000
The next 1½ months	14,705,000
The next 2¾ months	14,230,000
The next ¼ month	13,410,000
The next ¾ month	13,135,000
The next 1¾ months	12,315,000
The next 2 months	11,950,000

On the basis of these figures and proceeding by the same method as above, we obtain, as representing the total of full years, without allowance for the natural increase, the figure of 13,850,000. The natural increase from the middle of 1913 to the beginning of 1915 is 525,000, to which figure half of the increase for 1915, 175,000, must

[19] The accuracy of this calculation obviously is open to challenge because in reality the rate of natural increase of different age-groups is not uniform. However, as the natural increase is small as compared with the number of men-years, the possible error is of minor importance.

be added, or 700,000 in all. Adding this number to 13,850,000, we obtain a total of 14,550,000 full years, or 68.3 per cent of the total of 1913, spent at home by the men of the 18–43 age-group. The total effective loss equals 6,750,000, or 31.7 per cent.

TABLE 21

Approximate Civilian Time, 1916, by Men of Military Age.

Number of months spent at home	Number of men
First 1 month	11,940,000
Next 1⅚ months	11,670,000
Next 1⅔ months	11,300,000
Next 3⅓ months	10,700,000
Next ⅚ of a month	10,375,000
Next 1⅙ months	9,915,000
Next 2⅙ months	9,615,000

The total number of full years without introducing the necessary correction for the natural increase amounts to 10,750,000, but if the natural increase (1,050,000) is added to 11,800,000—or 55.4 per cent of the total of 1913—the total loss amounts to 9,500,000—or 44.6 per cent.

We can give no figures for the year 1917, for the irregular demobilizations that took place and the absence of statistical information frustrate all such attempts. The rise in the number of marriages that occurred in 1917 is connected with this irregular demobilization.

On the basis of our second computation (that is, assuming that the number of marriages of soldiers in peace-time was insignificant), we obtain for the year 1914 (the peace-time army being *excluded from* the initial total for 1913, *as well as from* the number of mobilized men) the figures in Table 22.

TABLE 22

Civilian Months, 1914, of Men of Military Age.

Number of months spent at home	Number of men
6⅗ months	20,300,000
⅛ of a month	17,810,000
2 months	17,170,000
¼ of a month	16,930,000
1½ months	16,370,000
1½ months	16,200,000

The total number of full years, without allowing for the natural increase, is 18,650,000; or with the necessary correction, it reaches 19,000,000, or 93 per cent of the figure for 1913 (20.3 millions). The total loss will thus be 1,300,000 or 6.4 per cent.

The number of men and months for the years 1915 and 1916 remains the same as in the first computation (since it is here immaterial whether the peace-time army is eliminated from the initial figure *or added to* the number of men mobilized in the first year of the War). The only change is that the initial figure is 20.3 millions instead of 21.3 millions. The proportion of "full years" (14,550,000) to that figure in 1915 will be 71.7 per cent. The total loss will accordingly be 5,750,000, or 28.3 per cent. The total of "full years" in 1916 (11,800,000) is 58.1 per cent, and the total loss 8,600,000, or 41.9 per cent.

Comparing the two calculations, we obtain the following contrasts :[20]

Indexes of Decrease of the Male Population Owing to Mobilizations (Measured in Man-years) (The Decrease as Percentage of the Number of Men in 1913).

Years	By first method of calculation	By second method of calculation
1914	8.5	6.4
1915	31.8	28.3
1916	44.6	41.9

As will be seen, the difference between the results is inconsiderable; we may therefore estimate with sufficient accuracy that the effective loss or decrease of the male population due to mobilizations in 1914

[20] As follows from the preceding, each of these indexes is computed by taking the decrease below 1913 status, *i.e.,* the difference between the number of given year and the number of 1913 and by calculating what percentage this difference is of the number for 1913. We see that this is not an index number in the proper and strict meaning of the word, for the last signifies the *ratio of two values of one and the same quantity* in two different points of time (in our case, for instance, the percentage of the number of men at home in 1915 to the number of them in 1913, and not the ratio of the difference between two numbers to the first of these numbers). But we hope to be able to use without misunderstandings the word index also in the last sense, that is, to use it in a wider sense of a *relative* in which sense it is often used.

ranged from 6 to 9 per cent; in 1915, from 28 to 32 per cent; and in 1916, from 42 to 45 per cent.

We are ready now for Table 23 which gives comparison of the relative decrease of the male population from 18 to 43 years of age with the relative decline in the numbers of marriages, both of which as compared with the pre-war year 1913—this is part of the problem we set before us for investigation.

TABLE 23

Indexes of Decrease of the Male Population Measured in Terms of Full Man-years for the Age-group, 18–43 Years, and Indexes of Decrease of the Number of Marriages.

Year	Loss of full man-years[21] (No. of men in 1913 = 100)	Decrease of marriages (No. of marriages in 1913 = 100)
1914	6 to 9	17
1915	28 to 32	58
1916	42 to 45	56 to 66

We thus see that in 1914 and 1915 the relative decrease in the number of marriages greatly exceeds the relative decline of the male population. In 1914 the decrease due to mobilization is approximately twice as large as the marriage decrease and in 1915 it is

[21] We have seen above (p. 52) that the marriage indexes of Table 23 can be considered as more or less characteristic for the territory of European Russia without provinces, adjacent to the front. The indexes of man loss, that are compared with them in Table 23, can be also considered as approximately characteristic for this territory, although they are based on the data for all fifty provinces of European Russia. Of course the excluding of the provinces adjacent to the front would reduce a little the indexes of man loss, because, as we have seen on pp. 30–31, in these provinces the percentage of mobilized men should have been to some extent higher than in other provinces. But as this last percentage generally varies little and, on the other hand, the provinces adjacent to the front are an unimportant part of European Russia, we can be sure that the average indexes of man loss would change very little by excluding the territory adjacent to the front. We can test it in computing, on the base of Table 5, the average index of changes in the female proportion for all forty-six provinces of this table, and then for territory remaining after excluding the provinces adjacent to the front: the first index is 124.2, the second 123.4, which is a negligible difference.

again almost twice as large. Though slightly less in 1916, the difference is still great.

The following consideration might lead us to make some corrections in our calculations. Among the mobilized men from 18 to 43 years old, the younger ages preponderate and these ages have a greater influence on the number of marriages than the others. On the other hand, the class of men of more than 43 years of age remained unaffected by military service and this fact has also a certain bearing on the number of marriages. To allow for these two factors in a precise manner is impossible, but the approximation that we give below will show that the corresponding corrections should not greatly affect the results of our calculation as regards the years 1914 and 1915.

We can apply the same method that we employed above to determine the number of full years spent at home and the loss in full years for the group of men of ages ranging from 18 to 43 years, to the group of men whose ages range from 18 to 26 years (though the degree of accuracy will be still less). This age-group comprises all soldiers of the peace-time army, the men of the 1914 to 1919 classes and a part of the territorials; it does not, on the other hand, include the reserves. We shall assume that this group constitutes slightly more than 15 per cent of the total male population of 1913 (according to the proportion established for 1897), or approximately 9 million men (the older group from 27 to 43 years will accordingly number 12.3 millions). The results of a calculation for the younger group (based on our first assumption) [22] are given in Table 24.

TABLE 24

Decrease of Number of Males in the Younger Age-group.

	Male population of the age-group 18 to 26 years		
Year	Number of full years spent at home (in thousands)	Net decrease of men compared to 1913 (in thousands)	Index of decrease (decrease as percentage of 1913 numbers)
1914	8,350	650	7.2
1915	5,500	3,500	38.9
1916	3,500	5,500	61.1

[22] *See* above, p. 54.

Compared with the former computation dealing with the age-group 18 to 43 years old (first method) the result will be as shown in Table 25.

TABLE 25

Decrease of the Number of Men Due to Mobilization.

Year	Decrease as compared with 1913 (Numbers)			Index of decrease (Decrease as percentage of 1913 numbers)	
	Age-group 18 to 43 years	Age-group 18 to 26 years	Age-group 27 to 43 years	Age-group 18 to 26 years	Age-group 27 to 43 years
	(in thousands)			(percentages)	
1914	1,800	650	1,150	7.2	9.3
1915	6,750	3,500	3,250	38.9	26.4
1916	9,500	5,500	4,000	61.1	32.5

As will be seen, the younger group in 1914 lost, proportionately, slightly less than the older one. In 1915, and especially in 1916, the losses of the younger class greatly surpassed those of the older class. This is to be explained by the fact that a great part of the men mobilized at the beginning of the War belonged to the reserves, that is to the group of men between 27 and 43 years of age, as well as to the fact that the levies of recruits in anticipation of the normal dates took place chiefly in the years of 1915 and 1916.

When computing the number of marriages, we should finally take into account the third group of men, those over 43 years of age, who were not called for service in the army.[23]

Table 26 shows to what extent the proportions of each of these three groups of men could influence the marriage index; this table is based on data for 1910.[24]

Taking into account the fact that in Russia the marriageable age begins with 18 years, we may assume that 96 per cent of the total number of male persons marrying belong to the group of men between 18 and 43 years of age, an age-group liable to military service. Within these age limits, 70 per cent, roughly, belong to the younger group between 18 and 26 years and 26 per cent to the older group between 27 and 43 years of age. Barely 4 per cent of persons

[23] This group probably sustained some loss, owing to an increased mortality, but it cannot greatly affect our calculation.

[24] Yakovenko, *Meditsinskaya Statistika* (*Medical Statistics*) [Moscow-Leningrad], p. 40.

TABLE 26

Percentage of Marrying Men, by Age-groups.

Age group	Percentage of marrying men of given age-groups to the total of men marrying in European Russia
20 and below	30.7
21 to 25	36.2
Total for the age-group below 26 years	66.9
26 to 30	18.8
31 to 35	5.7
36 to 40	3.2
Total for the age-group 26 to 40 years	27.7
Total for the age-group below 41 years	94.6
41 to 45	2.1
46 to 50	1.5
51 and above	1.8
Total for the age-group 41 years and above . . .	5.4

marrying belong to the group whose age exceeds 43 years and who were exempted from military service.

In order to estimate more accurately the influence of the decline

TABLE 27

Index for Decrease of the Civilian Male Population (1914).

Age-group	Index of decrease[25] (1)	Weights (age proportions among marrying men)[26] (2)	Index for decrease weighted for age (Read as percentage decrease below 1913 status) (3) (Col. 1 × 2)
18 to 26	7.2	0.70	5.04
27 to 43	9.3	0.26	2.42
44 and above	6.0	0.04	.24
Average weighted index of average decrease (per hundred)			7.70

[25] See Table 25.
[26] See Table 26 and following text for these weights.

in the male civilian population on the falling marriage index, it is necessary to weight the decrease sustained by each age-group with reference to the proportionate number of men of that age among those marrying. The weighted decreases are shown in Table 27.

Proceeding by the same method, the *weighted* index of average decrease compared with the *crude* index for the age-group 18 to 43 (according to the first method), reveals the following approximate results, omitting the decimal part of the index reading.

TABLE 28

Decrease in Male Population Weighted and Crude Indexes Compared.

Year	Weighted index of average decrease for the three age-groups (Read as percentage	Crude index of decrease for the age-group 18 to 43 decrease below 1913 status)
1914	8	9
1915	34	32
1916	51	45

As will be seen, the difference for the years 1914 and 1915 is not great—nor does it reach 6 per cent until 1916.[27]

If we base our estimate on our second method of calculation, the corrections would be still less important, since the elimination of the peace time army reduces materially the losses of the younger group.

Let us compare the weighted average index of decrease in the male population with the index of the marriage decrease. The reader should remember that we are using here the figures obtained by the first method which gives the higher rate of decrease of the male population.

[27] Since within each of the analyzed groups, the ages exerting the greater influence on the marriage index were also those most affected by the mobilizations, the question may arise, would not the corrections be considerably greater if we should subdivide the mobilized ages into smaller age-groups and make our calculations on the basis of the loss sustained by each of these smaller groups, taking into account the influence of each of them on the marriage rate. We have made such a calculation (distributing the total number of mobilized men into six groups), but the results differ but slightly and only for 1916 from those obtained by a division into two groups. The index of average decrease for 1914 is 8 per cent (no difference), for 1915 it is 34 per cent (no difference), and for 1916 it is 52 per cent (instead of 51 per cent).

TABLE 29

Decrease in Civilian Male Population and in Marriage Numbers (Weighted Index Numbers).

Year	Weighted average index of decrease in the civilian male population[28] (Read as percentage decrease from 1913 status)	Index of decrease in the number of marriages[29]
1914	8	17
1915	34	58
1916	51	56–66

We see that even when we use the weighted indexes for population decrease we discover a great excess in the fall of the marriage index as compared with the index of decrease in the civilian male population, for the years of 1914 and 1915; the difference for 1916 is smaller.

These computations, summarized in Table 29, enable us to state that the decline in the marriage number was due not only to the direct influence of the calling of a large number of men to the colors, but also to the abstention from marriage of the home-staying population since the decrease in the marriage index was so much greater than could reasonably be accounted for by the decrease in the male population due to mobilization.

The influence of the factor of abstention from marriage relatively to the direct factor of absence of men was greater in 1914 and 1915 than in 1916.

Let us now consider the territorial distribution of the declining marriage index. Chart VII gives for each province[30] the proportion of the number of marriages in 1915 to the number in 1913. Unhappily here our information is rather scarce. We may state on the whole, however, that the decline in the number of marriages affected chiefly the central industrial and agricultural provinces as well as two of the southern and southwestern provinces. It is less accentu-

---

[28] *See* Table 28.   [29] *See* Table 23.

[30] In addition to the twenty-seven provinces, the information for which is given for 1915, by the Narkonzdrav Commission, the chart includes also data for the provinces of Poltava and Chernigov, which we borrow from the publication of the Ukrainian Academy of Science, quoted above (*see* p. 6, n. 9). Data for the other provinces is given also in Appendix V.

ated[31] in those eastern and northeastern provinces for which we have data and in the extreme north (Archangel) as well as in Esthonia and Vitebsk in the northwest. Chart VIII shows the provincial index numbers for marriages in 1916 as compared with those in 1913, covering only the ten provinces for which we have data. This shows, so far as we can judge, that the general tendencies we observed in 1915 remained unaltered in 1916. The data for 1917, although for the six provinces only (not shown on any map), are very similar, though too limited in evidence to enable us to draw any full conclusions.

It is unnecessary as well as impossible to make for each province the computations regarding the decrease in the male population (expressed in "full years"), that we have made for the fifty provinces of European Russia taken as a whole, in order to obtain an explanation of these charts. The chief difficulty would lie in the lack of precise data concerning the successive drafts of men mobilized in each province (they depended on the age composition of the population and on the proportion of men fit for military service in each age-group). But we can make some calculations of correlation, in order to get an idea of the factors determining provincial differences shown by the marriage index. Some information can be derived from the correlation between the war-time index of the falling number of marriages and those indexes which show the decline of the civilian male population. This last information is implied in the index of the increased proportion of females in rural districts which we have already cited (see Chart III).[32] It is interesting, moreover, to investigate the question of whether there is a correlation between the index of the falling number of marriages during the War and the marriage rate per thousand population in pre-war times.

As regards the correlation between the war-time falling marriage index and the index of the decrease of males, this study will certainly not disclose any very new inferences. It presents, however, some points of interest, as it enables one to form an opinion as to the reliance that can be placed on the material with which we are working

[31] That is, showed the lowest indexes, lightest shading on the Chart VII.

[32] We remind the reader that the rural population constitutes more than 85 per cent of the total population of European Russia and that therefore the average demographical data for the country as a whole deal mainly with conditions of the rural districts.

(this, as mentioned above, requires to be constantly watched). The following question may certainly be raised: Is not the pronounced fall in the number of marriages that we observed during the War primarily due to the increasing defectiveness of marriage registration and to the inaccuracy of statistical records? The presence of a pronounced correlation would show that the data possess that self-consistency which would not have existed if the material used had been too imperfect to be of value. The investigation of the correlation with the pre-war marriage rates is also interesting from another point of view. If our above conclusion is correct, namely that the decline in the number of marriages during the War was not merely the direct result of the decrease of the male population but was also due to a voluntary factor, namely—abstinence from marriage by the male population while still at home—then it will be natural to expect that the provinces with a low pre-war marriage rate (which are generally characterized by a higher educational level and less patriarchal habitudes) would react more strongly to the unfavorable conditions of war-time by a greater abstinence from marriage than the provinces with a high pre-war marriage rate where the conditions of life were more patriarchal.[33]

This subject can be studied for 1915 alone, since the information for the succeeding years is recorded for too small a number of provinces. Moreover, the index of the increased proportion of females exists only for 1916 (on the basis of the agricultural census) and not for 1915. We shall thus be obliged to calculate on the basis of this 1916 index, assuming that there existed pronounced correlation between the provincial indexes of the decrease of the male population till 1915 and till 1916, on the strength of what we have seen existed in 1917 and 1916, by comparing Charts II and III. The territorial distribution of successive mobilizations over the territory of European Russia were more or less alike. Even if there were some deviations from this rule, the number of men mobilized in the first year of

---

[33] It might have been even more interesting to find out the correlation of the indexes of decline in the number of marriages during the War not with the pre-war marriage *rates,* but with the pre-war *indexes* of the *decline* in the marriage rate. The very casual character of the base figures for the computation of the pre-war decline in marriage rates (those for the years 1897 and 1899), however, makes it advisable to limit our investigation to the correlation with the marriage rates for 1909–1913. (*See* Appendix IV.)

the War was so great that it determined to a great extent the territorial distribution of the men called in the first and second years
taken together. We can, therefore, expect that the index of decrease
of the male population (or the index of the proportionate increase of
women) in 1915, if we had the data, would show in its territorial distribution, a pronounced likeness to this same index for 1916. For our
rough calculations the use of one or the other year's index is therefore admissible. In any case, if we find a correlation between the index of declining marriage number in 1915 and the index of decrease
in males for 1916 we shall draw, *a fortiori*, the conclusion that a similar correlation exists for the corresponding decrease of males index
in 1915.

That such a correlation exists between the proportionate increase
of females (1916) (or decrease of males) and the marriage index for
1915, can be surmised from a simple comparison of Chart VII with
Chart II. Corroborative evidence for twenty-seven provinces is
found in the correlation table (Table B[34]) compiled on the basis of
these two series.[35]

This Table B shows a rather significant inverse correlation between the index of marriages in 1915 as compared with those in 1913
and the index of the proportionate increase of females in 1916. Two
important exceptions only may be observed: one relating to the province of Esthonia and the other relating to Tambov.

We have already seen that the province of Tambov is in an exceptional situation as compared to neighboring provinces. We do not
know, but this deviation may be attributable to the inadequacy of
our data. As regards the province of Esthonia, though it is not immediately contiguous to the front, it is sufficiently near it to share in

[34] *See* above, p. 29, n. 34; Table B omitted here.

[35] The provinces of Kharkov and Vitebsk are eliminated from the table,
the first owing to the unreliability of the material, the second as being adjacent to the front. The region contiguous to the front is eliminated both in this
and in the further calculations, because as we have already seen (p. 52,
n. 13), the data of the natural growth of the population are least trustworthy
in these provinces and because they differ from all other provinces by their
peculiar situation because of an influx of men on military duty, who are only
partially isolated from the civil population. This fact may give quite unexpected results as regards the natural growth of the population, as will be
seen later, when the investigation of the birth rate is undertaken.

the conditions of such provinces.[36] At any rate we believe we are justified in excluding for computation of the coefficient of correlation these two provinces, which can obscure the general tendency of the remaining twenty-five provinces; a coefficient of correlation based on so few cases as we have to consider is greatly affected by any such extreme cases.

The coefficient of correlation (Table B[37]) for the twenty-five provinces is —0.55. This figure must be considered as indicating a moderate degree of correlation, but may also be considered of more significance if we take into consideration the fact that the correlation between the decline in the proportionate number of marriages in 1915 as compared with those in 1913 and the index for the decrease in the male population till 1916 is a secondary correlation achieved through the medium of a prior factor, namely the decrease in the number of males in 1915 (which we were unable to determine). In order that this secondary correlation should equal —0.55, the actual degree of correlation between the two series under consideration must be greater.

As regards the marriage index in 1915 and the pre-war marriage rate per thousand population we can again surmise a certain correlation between the two series, by comparing Charts V and VII. Correlation Table C[38] shows the correlation between these two series for twenty-seven provinces. (Data from Appendixes IV and V.)

We can see from this Table C a more or less definitely positive correlation again deranged by the same two extreme cases: the province of Tambov and that of Esthonia. Eliminating these extreme cases and calculating the correlation for the remaining twenty-five provinces, we obtain r = +0.56 which is also a significant coefficient of correlation, "positive" in character.[39]

The following question, however, may arise: Is not this a merely fictitious (spurious) correlation resulting from the influence of an intermediary variable—the index of decrease in the male population? We have seen that there is a rather strong degree of inverse correlation between the index of 1916 male population decrease and the

[36] *Cf.* p. 52, n. 13.
[37] *See* above, p. 29, n. 34; Table B omitted here.
[38] *See* above, p. 29, n. 34; Table C omitted here.
[39] "Positive" in the sense that the two variables seem to move in like direction.

1915 index of changes in the number of marriages. On the other
hand, the index of 1916 male population decrease has a marked degree of inverse correlation with the pre-war death rate. Since pre-
war death rates, birth rates, and marriage rates, all show a rather
uniform territorial distribution, it seems likely that a spurious correlation might exist between the 1916 index of decrease in the male
population and the pre-war marriage rate per thousand population.

Indeed, the coefficient of correlation between the pre-war marriage
rate per thousand, and the index of the decrease of the males up to
1916 for the same twenty-five provinces is negative (inverse) and
equals —0.24. (Data in Appendix IV.) It is clear, however, that
this correlation is not sufficient to have produced, jointly with the
correlation between the index of decrease of the males and the
changes in the number of marriages in 1915 (which equals —0.55),
the observed correlation between the pre-war marriage rate per
thousand population and the index of changes in the number of marriages in 1915 (with a coefficient of correlation of +0.56). (Table C
and text p. 69.) Operating on the basis of these three pairs of data
series and their coefficients of correlation, we find that the coefficient
of the partial (net) correlation between the war changes in the number of marriages (up to 1915) and the pre-war marriage rate is as
follows:

$$r_{1\,2\,3} = \frac{r_{12}-r_{13}\,r_{23}}{\sqrt{(1-r^2_{13})\,(1-r^2_{23})}} = \sqrt{\frac{+0.56-(-0.55)\,(-0.24)}{(1-0.55^2)\,(1-0.24^2)}} = +0.53$$

Thus, the positive correlation that we have observed between the
index of the number of marriages in 1915 and the average pre-war
marriage rate per thousand cannot be sufficiently explained by the
intermediary part we have tentatively assigned in our discussion
to the index of decrease in the civilian male population. The rather
high coefficient of direct correlation seems to corroborate our conclusion that the decline of the number of marriages during the War
was largely due not only to the calling in the army but also to the
abstinence from marriage on the part of the male population which
was not called in the army.

Marriages Among the Urban Population.

We have already seen from a comparison of the figures for Petrograd and Moscow with those for a group of provinces of European

Russia that the decrease in the number of marriages in large cities
was considerably smaller than in rural districts. We think this statement can be extended to cover the urban population as a whole,
though we possess but a small amount of trustworthy information
for the urban and rural population separately. It is available only
for several provinces of Ukraine.[40] In spite of the unreliable character of these figures (which is strongly emphasized by the editors of
the publication), they rather agree as to the general trend, in the
different decline of marriages in towns and in rural districts respectively.[41]

TABLE 30

*Number of Marriages in Villages and Cities of Ukraine, by
Provinces and Years.*

Province and year	Number	Index (1913 = 100)	Number	Index (1913 = 100)
Kiev:				
1913	31,395	100.0	6,140	100.0
1914	24,225	77.2	5,271	85.9
Kharkov:				
1913	27,286	100.0	4,931	100.0
1914	21,216	77.7	4,283	86.9
1915	9,530	34.9	2,768	56.1
Chernigov:				
1913	23,402	100.0	1,788	100.0
1914	17,812	76.1	1,234	69.0
1915	7,323	31.3	782	43.2

The smaller decline in the number of marriages in towns may be
explained, as indicated above, by the smaller percentage of men
drawn from the urban population into the army as a consequence of
the exemption from military service of men working for national defense. Such factories were chiefly concentrated in Petrograd and
Moscow, especially in the former, and this explains the slight effect
of the War in the number of marriages in that territory.

[40] *Cf.* above, p. 6, n. 9.

[41] As indicated in the Introduction, this source of information gives for
several provinces the figures for 1916 and 1917. They refer, however, to the
orthodox population, which prevents using them for comparisons with the
figures of previous years. They are moreover unreliable.

We possess for both capitals, in addition to the figures for the number of marriages, those referring to the numbers of the population during the War. The latter enable us to calculate the usual marriage rate per thousand population. (See Table 31.)

TABLE 31

Marriage Rates Per Thousand Population, Petrograd and Moscow, 1913 and War Years.[42]

Year	Petrograd	Moscow
1913	6.3	5.8
1914	6.0	5.5
1915	5.0	4.1
1916	4.7	3.9
1917	8.5	5.3

Both Petrograd and Moscow which, as we know, always had a low marriage rate,[43] showed a marked reduction even in this rate during the years of the War: in 1916, the rate in Petrograd dropped about 25 per cent and in Moscow, 33 per cent. But in 1917 we observe an increase: in Petrograd the marriage rate exceeds by a trifle over one-third the level of 1913—in Moscow it almost reaches it (about 91 per cent of the 1913 rate).

The absence of information regarding the number of men called to the colors from Petrograd and Moscow, as well as regarding the number and distribution according to sex of the population which crowded the capitals during the War, makes it impossible to calculate whether the decline of the marriage rate in any way corresponds to the change in the number of men. It seems likely, however, that this decline was chiefly due to the abstinence from marriage of the male population remaining in the cities. The portion of the male population of the capitals liable to military service and actually sent to the front was relatively very small and its loss was moreover com-

[42] Cf. *Materyali po Statistike Petrograda i Petrogradskoi Guberni (Statistical Returns for the City and Province of Petrograd)* [1921], V, 19; also *Krasnaya Moskwa (Red Moscow)*; also *Proceedings (Trudi)* of the Narkomzdrav Committee, p. 107.

[43] The low marriage rate in Petrograd and Moscow is chiefly explained by the important element of residents drawn from the rural population who usually returned to their native villages to marry.

pensated by the increase of the garrisons and the swelling of the institutions working for national defense. The available information on the sex distribution of the population of the capitals shows that while the proportion of men decreased slightly in Moscow, it even increased in Petrograd. The figures relating to Moscow are as follows:[44]

TABLE 32

Population of Moscow.

	Total population	Number of men	Percentage of men
According to census of 1912	1,617,700	878,000	54.26
As estimated on Nov. 20, 1915	1,983,700	1,049,000	52.88
As estimated on Feb. 1, 1917	2,017,200	1,017,000	50.43

For Petrograd with its suburbs, the figures for January 1, 1914, are 1,075,000 men, out of a population of 2,118,000, or 50.75 per cent males;[45] as estimated for November 1, 1915, these were 1,239,-000 men out of a population of 2,348,000 or 52.72 per cent males.

The Influence of the War on the Marital Status and on the Ages of the Couples Marrying.

On this point we possess but very scanty information. The available data regarding the rural population are for the Moscow province alone; for the urban population they are available only for Petrograd. Their analysis, however, is of some interest.

In the first place, as regards the previous marital status of the couple married in the rural areas of the province of Moscow, we find the following figures[46] (see Table 33).

[44] Calculated on the basis of the figures of *Krasnaya Moskwa* (*Red Moscow*).
[45] *Yearbook* of the Central Statistical Committee for 1914.
[46] The *Proceedings* of the Narkomzdrav Commission, p. 107.

TABLE 33

Previous Marital Status of Brides and Bridegrooms, by Years,
1913 to 1916 Inclusive, for Moscow.

| | Bridegrooms | | Brides |
| | Bachelors | Widowers | Widows |
Year	(Per hundred bridegrooms)		(Per hundred brides)
1913	90.8	9.2	5.2
1914	90.2	9.8	5.4
1915	80.1	19.9	11.6
1916	77.2	22.8	13.4

This Table 33 reveals a characteristic feature of the war period, the decreased proportion of bachelor bridegrooms and the increased proportion of widowers remarrying, probably because of the drop in the general supply of men and the correspondingly increased "demand" for widowers. On the other hand, as early as 1915, an important increase in the proportion of widows among the brides may be observed; this is evidently due to war-increased widowhood and a consequently increased "supply" of widows who under the stress of war-time living felt the necessity of remarrying.

If, on the other hand, we use as a basis of comparison the figures for Petrograd, we shall see that here the change in the previous marital status of the marrying couples is insignificant. (See Table 34.)

TABLE 34

Previous Marital Status of Brides and Bridegrooms, by Years,
1913 to 1917 Inclusive, for Petrograd.

| | Bridegrooms | | Brides | | |
| | | Widowers | | | |
Year	Bachelors	and divorced	Spinsters	Widows	Divorced
1913	90.9	9.1	91.6	7.5	0.9
1915	90.5	9.5	92.0	7.0	1.0
1916	89.3	10.7	91.9	7.0	1.1
1917	90.5	9.5	92.4	6.3	1.3

In Petrograd the proportion of bachelor bridegrooms decreased but slightly during the War down to 1916 and it increased in 1917. The proportion of widowers and divorced husbands shows little change; the proportion of widows did not increase at all; a persistent (though slight) increase falls to the share of divorced women. These figures confirm the statement that the War and service in the army had a comparatively small effect on the composition of the population of Petrograd.

This statement is also corroborated by the proportion of marriages according to the combined status of the contracting parties.[47]

TABLE 35

Combined Marital Status in Marriages—Petrograd.

Year	Marriages of bachelors with spinsters (per hundred marriages)	Other marriages (per hundred marriages)
1907–1909	85.1	14.9
1915	85.3	14.7
1916	84.3	15.7
1917	85.4	14.6

An increase is noticeable in the proportion of marriages where either the bridegroom, or the bride, had been divorced:

TABLE 36

Remarriage of Divorced Persons—Petrograd.

Year	Marriages in which one or both parties were previously divorced (per hundred marriages)
1907–1909	1.3
1915	1.7
1916	1.9
1917	2.1

The increase in the proportion of marriages with divorced men or women may also be noticed in the countries of western Europe. Its causes are the same as those leading to the so-called "difficult" marriages generally;[48] viz., the weakening of psychological restraints normally tending to prevent such marriages, such weakening being due to the War.

[47] *Materyali po Statistike Petrograda (Statistical Returns for the City and Province of Petrograd)*, V, 21.

[48] For an interesting treatment of this problem *see* A. A. Chuprov, *op. cit.*, pp. 128–129.

As regards the age of persons entering wedlock, we find again noticeable changes in respect of the population of Moscow.

TABLE 37

Age of Bridegrooms at Marriage, for Moscow, for the Years 1913–1916. (Percentages of Total Bridegrooms of Indicated Age-Groups in Years Indicated.)

| | | *Percentage of bridegrooms marrying* | | | |
Year	*Under 20 years*	*20 to 29 years*	*30 to 34 years*	*35 to 39 years*	*40 years and above*
1913	17.2	71.2	4.9	2.4	4.3
1914	17.8	69.3	5.4	2.8	4.7
1915	14.5	57.8	8.5	6.5	12.7
1916	12.6	53.0	10.4	7.2	16.8

The increase in the proportion of the older bridegrooms and the corresponding decrease in younger ages are strongly accentuated.

In Petrograd these phenomena are revealed only on a very reduced scale.

TABLE 38

Age of Bridegrooms at Marriage, for Petrograd, for the Years 1913–1917. (Percentages of Total Bridegrooms of Indicated Age-Groups in Years Indicated.)

| | | *Percentage of bridegrooms marrying* | | | |
Year	*Under 20 years*	*20 to 29 years*	*30 to 34 years*	*35 to 39 years*	*40 years and above*
1913	7.5	65.6	14.7	5.9	6.3
1915	7.3	65.1	13.6	6.6	7.4
1916	6.0	61.8	14.8	7.8	9.6
1917	6.6	66.8	12.6	6.5	7.5

In 1915 and 1916 the proportion of the bridegrooms under thirty years slightly diminished and that of bridegrooms older than thirty-six years correspondingly increased. But by 1917 the opposite tendency may already be noticed.

No important changes in the ages of the brides occurred.[49]

[49] See *Materyali po Statistike Petrograda (Statistical Returns for the City and Province of Petrograd)*, V, 22.

CHAPTER II

BIRTHS

RUSSIA has always been known for her high birth rate. In the five years immediately preceding the War (1909–1913) the average birth rate was 44.3 per thousand. From the end of the last century, however, the birth rate was declining in a marked degree as can be seen from the following figures relating to fifty provinces of European Russia.[1]

Periods	Average birth rate (per thousand population)
1894–1898	49.7
1899–1903	48.8
1904–1908	46.6
1909–1913	44.3

The territorial distribution of the birth rate in 1909–1913 may be seen in Chart IX, the territorial changes from the period 1895–1899 to that of 1909–1913 in Chart X.[2]

The general lines of the territorial distribution of the birth rate resemble those of the marriage rate. Whereas the highest rates are to be found in the eastern and southeastern provinces, they decrease in a westward direction. There are, of course, discrepancies in details;

[1] These computations are based on the data of the Central Statistical Committee taken from the yearbooks of the Committee and from Yakovenko, *op. cit.*, p. 36 (for the years for which the yearbooks are not available). As regards the population on which the computation of rates is based *see* above, p. 45, n. 1.

[2] Information on which Charts IX and X are based will be found in Appendix VI. It is the result of an investigation carried out by M. A. Edelson (Warsaw) and based on the figures furnished by the Central Statistical Committee and by the reports of the Chief Medical Inspector. M. Edelson kindly put the result of his investigation at the disposal of the author for the purpose of the present work. The birth rates for the period 1895–1899 are computed using the figures of the population of Russia in 1897. Information supplied by the reports of the Chief Medical Inspector is used in computing birth rates for the period 1909–1913. The final figures of the Chief Medical Inspector, as it was pointed out above, do not agree with those of the Central Statistical Committee as regards the size of the population, but the divergence between the territorial distribution of the figures is slight.

for instance, the concentration of marriage rates in several industrial provinces of the central area is not equally conspicuous in respect of the birth rates.

The territorial distribution of changes in the birth rate (Chart X), as compared with the distribution of the birth rate before the War, has the following particularities: In the western region several provinces of a low birth rate showed a small decrease; these were provinces of a traditionally low birth rate. On the other hand, a considerably declining birth rate is to be noticed in the provinces of the central agricultural area, which means that these provinces were quickly approaching the low birth-rate status of the western provinces. Lastly, the northern provinces show a great stability in their high birth rate, two of them (the provinces of Archangel and Vologda) even show an increase in the birth rate.

As regards the influence of the World War on the birth rate, it should be noticed that statistics concerning the number of births, as of marriages, during the war period, are not available for all provinces of European Russia, though the number of provinces for which the information exists is greater for the birth rate than for the marriage rate.

The *Proceedings* of the Narkomzdrav Commission give the rates for forty-one provinces in 1915; eighteen in 1916; and seven in 1917.

The provinces included in each of these groups of provinces can be judged from Appendix VII, which gives for separate provinces the total numbers of births for the years 1913, 1914, 1915, 1916, and 1917 and the indexes of these (ratio to the number for 1913).[3] Of a total of nine provinces for which information is lacking for the year 1915, eight are situated in the western region and one (Orenburg) in the east. The eighteen provinces included in the information available for 1916 are distributed as follows: one in the north (Archangel), three in the northwest, one in the southwest (Kherson), three in the southeast and ten in the central (chiefly the central industrial) region. The information available for 1917 extends only over five provinces of the central region, and also to the provinces of Kherson and Saratov.

We also possess birth data for the provinces and cities of Petrograd and Moscow for all these years. The author of the article in the

[3] *See* also Charts XI and XII.

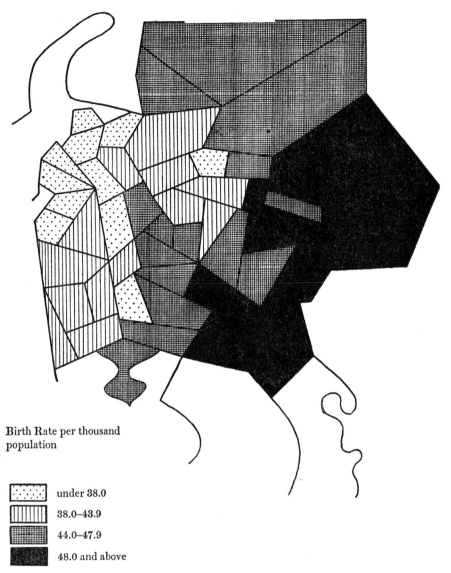

Birth Rate per thousand
population

- under 38.0
- 38.0–43.9
- 44.0–47.9
- 48.0 and above

CHART IX

*Birth Rates per Thousand Population in Fifty Provinces of
European Russia; Average Rates for the Period 1909–1913,
by Provinces.**

* Data from Appendix VI.

Proceedings of the Narkomzdrav Commission takes the latter figures
into account by adding them to the figures for the respective groups
of provinces.

The general results for the areas that are comprised in the available information may be seen from Table 39.[4]

TABLE 39

Number of Births, Provinces, and Cities, 1913 and War Years.

Number of births

Year	50 provinces of European Russia	41 provinces*	18 provinces*	7 provinces*
1913	5,252,805	4,542,698	1,934,384	742,806
1914	5,324,392	4,604,651	1,977,513	757,917
1915	....	3,930,100	1,692,097	655,433
1916	....	....	1,281,648	511,574
1917	....	....	....	400,369

* Including the province of Moscow and the cities of Moscow and Petrograd.

Assuming the figures for 1913 = 100, we obtain the index numbers for succeeding years as shown in Table 40.

TABLE 40

*Index Numbers for Births in War Years as Compared
with 1913 Births.*

Year	50 provinces of European Russia	41 provinces*	18 provinces*	7 provinces*
1913	100	100	100	100
1914	101	101	102	102
1915	..	87	87	88
1916	..	..	66	69
1917	..	..	..	54

* Including the province of Moscow and the cities of Moscow and Petrograd.

Judging by this table, the indexes for 1914–1915 for the various
groups of provinces are very similar. The group of eighteen provinces for which information is available for 1916 may be considered

[4] *Proceedings* of the Narkomzdrav Commission, p. 109.

as more or less representative of the whole territory of European Russia for the following reasons: the indexes of this group for the years 1914 and 1915 come very near to those of the forty-one provinces; the provinces included in this group are situated in various parts of European Russia, and comprise 40 per cent of the total number of births in European Russia; and lastly, taking into consideration their large population, it seems likely that the addition of the capitals did not exert a great influence on the birth rate, especially as the birth rate in Petrograd and Moscow does not differ from the general birth rate to the same extent as does the marriage rate. This may be seen from Appendix VII. As regards the group of seven provinces, we feel there is no justification for taking their birth rate as representative of the whole of Russia in 1917. The nine territorial units included in this group are situated in the same part of the Empire and within this group the birth index, compared to that of 1913, varies largely. These fluctuations are as shown in Table 41.

TABLE 41

Variation of Birth Indexes in the Provinces for Which Births Are Reported for 1917.

Name of province	Index of births in 1917 (1913 = 100)
Vladimir	41.9
Tver	57.7
Yaroslav	58.8
Nizhni-Novgorod	36.1
Kaluga	44.5
Tula	87.5
Kherson	34.5
Saratov	41.1
City of Moscow	66.4
City of Petrograd	76.7

The mean obtained from this series, noticeable for its wide range, can hardly be considered as representative of the European Russia as a whole. The average index of fifty-four for 1917, therefore, does not carry weight.

As regards the years 1915 and 1916, we have adequate reasons for believing index 87 (13 points decrease) for the former year and in-

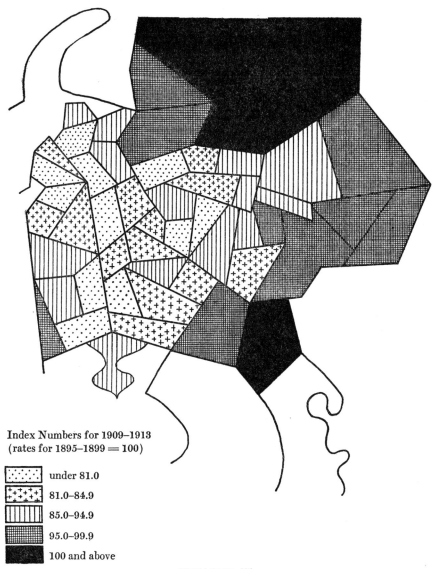

Index Numbers for 1909–1913
(rates for 1895–1899 = 100)

- under 81.0
- 81.0–84.9
- 85.0–94.9
- 95.0–99.9
- 100 and above

CHART X

*Birth Rates per Thousand Population, Indexes for the Years
1909–1913 as Compared with Indexes for 1895–1899.**

* Data from Appendix VI.

dex 66 (thirty-four points decrease) for the second year, are more
or less accurate.[5]

Let us now examine, as we have done for the marriage rate, the extent to which the decrease in the number of births was the direct result of the withdrawal to the front of a large number of men in the
prime of life and to what extent the decrease was due to birth control.[6]

Unfortunately the investigation of this extremely interesting
question of war demography, on the basis of the scanty available
material, is even more difficult than that of the part played by the
voluntary factor in the decline of marriage rates. We will, none the
less, attempt certain calculations, remembering, however, that they
are only crude and largely speculative.

For this object, we shall have to calculate, as we did before, the
decline in the civilian male population from 18 to 43 years of age,

[5] Since in the group of forty-one provinces, for which we have the data
for 1915, there are some provinces adjacent to the front, it is interesting to
calculate the total index without these provinces (*see* above, p. 52, n. 13).
This index is 86, which coincides closely with the total index for forty-one
provinces (87). Also for 1916, excluding from eighteen provinces the
Vitebsk province adjacent to the front, we obtain the same index (66) as for
all eighteen provinces.

[6] In addition to deliberate restriction of childbirth during marriage, the
voluntary factor exerts an influence on the number of births through the prevention of marriages. This latter factor, however, could not exert any appreciable influence on the number of births in 1915, 1916, and even 1917. Compared to the total number of births in a given year, the proportion of births
resulting from marriages concluded in the previous year or even two years is
so small that the reduction in this group of births can have but an insignificant influence on their total number for the year. Still less important is the
influence of the "deficiency" of marriages, due to the voluntary factor as opposed to the direct influence of the decrease in the male population.

It must also be observed, that besides the voluntary birth control, a certain
rôle in the birth decline could be played by the unconscious psychological
and physiological factors reducing reproductivity in the conditions created by
the War. But the general conditions of life in Russia (especially in rural districts) were, during the first two years of the War, not so bad as to let us
assume that this factor could be of great importance. In following pages,
speaking of birth control we will not repeat this observation, but it is to be
remembered that in so far as the reduction of births took place at all on the
part of those remaining at home the "unconscious" factors must have played
a certain part.

taking as the basis its number in 1913 and the number of full years that the men of this group spent at home during the successive periods of the War. While in the case of marriages we proceeded on the basis of calendar years, we shall now have to use the periods of conception corresponding to births in the calendar years; thus the decline in the number of births in 1915 will have to be compared with the decrease in the male population for the period from April 1, 1914, to April 1, 1915, etc. A more or less accurate calculation can be made only for the years 1915 and 1916, because, as shown above, no reliable statistics of births exist for 1917.

We shall base our estimates, as in the case of marriages, on two different assumptions:

First, that the peace-time army was a factor influencing the birth rate in the same degree as was the civilian male population, and

Second, that it had no influence on the birth rate. The truth will lie somewhere between the results of the two calculations. Let us begin by computing the decrease in the whole male population of the age-group liable to military service, that is between 18 and 43 years of age.

Without reproducing the details of our calculation (which is similar to that made for the marriage rate and based on the data of Appendix II and on those of the normal growth of the population), we give in Table 42 the results obtained.[7]

TABLE 42

Number of Full Years at Home and Decrease as Compared with 1913 Status.

Period	Number of full years spent at home	Male population, 18 to 43 years of age Decrease as compared with 1913	
		Number	Index
Method I:			
April 1, 1914, to April 1, 1915	18,100,000	3,200,000	15
April 1, 1915, to April 1, 1916	13,700,000	7,600,000	36
Method II:			
April 1, 1914, to April 1, 1915	17,800,000	2,500,000	12
April 1, 1915, to April 1, 1916	13,700,000	6,550,000	32

[7] We remind the reader that the total number of men of this group in 1913, according to our first assumption, equals 21.3 millions, and according to the second, 20.3 million men.

The decline for the period 1914–1915 ranges between the limits of 12 and 15 per cent, for that of 1915–1916 between 32 and 36 per cent. A comparison of this result with the decline in the birth rate during the calendar years 1915 and 1916 gives Table 43.

TABLE 43

Index of the Decline (below 1913 Status) in Births and Number of Males, 18–43 Years of Age, in the Years 1915 and 1916 and Corresponding Periods of Conception.

		Index of decrease	
Year	In number of births in the calendar years[8]	In number of males of 18–43 years, in corresponding periods of conception (Number for 1913 = 100)
1915	13	12 to 15
1916	34	32 to 36

This computation shows that, unlike the decline in the number of marriages the decline in the number of births comes very near to the proportionate decrease in the male population.

This result, however, cannot be considered as conclusive. The contribution to childbearing of men above 43 years and not affected at all by the service in the army is considerably greater than the contribution of this age-group to the number of marriages. On the other hand, within the age-group 18 to 43 years, the contribution of different ages to childbearing varies. Some corrections must accordingly be introduced in our computation, here, analogous to that correction already made in our computations with reference to marriage indexes. Herein our situation is even more difficult, since we have no precise information concerning the contribution of the various age-groups of men to childbearing, in other words we lack a distribution of births according to the age of the fathers, in European Russia. We shall have, therefore, to base our statements on certain assumptions, which will indicate only the very crude general outline of the subjects under discussion.

If the total number of men between 18 and 43 years is distributed into two groups: a younger from 18 to 26 years and an older from 27 to 43 years, and the approximate loss of "full years," as com-

[8] *See* p. 59, n. 20.

pared with 1913 is then calculated, the result on the basis of our first method[9] will be as follows (see Table 44):

TABLE 44

Decrease in the Number of Full Years as Compared with 1913.

| | Number (difference between the given period and 1913) | | | Index (1913 = 100) | |
Period	Age-group 18-43	Age-group 18-26	Age-group 27-43	Age-group 18-26	Age-group 27-43
1914–1915	3,200,000	1,150,000	2,050,000	13	17
1915–1916	7,600,000	4,200,000	3,400,000	46	28

In our calculation of the possible influence of the decrease of the male population on the birth rate, we must estimate the contribution to childbearing of each of these age-groups, as well as of the group above forty-three years. As mentioned above, we have no data on the distribution of births according to the age of the fathers, in European Russia. All we can do is to estimate the most probable distribution ensuing from the three following factors: (1) certain information about the distribution of births according to the age of the fathers in Petrograd;[10] (2) the distribution of births according to the age of the mothers (in European Russia);[11] (3) the relation between the ages of husbands and wives; and (4) the comparison of these data with information relating to certain European countries.[12]

The result is as follows:

Age-group of fathers	Percentage of births
18 to 26	15
27 to 43	75
Above 43	10

[9] Cf. above, pp. 54 sqq.

[10] *Materiali po Statistike Petrograda i Petrogradskoi Gubernii* (*Statistical Returns for the City and Province of Petrograd*), VI, 204 sqq.

[11] Cf. S. Novoselsky, "O Prilozhenii Metoda 'Standard Population' k Izmenenyu Rozhdaemosti" ("Application of the Method of 'Standard Population' to the Changes in Birth-rates"), in *Materyali po Statistike Petrograda i Petrogradskoi Gubernii* (*Statistical Returns for the City and Province of Petrograd*), III [1921], 28.

[12] Cf. for instance, Raseri, "Les Naissances en Rapport avec l'Age des Parents," in *Bulletin International de Statistique*, Vol. X.

For each group (especially for the first and the third) a certain error is of course possible; allowing for this error it will be more prudent to accept the following table (where the ratios are altered in opposite directions):

Age-group	Percentage	
18 to 26	15	20
27 to 43	70 or 70	
Above 43	15	10

In order to reduce the possibility of error to a minimum, we shall calculate on the basis of wider, rather improbable, deviations:

Age-group	Percentage	
18 to 26	25	10
27 to 43	70 or 75	
Above 43	5	15

We thus probably reach the limits of possible proportions.

The average weighted index of decrease in the male population will accordingly be as follows: (Method 1)

Years	Index of decrease in the male population	
	According to the most probable calculation	According to the extreme calculations
	(1913 = 100)	
1914–1915	14.7	14.1–15.2
1915–1916	27.9	25.6–31.1

The foregoing figures reveal that for the first period the average weighted index of decrease is moving in the very narrow limits of 14 to 15 per cent; for the second period it varies from 26 to 31 per cent.

A similar computation based on our *second assumption* (that the peace-time army had but an insignificant influence on the birth rate) gives the following results:

Years	Average weighted index of decrease in the male population (Method 2) (1913 = 100)
1914–1915	13–14
1915–1916	25–30

The limits thus obtained differ by 1 per cent from those obtained by the first method. *Taking both modes of calculation into account, we shall obtain slightly wider limits for the index of the decrease in* the male population, which is in Table 45, compared with the actual decline of the birth rate.

TABLE 45

Indexes of Decline in Births and Decrease in Males (Full Years) for Conception Periods and Years of Birth.

	Decline in the number of births (*1913 = 100*)	Decrease in the male population ("*full years*") in the corresponding period of conception (*1913 = 100*)
1915 (period of conception April 1, 1914—April 1, 1915)	13	13–15
1916 (period of conception April 1, 1915—April 1, 1916)	34	25–31

We thus see that the percentage decline in the number of births is, in 1915, very near to the decrease in the male population for the corresponding period of conception. In other words, the number of births fell not more (rather less) than it would have fallen as a direct result of the withdrawal of men.[13] In 1916 it fell slightly more than it should have fallen as a result of the same cause. We may, therefore, assume for the corresponding period of conception a certain, though probably not very large, influence of the restriction of childbirth by the civilian population.

The influence of the voluntary factor might be on the whole much smaller as regards the birth rate than it is in respect to the decline of the marriage rate. In 1914 and in 1915 (periods corresponding to the periods of conception from April, 1914, to April, 1915, and from April, 1915, to April, 1916), the decline in the number of marriages was almost twice as large as the rate of decrease of the male population, and only in 1916 does this discrepancy diminish. In the case of the number of births, the first period shows no excess at all and the second only a small excess.

Practically no data are available for 1917. The crude computation that we have made (which is not reproduced here) seems to show, however, that the influence of the deliberate restriction of births was no greater in 1917 than in 1916.

---

[13] A certain influence was obviously exerted by the granting of furlough, but this influence could not have been great.

Thus the part of deliberate birth control in the decline of births during the War does not seem to have been very important; it was certainly less than the influence of the voluntary element on the decline of the marriage rate. This might reasonably be expected in a country like Russia, where the rural population was numerically preponderant and where the patriarchal mode of life was preserved not only in the villages, but also in small towns. The voluntary factor in respect to abstention from marriage is entirely different from the deliberate restriction of childbearing in the sense of the neo-Malthusian practice. We may assume that the pre-war decline of the birth rate, as observed chiefly in the western and central provinces of European Russia, was due principally to the more advanced age of marrying couples and to the general decline of the marriage rate. The latest investigations show that the difference in the birth rates between the western and eastern provinces was chiefly caused by the difference in the marrying age, that is, in the age distribution of the married couples. In this connection we may quote again the investigation of the well-known Russian expert on demography, M. Novoselsky, already referred to above.[14] M. Novoselsky, applying the method of "standard population" to this problem shows that the "standard" or "normal" birth rates obtained after eliminating the differences in age distribution of married women are not higher in the eastern provinces of Russia than they are in the western provinces. M. Novoselsky arrives at the conclusion that "the fundamental cause of the difference in birth rates should be sought in the distribution of the population as to being married or unmarried and as to age, especially with reference to women." The birth rate is higher where the ratio of married women to the whole population is higher, and where among them predominate, as a result of early marriages, young women of the most fertile age.[15]

[14] *Cf.* above, p. 84, n. 11.

[15] For instance, in the province of Samara the ratio of married women from 15 to 49 years of age to the total number of females of this age-group is 75 per cent; in the province of Kovno, only 51 per cent; the ratio of married women from 15 to 29 years of age to those from 15 to 49 years of age in the province of Samara is 46 per cent, in the province of Kovno, 30 per cent. It is not surprising, therefore, in view of the vast difference in the age of married women and the duration of marriage, that the general birth rate (per thousand) in the province of Samara reaches 61.3, while in the province of Kovno it is but 35 (in 1896–1897). The standard birth rate (representing the

It would evidently have been very interesting (if the available material had allowed it) to apply the method of "standard population" to the birth rates for *successive* periods, and thus possibly to show that their decline in pre-war Russia was not caused by a neo-Malthusian practice but was chiefly due to the changes in the age composition of married couples, that is, chiefly to the increase in the age of marriage. But already the quoted geographical analysis corroborates this interpretation of the dynamics of the birth rate.

We do not mean to say that in pre-war Russia, birth control had no influence on the decline in the birth rate; in certain localities, especially in the large cities, it may have been an important factor. But for Russia taken as a whole, with her 85 per cent rural population, this factor was hardly important. It is therefore not surprising that during the War, especially during the first part of it, it did not exert a great influence, and that the decrease in the male population was probably the fundamental cause of the decline in the birth rate.

This conclusion is confirmed by an examination of the territorial distribution of the decline in the number of births during the War, combined with the territorial distribution of certain other factors that we shall now consider.

The territorial distribution of births-decline indexes is illustrated in Charts XI (for 1915) and XII (for 1916).

Chart XI, though it includes a greater number of provinces than the corresponding chart for the marriage rate (Chart VII), represents a less definite and more heterogeneous picture. The comparison of this chart with that of the territorial distribution of the pre-war birth rate, and the pre-war decline in the birth rate, will show a smaller number of points of similarity than between those of the war decline and pre-war rate of marriages. It also discloses to less extent the similarity we have observed between the territorial distribution of the indexes of the decline of the number of marriages and the indexes of decrease of the male population (represented by the index of the increased proportion of females, Chart III).

Attention should be drawn to the following fact: In several provinces adjacent to the front, the decline in the birth rate is insignificant and there are even instances of its increase (for example, in the

"net" fecundity after the elimination of the age factor) is, on the contrary, very much the same for the two provinces; it is 52.7 for Samara, and 49.7 for Kovno.

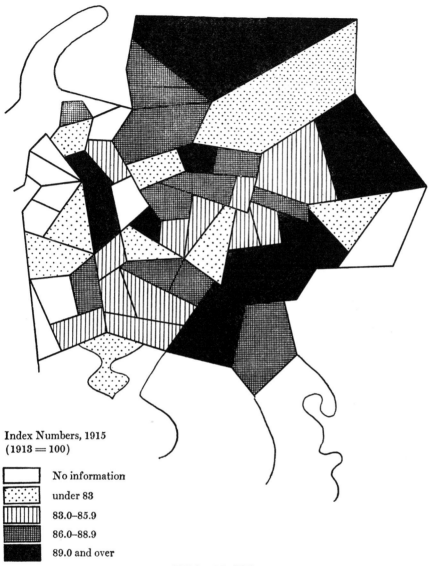

Index Numbers, 1915
(1913 = 100)

	No information
	under 83
	83.0–85.9
	86.0–88.9
	89.0 and over

CHART XI

*Index Numbers for the Number of Births in 1915 as Compared with the Number in 1913, by Provinces, for European Russia.**

* Data from Appendix VII.

province of Mogilev),[16] in spite of the important decrease in the civilian male population (Chart III represents the rural civil population only). This fact is to be attributed to the concentration in these provinces of soldiers who had been withdrawn from the civil population of these and other provinces. It is regrettable that the absence of information concerning the distribution of births according to legitimacy, for these years, prevents us from investigating this interesting problem.

The territorial distribution of the decline in the number of births for 1916 differs fundamentally from that of 1915 (as well as from the pre-war distribution of the decline in the number of births). The largest fall in the number of births is noticeable in the three eastern and southeastern provinces (Samara, Saratov, and the Don Territory). No satisfactory explanation can be found for this fact, which is not attributable either directly or indirectly to the withdrawal of the male population. It is possible that here we have simply the results of the incomplete registration, as the registration mechanism became more and more destroyed during the War.[17]

But let us investigate this subject more closely by constructing tables of correlation and calculating the coefficients of correlation. These calculations, however, we will make only for the year 1915, since the data for 1916 relate to too small a number of provinces.

In these calculations, we have eliminated the provinces adjacent to the front for the reasons already pointed out above. The tables[18] are established accordingly for thirty-five provinces only.[19]

[16] In some other provinces adjacent to the front (for instance, the provinces of Volhynia and Livonia) the decline of the birth rate was exceptionally marked; it is possible that this fact is due to incomplete registration, caused by the disorganization resulting from the War.

[17] Also the distribution of birth numbers in the seven provinces for which information is available for 1917 (*see* Table 41) cannot be satisfactorily explained. The order in which they stand as regards the falling number of births has no relation whatever to that in respect of the rate of mobilized men. This fact, though not completely destroying the credit to be accorded to these figures, gives rise to a natural suspicion. We must also point out that in 1917, the year of the Revolution, the disorganization of the registering bodies must have been very great, which is seen from the fact that information on the birth number is available only for seven provinces.

[18] The correlation tables are omitted here, *see* above, p. 29, n. 34.

[19] In addition to the five provinces adjacent to the front, we have also ex-

Table D illustrates the correlation existing on the one hand between the ratio of births in 1915 to that of 1913, and on the other, the index of the increased proportion of females (representing the index of decrease of the civilian male population) for 1916. We have already pointed out in respect to the marriage index, that the negative correlation between the decline in the marriage number from 1913 to 1915 and the decrease in the male population down to 1916 is a secondary correlation created through the medium of the direct correlation between the decrease in the male population down to 1915 and down to 1916. We have drawn attention to the fact that this secondary correlation must naturally be weaker than the primary correlation between the marriage rate in 1915 and the decrease in the male population during the same year, which cannot, however, be established for lack of information. These considerations apply with much greater force to the correlation between the number of *births* in 1915 and the decrease in the male population in 1916. In this case, a primary correlation should be established between the decline in the birth index in 1915 and the index of decrease in the male population in the period from April 1, 1914, to April 1, 1915, which embraces only the first eight and a half months of the War. It is clear that the correlation between the decrease in the male population during that period and the decrease in the male population down to the middle of 1916 must be weaker than the correlation between the decrease in the male population in 1915 and 1916 respectively. It is, therefore, not surprising that the secondary negative correlation between the birth index of 1915 and the index of the increased proportion of females in 1916 should be weaker (Table D)[20] than that same correlation in respect of the number of marriages in 1915 (*see* above, Table B).[20] The coefficient of correlation, calculated on the basis of Table D, is −0.30 (while the coefficient of Table B is −0.55). If the indirect character of connection between two varieties is taken into account, this coefficient should perhaps be considered as even more important than the corresponding coefficient of the marriage index.[21]

cluded Kharkov from the total of forty-one provinces for which information is available for 1915, the data for this province being unreliable.

[20] As stated above, all correlation tables have been omitted for reasons of economy in printing, but are on file for consultation.

[21] We must point out another reason why the coefficients of correlation given above for the marriage indexes and birth rates are not quite compa-

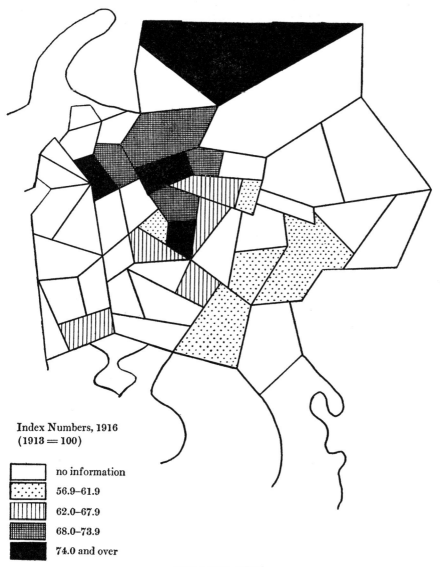

Index Numbers, 1916
(1913 = 100)

	no information
	56.9–61.9
	62.0–67.9
	68.0–73.9
	74.0 and over

CHART XII

*Index Numbers for the Number of Births in 1916 as Compared with the Number in 1913, by Provinces for European Russia.**

* Data from Appendix VII.

Table E illustrates the correlation between the decline in the number of births from 1913 to 1915 on the one hand, and the pre-war decline of the birth rate (according to Appendix VI) on the other. We see from this table that there exists a positive though weak correlation between the two phenomena.

The coefficient of this correlation (Table E) is +0.20, but there is reason to believe that even this weak correlation between the decline in the birth rate during and before the War is only a secondary one. In fact, as may be seen from Table F, there exists a rather stronger degree of inverse correlation between the pre-war decline in the birth rate and the index of the increased proportion of females in 1916 (the coefficient of correlation is —0.57). This is also an evidently secondary correlation caused principally by the correlation between the drafts of men down to 1916 and the morbidity of the population represented by the pre-war death rate, and also by the correlation, or rather "co-variation," between the pre-war death rate and the pre-war decline in the birth rate. Certain other factors of a fortuitous character also may have influenced this secondary correlation as, for instance, the greater difficulty of avoiding military service in the western provinces. These provinces were, as we have seen, also those where the decline in the birth rate was particularly pronounced before the War.

Whether this supposition be correct or not, the existence of a strong negative correlation between the index of proportion of females and the pre-war index of changes in the birth rate, combined with the negative correlation between the index of proportion of females and the birth index of 1915, is sufficient to create a little spurious positive correlation between the decline of the birth rate before and during the War.

In fact, if we calculate on the basis of these three coefficients of correlation: (1) the coefficient of correlation between the pre-war decline in the birth rate and the decline of birth number in 1915 (+0.20); (2) coefficient of correlation between the index of the increased proportion of females in 1916 and the decline of the birth

rable. The first is obtained after the elimination of two extreme cases strongly divergent from the general trend; on the contrary, Table D does not show any such strong divergence and, hence, no eliminations have been made in it. The coefficient resulting from Table D has, therefore, more weight than that resulting from Table B.

number in 1915 (—0.30) ; and (3) coefficient of correlation between
the index of the increased proportion of females in 1916 and the pre-
war decline in the birth rate (—0.57), the coefficient of the net
(partial) correlation between the pre-war and the war decline in the
birth number will be as follows:

$$r_{12.3} = \frac{+0.20 - (-0.57)\ (-0.30)}{\sqrt{(1 - 0.57^2)\ (1 - 0.30^2)}} = +0.04$$

The apparent correlation between the last two variables disap-
pears. We have reason thus to assume that there is no actual correlation between the territorial distribution of the decline in the birth
rates in 1915 and before the War. This corroborates our previous
statement that the voluntary element of birth control played but a
small part in the decline of the number of births during the War, at
least in its first period. If the decline in the birth rate during the
War were due to deliberate birth control, that is, if the conditions of
war-time had strongly increased the neo-Malthusian practice, which
had exerted but a slight influence in pre-war Russia, then the decline in the birth rate during the War would be greater in the area
with less patriarchal and more rationalized conditions, that is, in
the provinces with a strongly declining pre-war birth rate. There
should be in other words a direct correlation between the pre-war
and war-time decline of the birth number. If, on the contrary, as we
have assumed, the voluntary birth control was a factor of minor importance and the decline in the birth number was chiefly due to the
decrease in the male population, the situation will be entirely re-
versed. In this case, the remaining provincial differences in the birth-
number-decline during the War (in case of an equal ratio of decrease
of the male population) will depend on the one hand upon the differences in the age distribution of the male population in the separate
provinces and, on the other hand, upon the relative importance of
the married and unmarried groups of men. These two factors are
totally independent from and sometimes opposed to the influence
exercised by the age distribution of married couples upon the pre-
war birth rate. A greater percentage of married men of younger age
or, in other words, the younger age of the married couples, caused
before the War a higher birth rate. During the War the opposite is
true: the younger age of married men produced a more pronounced

decline of the birth number as a consequence of the greater effect of
military service on the younger age-groups. The result depends here
on the relation between the classes of men called to the colors and the
distribution of the population as to age and marriage, that is, on a
combination of factors totally different from the pre-war conditions
determining birth rate. It is clear that on the basis of our assumption
(small influence of birth control in war-time), there is no reason to
expect a correlation between the decline in the birth rate before and
during the War. We have seen that no such correlation seems to
exist.

All these considerations refer, as already stated, to Russia taken
as a whole, where the birth rate was determined by the predominance
of the rural population. The changes in the number of births in
towns, especially in large cities, was probably influenced more
strongly by birth control. Unfortunately, statistics of the births in
towns are very scanty, and we are almost entirely precluded from an
investigation of the causes of their variations, since no information
is available regarding the changes in the age and sex distribution of
the urban population.

According to the figures given by the Narkomzdrav Commission
for forty-one provinces of European Russia, for which information
is available to the end of 1915, the number of births in 1915 in the
rural areas declined by 15 per cent as compared with 1913, while in
the towns the decrease was only 9 per cent.[22] Among the eighteen
provinces for which information is available to the end of 1916,
classified figures of the urban and rural population are given only
for thirteen provinces. The number of births in 1915 and 1916 compared with that of 1913, on the basis of this information, is as follows (see Table 46) :

TABLE 46

*Changes in the Number of Births in 1915 and 1916 as Compared
with 1913 (1913 = 100).*

Year	Urban population	Rural population
1913	100	100
1915	95	86
1916	83	67

[22] *Proceedings* of the Commission, p. 112. The figures for the separate
provinces are, unhappily, lacking in the *Proceedings*.

While in the rural districts the number of births in 1915 declined by 14 per cent, the decrease in the towns was only 5 per cent; in 1916, however, the decline in the villages reached 33 per cent and in towns 17 per cent. A lower decrease in the towns may also be observed from the figures available for several provinces of Ukraine.[23] In all provinces without exception the birth number decreased less in towns than in rural districts as appears from Table 47.

TABLE 47

Changes in the Number of Births in 1915 as Compared with 1913 (Number of Births in 1913 = 100).

Name of the province	Urban population	Rural population
Kiev	89.2	86.8
Poltava	90.4	82.9
Kherson[24]	92.0	83.6
Chernigov	93.5	84.5

We also possess for 1917 the birth rate (per thousand) for the province of Kiev;[25] though the figures are of doubtful accuracy, they

[23] *See* above, p. 6, n. 9. We have omitted the provinces for which data are particularly questionable.

[24] The figures for 1916 are: 78.9 for the urban population and 63.8 for the rural population. These figures do not comprise the cities of Nikolaev and Odessa. For the city of Nikolaev the changes in the number of births as compared with 1913 are estimated as follows:

Year	Number of births (1913 = 100)
1913	100
1915	81
1916	110
1917	102

These figures are dealing with the orthodox population only; they do not inspire much confidence. Those for Odessa are as follows:

Year	Number of births (1914 = 100)
1914	100
1915	85
1916	80
1917	71

[25] *Cf.* M. R. Khodos, *Preavaritelnya Dannya o Estestvennom Dvizhenii Naselenya Kievskoi Gubernii za Vremya 1915–1920 Godi (Preliminary*

show distinctly the difference in the decline of the birth rate in towns
and villages. (See Table 48.)

TABLE 48

Birth Rate (per Thousand) in the Province of Kiev.

Year	Urban population	Rural population
Average for 1909–1913	25.2	37.4
1917	20.6	21.9

The general characteristic noted—the smaller decrease in the
birth number in the cities—is due to the above-mentioned fact that
smaller drafts of men were called to the front from the towns than
from the villages. In many cases even these drafts were to a certain
extent compensated by an increase in the garrison, by an increase in
the personnel of the institutions working for national defense, by the
influx of refugees, and so on.[26] Unfortunately, the absence of information makes it impossible to calculate the possible effect of these
factors and to compare them with the decline in the birth number in
the towns.[27] We cannot, therefore, estimate in figures the influence
exerted by birth control in the towns.

There are reasons for supposing that this influence existed in
Petrograd and Moscow. The male population of Petrograd suffered
but little from the calling of men to the colors; and owing to the
compensation of men withdrawn to the front by the influx of other
elements of the population, the proportion of males up to the end of
1915, if our figures may be trusted, would seem to have increased.
The birth rate, however, showed a considerable decline, as may be
seen from Table 49.

*Data on the Natural Changes in the Population of the Province of Kiev in
1915–1920)*, in the Bulletin of the Statistical Bureau of the Province of Kiev,
Nos. 4 and 5, 1922; also an article by the same author in *ibid.*, Nos. 4 and 5,
1925. Unfortunately, there are some unexplained contradictions between the
two articles by this author.

[26] The compensation for the withdrawal of men (husbands) to the army
by the influx of other male elements can influence the birth rate only within
rather narrow limits, but this factor is still of some importance.

[27] The only statistics of sex distribution in 1917 (according to the 1917
census) relate only to certain towns and are hardly comparable with the pre-
war data; it is unknown whether they include the garrisons, the suburbs, etc.

TABLE 49

Birth Rate per Thousand in Petrograd.[28]

1913	26.4
1914	25.0
1915	22.5
1916	19.1
1917	17.8

The birth rate fell in 1917 by 33 per cent and it is quite probable that this decline was greatly due to birth control.[29]

In addition to the general birth rate (per thousand population) we also possess for Moscow the specific rate per thousand females of the childbearing age (15 to 49 years). It must be noted that in times of war the latter partly lose their normal importance, since the lacking factor is not the women, but the men. The data[30] are as given in Table 50.

TABLE 50

General and Specific Birth Rate in Moscow.

Year	General birth rate per 1,000 population	Specific birth rate per 1,000 women aged 15 to 49 years
Average for 1910–1914	33.2	117.2
1915	27.0	91.5
1916	22.9	72.4
1917	19.6	58.6

The publication from which these data are quoted also contains the following comment: "The decline in the birth rate on such a large scale depends not merely on the decline in the number of marriages and on the withdrawal to the war of at least 100,000 men who had to leave their wives at home, for the departure of married men to the War was to a great extent compensated by the influx into

[28] Cf. *Materyal po Statistike Petrograda i Petrogradskoi Gubernii (Statistical Returns for the City and Province of Petrograd)*, V [1921], 19.

[29] Or perhaps, to some extent, to the psychological and physiological effects of difficult life conditions, that in this time were already felt in capital cities.

[30] *Krasnaya Moskwa (Red Moscow)*, p. 66.

Moscow of soldiers coming from villages and from other towns, who refilled the ranks of the Moscow garrisons. We have undoubtedly to do with a deliberate abstinence of the women from childbearing, occasioned by the general unfavorable conditions during the war." Indeed if we consider that in 1917 the general birth rate declined by 41 per cent and the specific birth rate by 50 per cent, the above comment seems to be well founded.[31]

Let us now give some figures (see Table 51) regarding the illegitimate birth rate during the years of the War in Petrograd, Moscow, and in the province of Moscow.[32]

TABLE 51

Illegitimate Births (per Thousand Births).

Year	City of Petrograd	Towns of the province of Moscow (excluding the city of Moscow)	City of Moscow	Rural districts of the province of Moscow
1913	14.7	7.3	20.8	3.1
1914	14.4	7.4	19.7	3.0
1915	14.6	8.4	21.3	3.4
1916	15.9	9.6	..	4.3
1917	15.8	..	..	..

Down to 1915 the increase of the percentage of illegitimate births was little; but in 1916 it was already pretty considerable; it is to be noticed that in the rural districts it is not fewer than in towns.

For Petrograd and Moscow we possess some information concerning stillbirths.[33] The ratio of stillborn children to the total number of births increased slightly during the War. In Moscow the average for the period 1910–1914 was 3.8 per cent, in 1915 it rose to 4.3 per cent. In Petrograd it was as shown in Table 52.

[31] Still, the authors exaggerate perhaps a little the possible influence of the influx of outside men elements on the birth rate in Moscow.

[32] *Proceedings* of the Narkomzdrav Commission, p. 112.

[33] *Ibid.*, p. 112.

TABLE 52

Stillbirths in Petrograd, 1913 and War Years.

Years	Percentage of children stillborn
1913	4.1
1914	4.3
1915	4.3
1916	4.7
1917	4.6

These differences in percentage, however, are not large nor is the registration of stillbirths accurate enough to enable one to treat these data as significant.

CHAPTER III

MORTALITY

FROM the end of the nineteenth century, the death rate in Russia, which was generally very high, began to fall. Table 53 gives the general death rates from 1890–1894 to the outbreak of the War.[1]

TABLE 53

Average Death Rate per Thousand Population by Five-Year Periods.

Period	Death rate
1890–1894	36.4
1895–1899	33.0
1900–1904	30.9
1905–1908	29.4
1909–1913	27.9

Chart XIII shows the territorial distribution of the pre-war death rate and Chart XIV, the changes in this distribution which took place in the period 1909–1913 as compared with 1895–1899.[2]

As may be seen from a comparison of these charts with Charts IX and X, the territorial distribution of mortality in the last five years before the War greatly resembles that of the birth rate of the same period. The chart of the changes in mortality from 1895–1899 to 1909–1913 likewise resembles the corresponding changes in the birth rate. There are discrepancies in the details, but the general characteristics of the territorial distribution of the birth rate described above[3] may equally be applied to the territorial distribution of the pre-war mortality and its changes.

The following statistics of mortality during the years of the War

---

[1] These figures are taken from M. Yakovenko, *op. cit.*, p. 43. For most of these years we have been able to compare them with the figures of the *Yearbook* of the Central Statistical Committee, with which they agreed.

[2] The figures on which Charts XIII and XIV are based will be found in Appendix VIII. All that has been said above (p. 77, n. 2) with reference to similar figures concerning the birth rate should also be applied in this case.

[3] *Cf.* above, pp. 77 *sqq.*

are available: 1914, for all the fifty provinces of European Russia; 1915, for forty-one provinces; 1916, for fifteen provinces, and 1917, for six provinces.

We have also information for the cities of Petrograd and Moscow for 1914–1917. The group of forty-one provinces for which information is available for 1915 is the same as that mentioned above with reference to the birth rate.[4] The fifteen provinces to which the material available for 1916 relates include one northern, three northwestern, five central industrial, three central agricultural, one southwestern and two southeastern provinces. The data for 1917 cover only six provinces, including four of the central industrial and two of the central agricultural areas.

The total number of deaths for these respective groups, including the cities of Petrograd and Moscow, are as shown in Table 54.

TABLE 54

Number of Deaths in Groups of Provinces, 1913 and War Years.[5]

	Number of deaths			
Years	*50 provinces of European Russia*	*41 provinces**	*15 provinces**	*6 provinces†*
1913	3,322,894	2,852,729	955,673	426,760
1914	3,273,059	2,816,011	930,515	405,400
1915	....	2,886,922	910,379	398,247
1916	....	....	852,303	384,760
1917	....	....	....	364,566

* Including the province of Moscow and the cities of Moscow and Petrograd.
† Including the cities of Moscow and Petrograd.

Taking the figure for 1913 = 100, the ratios[6] will be as shown in Table 55.

These figures reveal that, unlike the birth rate, the evolution of

[4] *Cf.* above, p. 78.

[5] *Proceedings* of the Narkomzdrav Commission, p. 113. The War losses of these years are not included; as indicated by the Commission, however, "the wounded and sick combatants who were evacuated to the rear and died in the hospitals and nursing homes were included in the figures of most provinces," but "in certain provinces this is not made clear."

[6] The number of deaths as well as the number of marriages being slightly higher in 1913 than the average, their decline in the following years, as compared to the figures of 1913, must necessarily be slightly exaggerated.

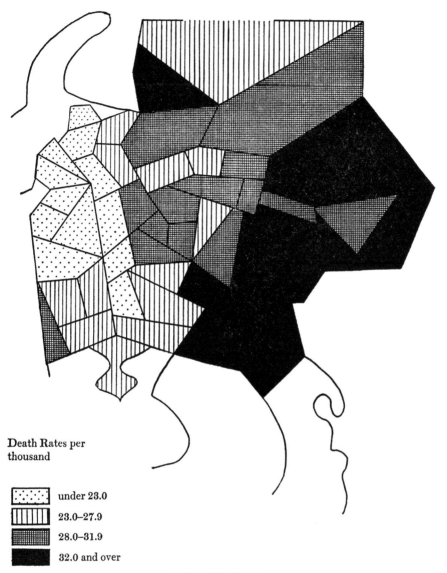

Death Rates per
thousand

░░░ under 23.0

‖‖‖ 23.0–27.9

▦▦ 28.0–31.9

██ 32.0 and over

CHART XIII

*Average Death Rate per Thousand for Pre-war Years,
1909–1913, by Provinces for European Russia.**

* Data from Appendix VIII, column 1.

TABLE 55

Index Numbers Showing Deaths during War as Compared with 1913 Deaths (1913 = 100).

Years	50 provinces of European Russia	41 provinces*	15 provinces*	6 provinces†
1913	100	100	100	100
1914	99	99	97	95
1915	..	101	95	93
1916	..	..	89	90
1917	..	..	..	85

* Including the province of Moscow and the cities of Moscow and Petrograd.

† Including the cities of Moscow and Petrograd.

the death rate in each of these groups is rather different: in 1915 the death rate increased in forty-one provinces by 1 per cent, in fifteen provinces it decreased by 5 per cent, and in six provinces it decreased by 7 per cent. The figures for fifteen and six provinces for 1916 are close to each other, but this is not proof that they are representative of the whole of European Russia. As may be seen from these statistics, as well as from Appendix IX and Charts XV and XVI, the territorial distribution of changes in mortality for 1915 and 1916 are much less uniform than in the number of births. The range of the provincial indexes is much wider. The foregoing selected figures cannot therefore be considered very reliable as regards their representative character either for 1917 or for 1916. The group of the six provinces, plus the two capitals, shows the following variations in the local indexes for 1917. (See Table 56.)

TABLE 56

Index Numbers of Deaths in Certain Provinces and Cities, 1917.

Name of province and city	Index numbers 1917 (1913 = 100)
Vladimir	69
Nizhni-Novgorod	55
Tver	82
Yaroslav	97
Kaluga	74
Tula	91
City of Moscow	106
City of Petrograd	134

As may be seen from the figures of 1915, the six provinces included in this group were in a more favorable condition than the average in respect of mortality. This explains why the entire group with the capitals, in spite of the high death index prevailing in the latter, shows a lower index than that for the forty-one provinces. The same is partially true in respect of the group of fifteen provinces. We have need therefore of great caution in calculating on the basis of the above quoted indexes for 1916 and 1917, and we have no reason to consider them as representative of the entire territory of European Russia.

As to the year 1915, its index computed for forty-one provinces (that is 101) can be considered just as representative for the whole European Russia (fifty provinces) as for the territory of European Russia without the provinces adjacent to the front, because the excluding of those adjacent provinces does not change the average index even for one unit.

It appears from the above figures that a gradual decrease in the total number of deaths took place during the War in the groups of provinces indicated. This decrease does not imply an amelioration of mortality conditions. It was caused partly by a decrease of the population, due to the withdrawal of a great number of men to the front, and partly to the decline in the birth rate, that is to the decrease in the number of infants, who, as a rule, furnish a large proportion of the death number. It would be interesting to calculate to what extent the decrease in the number of deaths is due to the action of these two factors alone (alteration in the age distribution and in the number of the population) and to what extent it shows the actual decrease of the mortality, i.e., the decline in the death rate for each given age-group.

We have no means of answering these questions with accuracy, but by using approximate calculations we can throw some light on them.

The first question to be elucidated is the extent to which the calling of a large number of young men to the colors should have influenced the number of deaths of the civil population. The figures of this loss expressed in "full years" have been computed above for the consecutive periods of the War. When calculating the death rates, we shall have to deal with calendar years, and only the first method of calculation shall be used.[7] The calculation based on our second

[7] *Cf.* pp. 53 *sqq.*

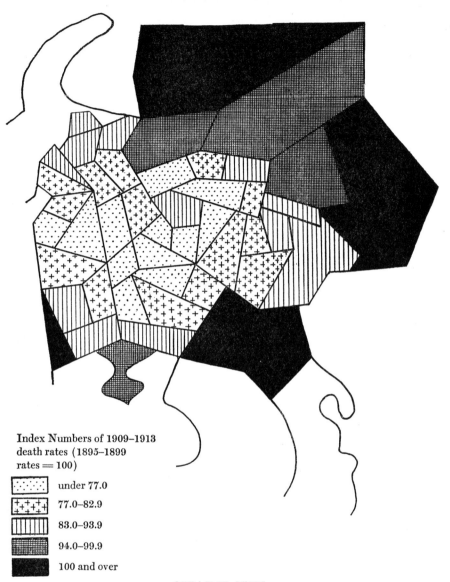

Index Numbers of 1909–1913
death rates (1895–1899
rates = 100)

under 77.0	
77.0–82.9	
83.0–93.9	
94.0–99.9	
100 and over	

CHART XIV

*Index of Pre-war Death Rates (1909–1913) Compared with
the Rates for the Years 1895–1899.*

* Data from Appendix VIII, column 2.

assumption (the peace-time army being excluded both from the de-crease in the male population and from the pre-war male popula-tion) has no bearing on the estimate of mortality, since the death rate among soldiers in peace-time shows no particular divergence from the general death rate and is included in it.

We remind the reader that the net decrease of the male popula-tion of the age-group 18 to 43 as compared with the figures for 1913 and expressed in "full years" according to the first method, is 1,800,000 in 1914, 6,750,000 in 1915, and 9,500,000 in 1916. No calculation can be made for 1917 owing to the random character of the demobilization which took place then.

What was the effect of the withdrawal of a large number of men upon the general death number?[8]

The death rate per thousand males of separate age-groups can be tabulated as in Table 57, on the basis of the data given by M. Novo-selsky for European Russia.[9]

TABLE 57

Death Rates by Age-groups, 1897.

Age-group	Death rate in 1897 (per 1,000 males)
20 to 24	7.3
25 to 29	7.7
30 to 34	8.3
35 to 39	9.8

These are approximately the age-groups liable to military service. We see that the death rate does not vary greatly.[10] If we calculate the probable decline in the number of deaths due to the decrease of the male population, firstly, on the basis of the lower figure, that is 7.3, and then on that of the higher, 9.8, we should obtain sufficiently

[8] Our calculation can only refer to the civil population; we must ignore the element of error resulting from the fact that in many provinces the fig-ures of the number of deaths included either totally or partially the deaths of soldiers evacuated to the rear.

[9] These data refer to 1897; they are borrowed from Yakovenko, op. cit., p. 109.

[10] We may ignore the death rate for the age-group 40 to 43 years, since this group constitutes a very small portion of the number of mobilized men, approximately 2.5 per cent.

reliable limits within which we may place the actual decrease of the number of deaths caused by the withdrawal of men to the army.

This computation will give the following results: In 1914 the loss of 1,800,000 men entails according to the death rate of 7.3 (per thousand males) a reduction of 13,140 in the number of deaths. The total number of deaths for 1913 for fifty provinces of European Russia was about 3,300,000 and 13,140 represents 0.4 per cent of this total. On the basis of the lower death rate (7.3), therefore, we thus obtain a reduction of 0.4 per cent.

On the basis of the highest death rate (9.8 per thousand males), the decline in the number of deaths due to the withdrawal of men will be 17,640, or about 0.5 per cent of the total number of deaths.

Thus the withdrawal of men to the front could have produced in 1914 a reduction in the number of deaths ranging from 0.4 to 0.5 per cent of the figure of 1913. This reduction is unimportant and its limits are very narrow.

Proceeding by the same method we find that, as compared with 1913, the decline in the number of deaths due to the decrease in the civilian male population, was between 1.5 and 2 per cent in 1915, and 2.1 and 2.8 per cent in 1916. Since the limits obtained are very narrow even for 1916, and the effects of the factor under consideration upon the number of deaths small, we may choose for each year an average rate between the two extreme rates as seems the most probable. We may, therefore, calculate on the basis of the death rate, 8 per cent (nearer 7.3 than to 9.8) because among the men called to the colors younger ages prevailed.[11] The approximate reduction in the number of deaths in the civil population, due to the withdrawal of men to the front will then be 0.4 per cent for 1914, 1.7 per cent for 1915, and 2.3 per cent for 1916. It should be observed that even these very small percentages are exaggerated, being based on the death rates of 1897 which had since declined.

The mobilization affected differently the several areas; the various groups of provinces on which we based our calculations might therefore differ in respect of the effect of the decrease of the male population upon the number of deaths. But as the action of this factor is so slight, we may be satisfied with the use of the same percentage of reduction for all provinces.

[11] This is not quite correct in respect of 1914; the presumable decline in the death rate caused by the loss of men is, however, so insignificant that the possible margin of error is of no importance.

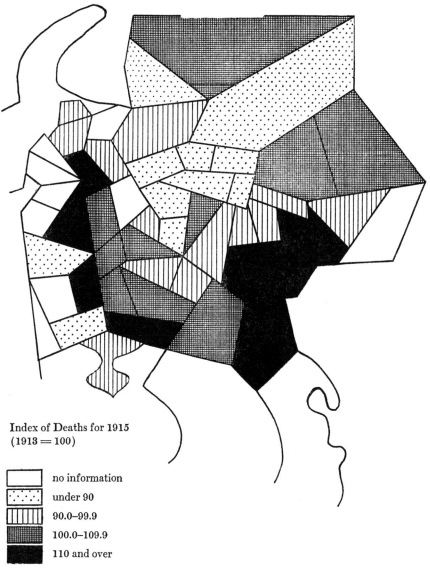

Index of Deaths for 1915
(1913 = 100)

☐	no information
⠿	under 90
▦	90.0–99.9
▩	100.0–109.9
■	110 and over

CHART XV

Index Numbers of Deaths in 1915 as Compared with Deaths
*in 1913, by Provinces for European Russia.**

* Data from Appendix IX, column 6.

In view of the unimportant action of this factor, a calculation for
1917 would be useless, even if it were possible. The direct effect of
the increasing number of men at home (due to demobilization) on
the number of deaths must have been insignificant, as compared with
the rise in the death rate of that age-group caused by infectious diseases brought home from the front, by the general economic depression prevailing in the revolutionary year, and so on.

Let us now consider the action which the *change in the number of
births* may have had on the reduction of the number of deaths. We
can, in this case, make our calculations for separate groups of provinces, since we know the number of births in each of them. We must,
however, base the argument on some general assumption as to the
part of infant mortality in the general pre-war mortality level.

When calculating the effect of the decline of the birth number on
the reduction in the number of deaths we shall assume, as is generally
done in statistics of mortality, that the number of dead infants below one year comprises approximately two-thirds of those born in
the same calendar year and one-third of those born in the preceding
calendar year. For children dying between one and two years we
shall assume that half of them were born in the last preceding calendar year and the other half in the previous year. It follows, therefore, that while computing the effect upon the decrease in the number of deaths of infants under one year in a given calendar year, the
decline in the birth number in the same year must be given a weight
of two-thirds, and that of the preceding year, of one-third. On the
other hand, in the case of infants from one to two years the decline
in the birth number in the last preceding year affects the reduction
in the number of infant deaths in the same degree as the decline in
the birth number of the previous year and therefore a weight of one-
half shall be used for each of these two years. The decrease in the
number of infant deaths of each given calendar year, caused by the
decline in the birth number of that and of the preceding years, will
have to be examined in the first place on the basis of these assumptions. We shall then calculate the influence which the decline in the
infant death number may have exerted on the relative decrease of
the total number of deaths. For that purpose it is necessary to know
the pre-war ratio of infant deaths to the general number of deaths.
No statistics concerning the age distribution of mortality in the
years immediately preceding the War are available. We might use
the figures of the years 1896 and 1897 included in the latest mor-

tality tables of European Russia compiled by M. Novoselsky. We prefer, however, to adopt the figures of the age distribution of deaths in Ukraine for the years 1896 and 1897 as used in the latest tables of mortality by M. Ptukha.[12] Mortality in the provinces of Ukraine in the years 1896 and 1897, especially infant mortality, was below the average of the fifty provinces of European Russia, and, therefore, nearer to the lower death rate in the latter at the beginning of the War. The average general death rate in European Russia declined as indicated above from 1895–1899 to 1910–1914 from 33 to 27.9 per thousand. As early as in 1896–1899 the average death rate in the ten provinces of Ukraine was 29.7 per thousand. It is also worth noticing that the difference between the death rate for European Russia as a whole and for Ukraine was particularly marked with reference to infant mortality[13] and that it was the latter that shows the strongest decrease in the last twenty years preceding the War.[14]

According to the Ukrainian statistics for 1896–1897, the proportion of deaths of infants under one year and from one to two years to the total number of deaths was as follows, in Table 58.

TABLE 58

*Ukrainian Infant Deaths—Proportion to Total Number of Deaths, 1896–1897.**

Age	Percentage of the total number of deaths
0 to 1	36.5
1 to 2	10.4

* N. Novoselsky gives the following data on infant mortality for fifty provinces of European Russia in 1896–1897:

Age	Percentage of the total number of deaths
0 to 1	41.2
1 to 2	10.2

S. A. Novoselsky, *Smertnost i Prodolzhitelnost Zhizni v Rossii* (*Mortality and Longevity in Russia*) [Petrograd, 1916], pp. 100–103.

[12] M. V. Ptukha, *Tablitsi Smertnosti dlya Ukraini 1896–1897 Rokhu* (*Mortality Tables for Ukraine, 1896–1897*) [Kiev, 1923].

[13] *Ibid.*, p. 45. [14] Yakovenko, *op. cit.*, p. 99.

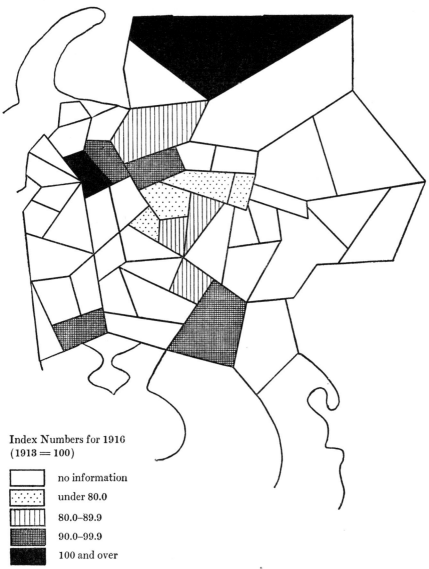

Index Numbers for 1916
(1913 = 100)

☐	no information
⋰	under 80.0
�III	80.0–89.9
▦	90.0–99.9
■	100 and over

CHART XVI

*Index Numbers of Deaths in 1916 as Compared with Deaths
in 1913, by Provinces for European Russia.**

* *Data from Appendix IX, column 7.*

We shall base our computations on these figures. But let us now proceed with the calculations themselves.

Group of forty-one provinces.[15] In 1914 the number of births (compared to that of 1913) was indexed by 101; in 1915 it fell to 87. In order to calculate the influence which the decline in the birth number may have exerted on the number of deaths of infants below one year during 1915, we must attach to the index of 1914 (101) the weight of one-third and to that of 1915 (87) the weight of two-thirds. We can therefore expect the percentage of decline in the number of deaths of infants below one year to equal:

$(101 \times \frac{1}{3}) + (87 \times \frac{2}{3}) = 91.7$; that is to say, the number of deaths of infants below one year should have diminished by 8.3 points in the index series.

The deaths of infants under one year constitute, according to our assumption, 36.5 per cent of the total number of deaths; their relative decline equaling 8.3 signifies a relative decline in the total number of deaths equaling $8.3 \times 36.5 = 3.01$ per cent. We are, therefore, entitled to expect a decrease in the number of deaths of this group of provinces in 1915 equaling 3 per cent of the figure of 1913.

As calculated above, a further decrease of 1.7 per cent in the number of deaths in this group of provinces is due to the withdrawal of adult men to the front. The total reduction in the number of deaths due to changes in the number and age distribution of the population should accordingly reach 4.7 per cent of 1913.

In fact, the number of deaths in 1915 in that group of provinces not only did not diminish, but increased by 1 per cent. We are, therefore, entitled to presume that the general conditions of mortality as expressed in death rates for separate age-groups (which are unknown to us) became slightly less favorable in this group of provinces than it was before the War.

Group of fifteen provinces, including the cities of Petrograd and Moscow. The expected reduction in the mortality of infants below one year in 1915 as compared with 1913 will be as above, 8.3 per cent, and the reduction of the total number of deaths, 3 per cent. Adding the reduction resulting from the loss of men (1.7 per cent), we obtain, as above, a presumable reduction of 4.7 per cent.

[15] We remember that the excluding from this group the provinces adjacent to the front does not change materially the average indexes as well for births as for deaths.

The actual reduction reached exactly this figure, 4.7 per cent, and we may therefore assume that in this group of provinces on the average no change in the mortality conditions occurred.

Let us now take 1916. We must allow for deaths of infants below one year and from one year to two years, and also take into account the birth rate for the three years of 1914, 1915, and 1916. The rates of births compared with 1913 are as shown in Table 59.

TABLE 59

Indexes of Births in 1914, 1915, and 1916 Compared to 1913.

Year	Index number of births (1913 = 100)
1914	101
1915	87
1916	68

The effect of these changes on the reduction of the number of deaths of infants below one year in 1916 compared with the corresponding figure for 1913 is accordingly:

$(87 \times \frac{1}{3}) + (68 \times \frac{2}{3}) = 74$ per cent; the decline in the number of deaths of infants below one year is thus 26 per cent. The resulting relative reduction in the total number of deaths will therefore be 26×36.5 per cent $= 9.5$ per cent.

The expected reduction of deaths for infants between one and two years is $(101 \times \frac{1}{2}) + (87 \times \frac{1}{2}) = 94$ per cent. The reduction is then 6 per cent.

The ratio of deaths of infants of that age to the total number of deaths is 10.4 per cent; the resulting reduction in the total death number will thus be 6×10.4 per cent $= 0.6$ per cent.

The total expected reduction of the number of deaths in 1916 due to the changes in the birth rate in 1914–1916 will therefore be 9.5 per cent plus 0.6 per cent $= 10.1$ per cent, to which must be added the reduction due to the loss of men, 2.3 per cent, or 12.4 per cent in all.

The actual decline in the number of deaths was 11 per cent.[16] This percentage is near enough to the theoretical figure to authorize the inference that the unfavorable turn in the average trend of mor-

[16] The excluding of the province of Vitebsk, adjacent to the front, gives 11.6 per cent.

tality in 1916 in this group of provinces, if it existed at all, was
slight.

Group of six provinces. We shall here eliminate the cities of Petrograd and Moscow, since otherwise the peculiar trend of mortality
in the capitals would exert too great an influence on the total figures,
owing to the exiguity of the territory under consideration. The
change in the number of births compared with 1913 was as follows:

| | *Index number of births* |
Year	*(1913 = 100)*
1914	102
1915	86

$(102 \times \frac{1}{3}) + (86 \times \frac{2}{3}) = 92$ per cent; the expected reduction in
the number of deaths of infants under one year is accordingly 8 per
cent. In proportion to the total number of deaths this will constitute
2.9 per cent. The reduction due to the decrease in the male population is 1.7 per cent, which makes a total of 4.6 per cent. The actual
decrease was, however, 14 per cent.

In 1916 the total number of births constitutes 70 per cent of the
number for 1913. The expected reduction in the number of deaths
due to deaths of infants under one year will be $(86 \times \frac{1}{3}) + (70 \times
\frac{2}{3}) = 75$ per cent, hence the reduction is 25 per cent. The resulting
reduction in the total number of deaths is 25×36.5 or 9.1 per cent.
The same calculation for the age-group one to two years is: $(102 \times
\frac{1}{2}) + (86 \times \frac{1}{2}) = 94$ per cent. The reduction is thus 6 per cent,
and in proportion to the total number of deaths $6 \times 10.4 = 0.6$ per
cent. The total reduction of deaths due to the changes in the birth
rate should therefore be $9.1 + 0.6 = 9.7$ per cent, and the reduction
due to the loss of men 2.3 per cent or 12 per cent in all. The actual
reduction of the number of deaths was 18 per cent.

For the year 1917, we should take into account the deaths of infants from two to three years and the change in the birth rate for
four years but since these deaths have but a small influence on the
total figure of mortality (according to the Ukrainian figures they
constitute 5.7 per cent of the total number of deaths) we may ignore
them for the error will be less than a fraction of 1 per cent.

The number of births in 1917 constituted 54 per cent of the total
number of births in 1913. The expected reduction of the number of
deaths of infants under one year is therefore $(70 \times \frac{1}{3}) + (54 \times \frac{2}{3})$

$= 59$ per cent; the reduction will accordingly be 41 per cent and its proportion to the total number of deaths $41 \times 36.5 = 15$ per cent. The same calculation for deaths of the age-group one to two years gives $(86 \times \frac{1}{2}) + (70 \times \frac{1}{2}) = 78$ per cent; the reduction is accordingly 22 per cent and its proportion to the total number of deaths is 22×10 per cent $= 2.3$ per cent. The total expected reduction in the number of deaths due to the changes in the birth rate will thus be $15 + 2.3 = 17.3$ per cent.

The decline in the death rate due to the decrease in the male population cannot be estimated for 1917, but it will certainly be less than the corresponding figure for 1916. We may therefore assume that the total theoretical figure for the reduction in the number of deaths did not exceed 18 per cent. The actual reduction in the number of deaths in 1917 reached, however, 24 per cent. Tabulating the theoretical and the actual reduction, we obtain for this group of provinces during three years the following figures:

TABLE 60

Actual as Compared with Theoretical Decline in Deaths
(Group of Six Provinces).

| Year | Percentage decline in the number of deaths (1913 = 100) | |
	Theoretical	Actual
1915	4.6	14.0
1916	12.0	18.0
1917	18.0	24.0

We see that in this group of provinces the actual decline in the number of deaths is greater than that expected, but the relative excess of the actual over the theoretical reduction diminishes from year to year. We may therefore assume that, though our approximate calculations show in this group of provinces a certain *improvement* in the conditions of mortality during the War (compared with the pre-war years), this improvement was rapidly diminishing with every year.

We may infer from the above figures that neither the group of fifteen nor the group of six provinces was typical of the whole territory of European Russia, whether in respect to apparent evolution of their death numbers during the War or in regard to the average conditions of mortality. Whereas there is reason to believe that the conditions were not less favorable than before the War in the group of fifteen provinces including both capitals, and that in the six provinces they became more so; they tended on the contrary in the average for the whole territory of European Russia to grow worse (and this is so, whether we exclude the provinces adjacent to the front or not) in 1915 judging by the figures available for forty-one provinces. Since they deteriorated in 1915, there is every reason to believe that they became even less satisfactory with every succeeding year. This is corroborated, moreover, by the information available for the groups of fifteen and six provinces respectively which allow us to infer the rise of the real mortality trend as the War went on.

This conclusion obviously refers only to the *average* for the territory included in the fifty provinces of European Russia; within these limits there are numerous pronounced differences in the conditions of mortality. It is therefore especially interesting to investigate the details of the territorial distribution of the changes in the number of deaths.

Before studying this point, however, we shall make a cursory observation in respect to the influence that may have been exerted on the increase of the number of deaths by the inclusion in the figures for 1915, for a series of provinces, of the so-called "hospital" mortality, that is the deaths of combatants in the hospitals at the rear. As indicated above, not all these deaths are included in the total figures: for several provinces it is not clear whether they are included; for others, however, they are included. When we study the mortality of the civilian population, these deaths should of course be eliminated.

The number of deaths of sick and wounded soldiers in the hospitals at the rear may be approximately estimated on the basis of the figures published by the Narkomzdrav Commission with regard to Russian war casualties. These statistics,[17] extending from the beginning of the War to October, 1916, indicate that approximately 1,500,000 sick and 2,500,000 wounded soldiers were evacuated from the front to the hospitals in the rear. On the basis of the death rate among soldiers in hospital estimated by the Commission, the number of deaths would lie between 200,000 and 250,000. About 40 per cent

[17] Cf. *Proceedings,* especially pp. 145, 147, 163, and 164.

of these occurred in the year 1915, that is approximately from 80,000 to 100,000 for the entire territory of Russia. Since the hospitals were not located in European Russia alone and since the deaths that occurred in the hospitals were not all included in the general death rate, we shall certainly not underestimate the influence of "hospitals" deaths if we assume that the total number of such deaths that were included in the general death rate was between 50,000 and 75,000.[18] The difference between the actual and the expected number of deaths for 1915 in forty-one provinces of European Russia, if the conditions of mortality had remained unaltered, is about 6 per cent of the 1913 figure. It would have been 95.3 per cent and was actually 101 per cent (see p. 107 above). The total number of deaths in 1913 for the whole of European Russia was 3,300,000; thus, worse mortality conditions could cause an increase in the death number equal to 200,000 deaths (6 per cent of 3,300,-000). If we deduct from this figure the 50,000 to 75,000 deaths which occurred among evacuated soldiers, there still remains between 125,000 and 150,000 deaths, being presumably due to the increase in the mortality of the civilian population. This increase is not large enough to justify the assumption that the general mortality trend was made seriously worse, especially as our calculations have not been made with absolute precision. A certain, though not a great, change for the worse in the average mortality conditions in European Russia is, however, likely.

The territorial distribution of the changes in the number of deaths as seen in Appendix IX (to some extent in Charts XV and XVI) show that as indicated above, the death indexes of 1915 and 1916 (1913 = 100) vary considerably more from one province to another than the corresponding birth indexes. Side by side with cases of a decline in the number of deaths reaching from 70 to 80 per cent of the 1913 figure, we have in 1915 cases where the death numbers increased by a substantial percentage (for instance 35 per cent in the province of Samara). Seventeen provinces out of a total of forty-one showed an increase in the death numbers. Three Volga provinces are especially prominent in this respect: these are the provinces of Samara, Saratov, and Astrakhan. Similar conditions prevailed in the provinces of Ekaterinoslav and a series of provinces near to the

[18] For the territory of European Russia without provinces near to the front this figure must be even much smaller.

front (especially those of Minsk, Vitebsk, and Kiev). The death number also increased, though to a smaller extent, in two northeastern provinces (those of Vyatka and Perm) in that of Archangel, in a group of western and southern provinces (Mogilev, Chernigov, Poltava, Kharkov) and in the provinces of the agricultural center (Orel and Ryazan). A decrease in the death number is especially noticeable in the central industrial provinces and in those of Olonets, Vologda, and Kherson. In the province of Volhynia where the death index shows a strong decline the records are obviously incomplete. The statistics for 1916 are only fragmentary (central provinces prevail), but, on the whole, they do not disagree with those of 1915.

We shall now make some comparative calculations in order to test the validity of the figures submitted for the individual provinces. Table G[19] illustrates the correlation existing between the change in the number of deaths in 1915 as compared with 1913 deaths and that of the number of births, 1915 compared with 1913. A direct though not strong degree of correlation can be detected; the coefficient of correlation is +0.26. As may be inferred from the foregoing statements it must not be great. The decline in the number of births, for example, by 20 per cent (which is an exception in 1915) must cause a reduction in the number of deaths among infants under one year, in the same calendar year, of 13 to 14 per cent; which corresponds to a maximum reduction in the total number of deaths of 5 per cent. This slight influence can easily be counterbalanced or concealed by the interference of the other factors.

Table H[19] gives data for the correlation between the index of the changes in the number of deaths and the index for the increased proportion of women. The correlation is inverse and the coefficient of correlation is —0.34. The decrease in the male population must cause a decline in the number of deaths of the remaining population. But, as indicated above, this effect is so slight (it is even less than the influence exerted by the changes in the birth numbers) that it can hardly explain the correlation represented in Table H.[20] This correlation is partly a secondary one (through the medium of the change in the birth numbers) but even if this medium were eliminated the coefficient of the negative correlation is still —0.28.[21] We

---

[19] Correlation tables omitted here; see above, p. 29, n. 34.

[20] Correlation tables omitted here.

[21] This correlation cannot be due to the medium of pre-war mortality since

may possibly have to deal with a purely fortuitous phenomenon, but we may perhaps also assume a certain real positive influence exerted by the high ratio of withdrawal of the male population on the reduction of the death number of the remainder. However paradoxical the statement may seem, the withdrawal of a large number of men under the special conditions prevailing in Russia was capable in certain (especially rural) localities of causing an improvement in the economic situation of the remaining population. We shall have to deal with this question later.

The most conspicuous feature revealed by a comparison of Charts XV and IV, and seen in correlation Table I,[20] is the marked relation between the increased death number and the presence in a given area of refugees. Four provinces where the death index was greatest, except the provinces adjacent to the front and that of Kharkov (for which the records are unreliable), namely the provinces of Samara, Saratov, Ekaterinoslav, and Astrakhan, are also prominent (next to two or three others) as having the largest proportion of refugee households (according to the census of 1917).[22] A certain, though minor, influence was probably exerted by the presence of civilian prisoners. Among the provinces with a high death rate, the provinces of Vyatka[23] and Astrakhan are also notable as including a large percentage of the households of civilian prisoners. Last, but by no means least, must have been the influence exerted by the influx of prisoners of war, especially in the camps where they were assembled and which often acted as foci of infectious diseases. It cannot be merely accidental that the province of Samara shows a very high death index, where a large camp of prisoners of war was located,

the changes in the mortality during the War are only slightly correlated with the pre-war changes.

[22] The largest part of them, without doubt, were there since 1915.

[23] *Cf.* K. Bukhman, *K Voprosu o Monografcheskom Izuchenii Estestvennago Dvizhenya Naselenya za Poslednie Godi* (*A Monographical Investigation of the Natural Change in the Population during Recent Years*), in *Vestnik Statistiki,* Vol. XII [1922]; M. Bukhman gives an investigation of the changes in the population of three rural districts (volost) of the province of Vyatka. These records show that the increase in the death rate was principally due to epidemics. This monograph would present considerable interest if the figures quoted by the author were not in many instances obviously inconsistent.

and an epidemic of typhus levied a toll of many thousand victims.[24]
There are no doubts that the high death index of the province of
Archangel was also partly due to the presence of a large number
of prisoners of war employed in the construction of the Murman
railway. Unfortunately the distribution of prisoners of war among
the different provinces is not available. That the increased real trend
of mortality in the provinces where it took place was due greatly to
the epidemics can be inferred from the data given by Professor
Tarassevitch in his report to the League of Nations on the "Epidemics in Russia Since 1914."[25] The epidemics had not generally become widespread in 1914, 1915, and 1916; this was due chiefly to the
splendid work of the medical organizations, especially those of local
government and their unions. But the situation became worse from
one year to the other and became very critical after the revolution,
with the rapid disorganization of economic and social life, and especially of medical assistance. Typhus, cholera, smallpox, scurvy, were
the chief epidemics spread during the War. Besides this, the army
suffered from typhoid fever, remittent typhoid fever, and dysentery
(see p. 136, n. 8).

If we compare the principal nests of the epidemics with Charts XV
and XVI, giving the death indexes of 1915 and 1916, we shall observe a great correspondence. So, between the provinces most attacked by typhus we find the group of four southeastern provinces
(Astrakhan, Don, Ekaterinoslav, Samara), then the provinces of
Taurida, Kherson, Kiev, and Kaluga. Five of these provinces (especially the four southeastern ones) have death indexes of 1915 greater
than 100 per cent (and have also the percentage of refugee households in 1917 higher than 1.5 per cent).

[24] *Cf.* Zhdanov, *op. cit.,* p. 292.

[25] "Les Epidémies en Russie depuis 1914." *Renseignements Epidémio-
logiques,* Nos. 2 and 5, League of Nations [Geneva, 1922]. Professor Tarassevitch gives considerable statistical data on epidemical cases by provinces
during the War and revolution (compiled by Dr. Kouvshinnikov), yet he
himself warns us of its considerable incompleteness which varies from one
year to the other and from one province to the other. Accordingly we renounced the calculation of provincial indexes of epidemics analogous to those
which we have computed for mortality, and we shall use for comparison, but
the information as to the fact in which provinces were to be found the epidemical nests during the War we take this information from the tables of Dr.
Kouvshinnikov, in Professor Tarassevitch's report, Part I, p. 34 *sqq.*

The cholera was more common in the provinces near to the front, that is, the second group of provinces, marked by the highest death indexes. We find here the provinces of Minsk, Mogilev, Kiev, Chernigov; we find further Kharkov, Poltava, Saratov and some others. All provinces just named have the death indexes of 1915 higher than 100 per cent.

The smallpox had a wider field of action, but this field embraced at all events the great majority of provinces with death rates above 100. Finally, the scurvy, besides in the army, was spread chiefly in the Archangel and Perm provinces.

What follows from our data about all the epidemics is that they did not attack in a greater extent the provinces of the central industrial region, that is, the provinces where we have found the lowest death indexes.[26]

Of course, there are also certain discrepancies between the territorial picture of epidemics and of our mortality indexes, but the observed general correspondence of the two pictures (based on different statistical data furnished by different organs) is sufficient to corroborate the conclusion that our mortality data are not so inaccurate as it might have seemed. The supposition that the correspondence is due to the parallelism in the *degree of incompleteness* of data, caused by the disorganization of the registering apparatus, is little plausible, because this disorganization should be of course more strongly felt in the distant southeastern or northern provinces than in the center, and just the last has the lowest death indexes.

What is, on the contrary, probable is the connection of the higher death indexes of these distant provinces with progressive disorganization of the *public health-service*, that was probably greater in distant provinces than in the center.

Finally, in some provinces, the high death index might partly be the result of poor crops (for instance in the provinces of Ekaterinoslav, Saratov, and Archangel), though on the whole the harvests of the years of the War were not bad, and as may be seen by a compari-

[26] If we disposed with epidemical statistics for the *towns* separately, we would discern probably an increased epidemical urban morbidity also in this most favorably situated region, as well as we state below an increased urban mortality even in a territory in which the total mortality indexes are favorable. We must always remember that our total data are by 85 per cent determined by rural conditions.

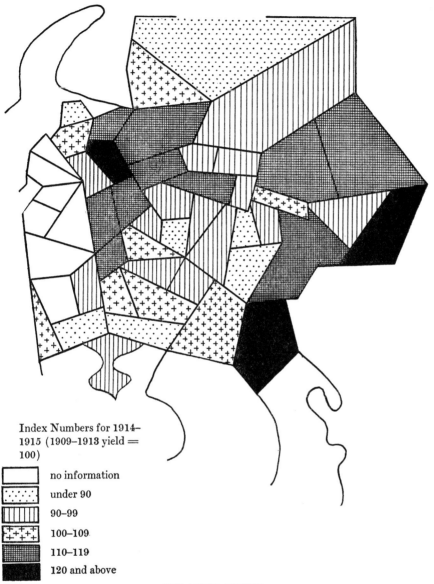

Index Numbers for 1914–
1915 (1909–1913 yield =
100)

	no information
	under 90
	90–99
	100–109
	110–119
	120 and above

CHART XVII

*Index Numbers of the Average Yield of Harvests of 1914
and 1915 as Compared with the Yield for the Period 1909–
1913.*

son of Charts XV and XVII, no correlation can be traced between
the yield of the harvests and the death indexes.

The above causes may explain to some extent (a full explanation
is not attempted here) the local peculiarities of the increase in the
death numbers. But how are we to explain the decline of the death
number which occurred in several provinces, especially in the central ones? As we have seen, this decline cannot be attributed to the
changes in the age distribution of the population alone, and we are
justified in assuming that there was here an improvement in the real
trend of mortality. Nor can we attribute it to defective registration,
for as it was just mentioned the disorganization was certainly less in
the more civilized centers than on the outskirts of European Russia.

In order to understand the situation, we must bear in mind that
the general death indexes, which are here used, are principally determined by the conditions of the rural districts, since the proportion of the urban population is small. It is important to note that a
decline in the number of deaths occurred only in the rural districts.

For thirteen provinces (out of a group of fifteen provinces on
which we worked above for the years 1915 and 1916) the mortality
figures are available separately for towns and for rural districts.
The following figures (Table 61) show the variations in the indexes
as compared with 1913.[27]

TABLE 61

*Mortality Indexes (Thirteen Provinces) for Urban and Rural
Population, 1913 and War Years.*

Years	Urban population	Rural population
1913	100	100
1914	100	95
1915	116	89
1916	119	82

These figures show that the number of deaths in this comparatively favorably situated group of provinces declined only in rural
districts and that in towns it had already increased in 1915 by 16
per cent.[28]

[27] *Proceedings* of the Narkomzdrav Commission, p. 115.
[28] The figures available for the majority of the Ukrainian provinces show
likewise an increase in the death rate in towns.

About the rural districts, it is possible to discover, especially in the central provinces, a number of causes tending, during the War, to improve the conditions of the rural population remaining at home and thus to bring about an actual decline in mortality. The improvement in the economic conditions of the Russian village in the first year and a half or two years of the War is a well-known fact. This was due, first, to the allowances granted to the families of mobilized men. These allowances were paid in cash and amounted to a considerable sum. The poverty of the Russian village and the weak development of monetary economics in it gave to these grants special importance, the more, that the families receiving the allowances had lost at the same time their principal consumers. It is true that they were also deprived of their principal bread earner, but, as is well known, the Russian village never suffered from a scarcity of labor, which was on the contrary, generally in excess of the demand. The loss of labor caused by military service was therefore of comparatively little importance in the village; it was, moreover, to some extent compensated by the cheap labor of the prisoners of war.

An essential factor in the improvement of the economic as well as of the health conditions of the village during the first years of the War was the compulsory temperance resulting from prohibition of the sale of intoxicants, introduced by the Government from the very first days of the War. All who are familiar with the life of the Russian village during these years, lay special emphasis on the excellent influence of this measure. It must be admitted that, as time went on, the population learned to replace the *vodka* by other substitutes. Drunkenness, accordingly, reappeared, but during the first one or two years of the War it undoubtedly decreased very substantially.

During the same period the wealth of the rural community greatly increased, owing to the exploitation of the economic difficulties experienced by the cities and to the high prices of grain. This was especially true of the central provinces, situated in the neighborhood of the large centers of consumption. Owing to the difficulties of transport, great differences in the price of grain existed between the so-called consumption centers (particularly the central industrial area) and the producing regions (the south and the southeast). The profits of the rural population, due to the disorganization of national economy must have been especially noticeable in the central industrial area.[29]

But other factors already cited must also have had a marked influence on the economic life of these provinces. For instance, the larger proportion of mobilized men in these provinces must have brought more considerable allowances to those remaining at home.[30]

These cursory remarks should to a certain extent explain the territorial peculiarities in the changes of mortality. A complete and detailed explanation of this phenomenon is impossible, owing to the absence of the necessary data; it would, moreover, exceed the scope of the present work.

Let us consider, in conclusion, in greater detail, the mortality of the urban population. The foregoing figures certainly show an increase in the total number of deaths in towns; this is true even for the group of provinces where the conditions as to mortality were comparatively favorable. But does this imply a higher death rate for separate age-groups, and if so, to what extent? In other words, does it mean an actual increase in the trend of mortality? It is impossible to answer this question for we lack the necessary information as regards the changes that occurred in the number and age distribution of the urban population. We know merely that the urban population greatly increased, owing to an influx of refugees, who, as indicated above, congregated principally in the towns. The total number of refugees has been estimated above at 3,300,000 persons (this figure is without doubt exaggeratedly small) ; only an insignificant part of this number settled in the rural districts. If we take into consideration that the total number of the urban population of European Russia was 17 to 18 millions, the influence of the refugee masses must have been great. Another factor influencing the number of deaths among the urban population is the mortality in military hos-

[29] At a later date the economic disorganization created by the War began to tell also on the village, especially when the currency rapidly depreciated; for it was the medium in which the village accumulated its savings and it was also the medium of payment of the allowances. This remark, however, applies only to the second half of 1916 and especially to 1917.

[30] This may be the cause of the negative correlation between the ratio of the decrease in the male population and the changes in the death rate referred to above.

pitals, which, of course, should not be included in the mortality of the civilian population, but which is still partly included.

In towns undoubtedly in very many cases we have to deal not only with an increase in the total number of deaths, but also with an actual alteration for the worse in the trend of mortality, represented by higher death rates for separate age-groups. This is certainly the case in the towns of those provinces where the conditions in the villages had become worse. If the trend of mortality in the villages became worse, it must have done so even more in the towns. It is probable also that even in the areas where conditions in the villages were more favorable, they altered for the worse in the towns. The mere influx of refugees created a menace to the health of towns. Those very conditions which enriched the village caused economic difficulties in the towns, an increase in the cost of living and a reduction in its general standard. The economic difficulties increased every year. There were, no doubt, other factors counteracting this influence, such as the prohibition of intoxicants. In several towns the situation was certainly different, but lack of information prevents us from describing the conditions even as they prevailed in the majority of towns. For Petrograd and Moscow, however, information is available which permits us to throw some light on the real trend of mortality there during the War. But the capital cities are not fully typical for other towns and it should be also noticed that the conditions are different in the two capitals. In Petrograd, mortality among the civil population was rising. The death rate, excluding soldiers, was as follows:[31]

TABLE 62

Death Rates per Thousand (Excluding Soldiers), Petrograd, 1913 and War Years.

Year	Death rate (per 1,000)
1913	21.6
1914	22.1
1915	22.2
1916	23.4
1917	24.0

[31] *Proceedings* of the Narkomzdrav Commission, p. 116.

In 1917 the death rate of the civil population had increased by 11 per cent as compared with 1913.[32]

Infant mortality also increased in Petrograd; the number of infants under one year who died, per thousand births, was as follows[33] (Table 63).

TABLE 63

Infant Mortality Changes in Petrograd, 1913 and War Years, Death Rates per Thousand Births.

Year	Death rate of infants under one year (per 1,000 births)
1913	23.1
1914	24.9
1915	25.3
1916	28.4
1917	28.7

Mortality from tuberculosis also showed an increase (before the War it was markedly decreasing).

TABLE 64

Tuberculosis Mortality Rates per Thousand, Petrograd, 1912–1917.

Year	Death rate from tuberculosis per 1,000 (excluding soldiers)
1912	28.8
1913	28.3
1914	29.4
1915	30.8
1916	30.9
1917	31.6

[32] This increase cannot be attributed to the withdrawal of adult men (the healthiest element of the population) since we have seen that this withdrawal was not numerically important in Petrograd.

[33] *Proceedings* of the Narkomzdrav Commission, p. 116.

These figures leave no doubt as to the actual trend of mortality.[34] The city of Moscow presents an entirely different picture. Below we give the general death rates per thousand population (excluding soldiers).[35]

TABLE 65

Moscow General Death Rates, Average, 1910–1914, and Years 1915, 1916, and 1917.

Years	Death rate (per 1,000)
Average for 1910–1914	23.1
1915	22.1
1916	20.2
1917	21.2

We have no statistics for the separate years of the period 1910–1914. Since mortality was decreasing before the War, it is possible that the average for 1910–1914 exceeds the figure for 1913 and that the comparison is therefore unduly favorable to the pre-war years.

Even allowing for this possibility, these figures give no ground for supposing that the death rate of the civilian population in-

[34] It is interesting to point out that the number of deaths due to accidents, suicides, and homicides declined during the War, as can be seen from the following figures:

Year	Number of deaths (per 1,000,000)		
	Accidents	Suicides	Homicides
1912	53.6	31.2	6.7
1913	55.9	27.7	7.0
1914	46.4	21.1	4.2
1915	37.9	10.7	2.8
1916	44.0	11.0	3.4

Prohibition is partly responsible for this decline, but as regards suicides and homicides, psychological causes connected with the War and especially prevalent during its first period must also have exerted an appreciable influence. (*Statistical Returns for the City and Province of Petrograd,* V, 42.)

[35] These and the subsequent figures on mortality in Moscow are borrowed from the above mentioned publication *Red Moscow.* When calculating the general death rate the authors have eliminated infant mortality which occurred in the "Moscow Home for Children," a large institution to which many thousand infants were brought from the suburbs and surrounding villages; they remained there often for only a short time, whence they were taken back to their village.

creased; on the contrary a small decline in this rate should be admitted.

The decline was partly connected with the decrease in the birth rate and, accordingly, with the corresponding reduction in the proportion of infants in the population. Table 66, however, will show that even after the elimination of this factor no increase occurred in the death rate in the first years of the War, but, on the contrary, it went down.

TABLE 66

Moscow Death Rates, Excluding Infants Under One Year of Age.

Years	Death rate per 1,000 population aged one year and over
Average for 1910–1914	15.6
1915	15.7
1916	14.9
1917	16.1

In 1915 there is a slight increase in the death rate; in 1916 the rate is lower than it was in 1913; and only in 1917 does the death rate substantially increase and exceed the pre-war level.

Table 67 gives a more detailed picture of the death rate according to age-groups:

TABLE 67

Moscow Death Rates by Age-groups of the Population.

(*Death rate per 1,000 of each age-group*)

Year	Under 1 yr.	1–14 yrs.	15–49 yrs.	50 yrs. and over
Average for 1910–1914	269	20	9	49
1915	267	25	8	46
1916	262	18	8	49
1917	281	16	7	59

Infant mortality declined only in 1916 and increased again (above the average pre-war rate) in 1917. The death rate of the age-group from one to fourteen years showed a strong increase in 1915 and then fell in 1916 and 1917 below the pre-war rate. For the age-group between fifteen and forty-nine years, the death rate in all these years is somewhat lower than the pre-war rate. The death rate of the age-group above fifty years, while remaining unchanged in

1915 and 1916 at approximately the pre-war level, exceeds it greatly in 1917.

This rather motley picture does not justify the assumption that mortality in Moscow increased during the War, except that in 1917 the death rate of children and old men showed an important increase.

There is certain reason to believe, however, that the above records, so far as the mortality from infectious diseases is concerned, are not fully complete. In the same publication,[36] we find information as to the progress of epidemics of typhus, typhoid fever, recurrent typhoid fever, and dysentery, which show that these epidemics developed greatly during the War.[37]

TABLE 68

Epidemics, Moscow, 1912–1917, by Years.

Name of disease	Number of cases per 1,000,000 population					
	1912	1913	1914	1915	1916	1917
Typhoid fever	649	778	1,237	5,810	3,050	2,475
Typhus	259	284	219	487	1,920	830
Remittent typhoid	648	54	27	798	9,060	2,220
Dysentery	2,278	2,176	2,531	5,645	7,610	4,985

The progress of these four diseases, if doubtful in 1915, is certainly conspicuous in 1916 and 1917. It is true that the records make the comment that these diseases attacked almost exclusively refugees, and that local residents were scarcely affected by them. The distribution of the cases of typhus, typhoid fever, and dysentery between the permanent residents of Moscow and the refugees was as shown in Table 69.

TABLE 69

Epidemics, Moscow, Among Residents and Refugees.

Name of disease	Number of cases	
	Residents	Refugees
Typhoid fever (1915)	1,283	9,290
Typhus (1916)	1,166	1,634
Dysentery (1916)	2,929	12,133

[36] *Red Moscow,* p. 411.   [37] *Ibid.*

These figures throw a strong light on the sanitary conditions of the life of the refugees. But on the other hand, and contrary to all expectation, they show that the epidemics among the refugees had but a small influence on the health of the local residents of Moscow. This is hardly true for other cities, as may be seen from the above quoted figures of the mortality in Petrograd.

The increase in the number of children who died from congenital debility during the years of the War is worth noticing. We possess on the subject only the figures relating to the Moscow Home for Children, but they are sufficiently significant.

TABLE 70

Infant Deaths Caused by Congenital Debility in the Moscow Home for Children.

Year	Percentage of total infant deaths in the home
1914	5.3
1915	6.2
1916	17.0
1917	27.1

This result is principally due to "undesirable" fathers. The departure of the stronger and healthier elements left the field clear for the weaker to propagate. This is one of the painful demographical effects of the War, which will be felt long after the fighting is over. The "undesirable" fathers not only affected the number of children who died from congenital debility, but also the weakness and organic defects of the children who survived, that is to say, it affected ultimately several generations of the post-war period.

CHAPTER IV

THE NATURAL INCREASE AND DECREASE OF THE POPULATION

THE result of the changes in the number of births and of deaths that have been described above are summarized in Table 71, showing the natural net increase (or decrease) of the population.[1]

TABLE 71

Natural Increase (or Decrease) of Population of European Russia, 1913–1917.

Year	50 provinces of European Russia	41 provinces*	15 provinces*	6 provinces†
1913	1,929,911	1,689,969	504,434	164,385
1914	2,051,333	1,788,640	561,572	195,699
1915	....	1,043,178	361,735	118,010
1916	....	....	147,115	35,871
1917	....	....	....	—26,503

* Including the province of Moscow and the cities of Moscow and Petrograd.

† Including the cities of Moscow and Petrograd.

Taking the figures of 1913 as = 100 we obtain indexes as shown in Table 72.

We see from this table that the indexes of the different groups of provinces are not entirely uniform, and especially that those for the groups of fifteen and six provinces are not adequately representative. On the whole the figures of the natural increase of these provinces are larger (and the decrease smaller) than for the whole of European Russia. But even in these groups the natural increase fell already in 1916 to between 20 and 30 per cent of the increase in

[1] The groups of provinces are the same as those chosen for mortality. The totals of the natural increase given in the *Proceedings* of the Narkomzdrav Commission, p. 119, omit for the group of fifteen provinces the province of Kherson, though the figures of its birth and death numbers are used in the text. Our figures include the province of Kherson. We have also corrected some minor errors, which had crept into the totals calculated by the Narkomzdrav Commission.

TABLE 72

Index Numbers for Natural Increase (or Decrease) of Population, European Russia, 1913 and War Years.

Year	50 provinces of European Russia	41 provinces*	15 provinces*	6 provinces†
1913	100	100	100	100
1914	106	106	111	119
1915	..	62	71	72
1916	..	..	29	22
1917	..	..	..	16

* Including the province of Moscow and the cities of Moscow and Petrograd.

† Including the cities of Moscow and Petrograd.

1913; in 1917 an actual decrease is seen. This decrease extends to all the six provinces except that of Tula. In the capitals a decrease of population had already occurred in 1916.

On the basis of the above figures (Table 72) we may make the following estimate of *the loss in the growth of the population of the fifty provinces of European Russia* for the three years of the War *as compared with the normal growth of 1913.*[2] (See Table 73.)

TABLE 73

Estimated Loss in the Growth of Population in Fifty Provinces of European Russia during the War.

Year	Difference between the normal growth (1913) and the growth of given year[3]
1915	733,000
1916	1,370,000
1917 (absence of increase plus actual decrease)	2,239,000
Total	4,342,000

[2] *Proceedings* of the Narkomzdrav Commission, p. 119; our total differs slightly from that given by the Commission, owing to small corrections.

[3] Call G_0 the "normal" growth of the population (say, that of 1913) and G_1 the growth of the given year; B_0, the normal birth number; B_1, the birth number of the given years; and D_0 and D_1, the analogous numbers of deaths. Then the loss (deficit) in natural growth of the population in a given year,

The estimated loss in natural growth of the population is strictly based on the decline of the birth number, since the number of deaths only in the year of 1915 rose a little and in 1916 and 1917, according to our data, did not rise, but decreased, thus more than compensating for the rise in 1915.[4]

The proper decline in the birth number was approximately as follows (see Table 74):

TABLE 74

Estimated Decrease in the Number of Births in European Russia during the War.[5]

Year	Difference between the number of births in 1913 and the number of births in the given year
1915	683,000
1916	1,786,000
1917	2,416,000
Total	4,885,000

When comparing these figures with Table 73, giving the total loss of natural growth of the population during these years, we see that in 1915 the total loss is greater than the decrease of the birth number (to the decrease of births is joined an increase in deaths). On the contrary, in 1916 and 1917 the total deficit in the growth of the population is smaller than the decrease in births; the last is to some extent compensated by the decline of the death number. Owing to this pretty noticeable decline of the death number the total three-

compared with the normal, will be $G_0 - G_1$. As $G_0 = B_0 - D_0$ and $G_1 = B_1 - D_1$, the loss in natural growth (say, L) can be written: $L = B_0 - D_0 - B_1 + D_1 = (B_0 - B_1) - (D_0 - D_1)$. Thus, the loss in the natural growth is equal to the decrease of birth number less the decrease of death number (or *plus* the increase of death number).

[4] It must be always remembered that here we deal with mortality *without war losses* and the reduction of the number of deaths was partly due to the withdrawal of a great mass of men mobilized and the reduction of the number of births (*see* the foregoing chapter).

[5] *Proceedings* of the Narkomzdrav Commission, p. 110. These figures are calculated according to the indexes reckoned for the groups of provinces known to us (*see* Table 40, p. 79).

year deficit in growth of the population is even smaller than the deficit of births alone.[6]

It should, however, be remembered that the above calculation of the deficit in the growth of the population for 1916 and 1917 is underestimated, since it is based on the figures of the groups comprising fifteen and six provinces respectively, together with the capitals. These groups, judging by the figures of 1915, were in a more favorable condition in respect to mortality (the group of six provinces also in regard to the birth rate) than the entire territory of European Russia (see p. 110). There will hardly be any exaggeration in estimating the deficits in the natural growth of the population of European Russia at 4.5–5 million people for the three years of the War; in other words the *net* increase amounted probably to about 800,000–1,300,000 instead of 5,800,000. For the whole territory of the former Russian Empire the loss probably exceeds six million persons. This relates to the deficit in the natural growth of population. In order to estimate *the total loss of human lives*, that Russia bore as a result of the War, we must add to this quantity the *direct* war losses of Russia, i.e., the number of deaths among the mobilized men. This question (which is not strictly connected with vital statistics) we will deal with shortly in the next chapter.

[6] Speaking strictly, Tables 73 and 74 are not quite mutually comparable, since the index of 1916, on which the figure for this year in the first table is based, is computed according to the data for fifteen provinces, while the second table is based on the data for eighteen provinces; similarly the index for 1917 used in the first table is related to six provinces and in the second table to seven provinces. But this fact cannot much change the general picture.

PART III

THE WAR LOSSES OF RUSSIA

THE WAR LOSSES OF RUSSIA

As indicated in the Introduction, the available statistical material about the direct war losses of Russia is hardly more complete than that relating to the natural growth of the population. A great deal of statistical material exists on cards, and it is preserved in the archives of the institutions concerned. But it is as yet scarcely analyzed and is preserved in a rather chaotic condition, which renders the work of compilation very difficult.

Three documents based on this material have been published. They contain a partial analysis of the available material. They are the following: (1) *Russia in the World War*,[1] often quoted in this work; (2) the appropriate chapters of the *Proceedings* of the Commission for Investigating the Effect of the War on Public Health,[2] and (3) an article by Dr. V. Avramov on Russian war losses.[3] The latter represents an independent attempt to estimate the number of victims of the War based on the material of the Army Health Department.[4]

The *Proceedings* of the Narkomzdrav Commission contain two articles on the war losses of Russia. One was compiled by Dr. Binshtok; the other by L. I. Sasonov. Each author approaches the problem of the war losses from a different point of view. The latter calculates the general losses of the army, that is to say, he estimates the number of soldiers who left the ranks owing to various causes and does not consider their ultimate fate (so that, in the losses are counted also the wounded soldiers who, after being cured, returned to the ranks). The former attempts to establish the *net* losses of Russia, that is, to trace among those who left the ranks of the army the actual number of deaths. From the demographical point of view the latter conception of war losses is certainly of greater value. But the first is

---

[1] *Cf.* above, p. 8.   [2] *Cf.* above, p. 4, n. 4.

[3] V. Avramov, *Zhertvi Imperialisticheskoi Voini v Rossii* (*Victims of the Imperialistic War in Russia*) in *Izvesia Narkomzdrava* (*Bulletin of the People's Commissariat of Public Health*), Nos. 1 and 2 [1920].

[4] We were unable to obtain a copy of Dr. Avramov's article and are using here the excerpts which appeared in *Russia in the World War* and in the *Proceedings* of the Narkomzdrav Commission.

not devoid of importance, and we shall begin with it as containing the more general information.

The Narkomzdrav Commission, represented by M. Sazonov, does not give any final figure of the war losses. It produces cautiously a series of calculations based on various sources, commenting upon them critically, and indicating which of the various estimates it considers most trustworthy. As indicated above, the calculations of the Central Statistical Office, published in *Russia in the World War*, are also available and include two distinct estimates: one based on the figures of the former General Headquarters, and the other on the records of the General Staff, independently analyzed by the Central Statistical Office. Lastly we have the above-mentioned computation of Dr. Avramov.

It is of course impossible to give here an independent analysis of all these frequently contradictory estimates, or to arrive at a satisfactory final figure. This can be done only by specialists of war science. We can only compare the existing estimates and draw the most obvious inferences from this comparison. For an appreciation of them we shall only have to utilize the critical comments of the Narkomzdrav Commission on the one side and of certain other specialists on the other.[5]

The estimates referred to may be tabulated as in Table 75, for purposes of comparison:

The differences in the estimates of the number killed are relatively immaterial except as regards estimate IV, which is considered by the Commission itself as unduly low. The figure may be taken as between 600,000 and 650,000.[6]

[5] We mean chiefly the public lectures given in Paris by General N. N. Golovine, one of the best war specialists of Russia, on the "War Efforts of Russia." Regrettably, we can quote them only according to a report in the Russian newspaper *Vozrozhdienie* [Paris, January 26, 1927]. *Cf.* also General N. N. Golovine, *The Russian Army in the World War* [Yale University Press, 1931], in this series of the "Economic and Social History of the World War." General Golovine's was published when the present volume was already in the press.

[6] The number of killed was estimated by foreign investigators at 1.5 or even 2.5 million. The Central Statistical Office's comment on these figures is that they are obviously exaggerated. They are based on calculations, which are not confirmed by the material at the disposal either of the Central Statistical Office or of the Narkomzdrav Commission.

TABLE 75

Various Estimates of Russia's War Losses.

Casualties	General losses of the army					
	I	II	III	IV	V	VI
	According to the figures of the General Staff for December 31, 1917 (Russia in the World War, Tables 22 and 23)	According to the figures of the General Headquarters for September 1, 1917 (ibid., Table 5)	According to the figures of the Narkomzdrav Commission based on the data of the General Headquarters and General Staff for October 1, 1917	According to the figures of the Narkomzdrav Commission based on subsequent research in State Archives (1914–1918)	According to the figures of Dr. Avramov for October 1, 1917 (as quoted by the Narkomzdrav Commission)	According to the figures of Dr. Avramov with corrections introduced by the Narkomzdrav Commission
Killed	228,838	} 775,400	600,000	511,068	646,512	646,512
Missing	626,440		200,000	200,000	2,333,375	200,000
Wounded and shell-shocked	2,715,603	2,844,500	3,000,000	2,830,262	3,748,669	3,748,669
Died of wounds before evacuation	17,174	....	....	35,185	18,378	18,378
Died of wounds, shell-shocks, and disease	....	....	200,000	....	....	....
Released from service on account of wounds, shell-shock, and disease	....	348,500	700,000	....	....	....
Gassed	38,599	....	40,000	....	65,158	65,158
Prisoners	3,409,433	3,343,900	2,043,548	3,759,000	....	3,750,000
Total	7,036,087	7,312,300	6,788,548	7,385,515	6,812,092	8,428,717

The number missing is also more or less uniform and is estimated at about 200,000: an exception is to be made for the computation of Dr. Avramov who gives the colossal figure of 2,333,000 missing. The Narkomzdrav Commission thinks that this estimate includes, in addition to the "missing" proper, losses which should be included in other categories, and particularly men taken prisoners. Dr. Avramov gives no figure for these. The number of prisoners is estimated at 3,000,-000 to 3,750,000, except in estimate III based on the figures of the General Headquarters (2,043,548). The figure of the latter is considered by the Commission (L. I. Sasonov) to be an obvious underestimate. The most probable figure, according to the Commission is 3,750,000. On the contrary, Gen. N. N. Golovine in his lectures quoted above,[7] estimates the number of Russians taken prisoners as only 2,440,000. As his estimate is also based upon data procured from German and Austrian archives, it merits perhaps more confidence than the other estimates. Lastly, the figure of those gassed lies within two not widely divergent limits of 40,000 to 65,000.

The greatest discrepancies occur with reference to the number of wounded and shell-shocked soldiers. These are only partly due to material discrepancies and partly caused by lack of uniformity in distributing the figures among the various headings.

Estimate III, distinguishing out of the total number of wounded and shell-shocked men, those who died from injuries, adds to them those who died from *diseases* (together 200,000 men—a figure inspiring little confidence). In other estimates those who died from diseases are not included and generally our table does not count the sickness casualties.[8] From these last the estimates II and III include also the sick, *released from service* (together with men released on account of wounds and shell-shock). In other estimates this is not so, and the wounded, released from service, are even not discerned out of the total number of wounded. This is the case also in the estimate of Dr. Avramov, which is considered by the Narkomzdrav Commis-

[7] See *Vozrozhdienie,* January 26, 1927.

[8] The total number of sickness cases in the army is estimated by Dr. Avramov as 5,069,000, from which the numbers of chief infectious sickness casualties are as follows: typhus 21,093, typhoid fever 97,522, remittent typhoid fever 75,429, dysentery 64,364, cholera 30,810, smallpox 2,708, scurvy 362,756 (see *Proceedings,* p. 144).

sion to come nearest to the truth,[9] subject to correction in respect of the missing and the prisoners. Such a corrected estimate is presented in the last column of our table. It puts the total losses of the army at some 8.5 millions, distributed as follows: 3,750,000 prisoners of war, an equal number of wounded and shell-shocked soldiers, approximately 65,000 gassed, and finally about 865,000 killed and missing.

If we do not admit the correction of the Commission as to the number of prisoners and estimate it with General Golovine as to be about 2,500,000, we arrive to the figure of 7.2 millions representing the total losses of the army.

Thus, the total losses of the army represent from 7.2 to 8.5 millions, that is, from 45 to 54 per cent of the total number of mobilized men (approximately 15.8 millions); the killed and missing amount to 10–12 per cent of the total loss and about 5.5 per cent of the total number of mobilized men.

Let us now consider the number of *fatal casualties* (killed, died of wounds and sickness, died in captivity, and reported missing). Not only deaths caused by wounds and sickness among men with their units, but also those which occurred among men in the hospitals behind the lines should be taken into account for this purpose. The calculation becomes accordingly even more complicated and less reliable. The Narkomzdrav Commission, represented by Dr. Binshtok, has attempted such a computation on the basis of more or less trustworthy assumptions regarding the rate of mortality among wounded and sick soldiers. The Commission itself considers the result very conjectural. It is as follows (see Table 76):

TABLE 76

Fatal Casualties among Soldiers of Russia

Casualties	*Number of men*
Killed	664,890
Died of wounds with their units	18,378
Died of wounds in the hospitals	300,000
Died of diseases in the hospitals	130,000
Died in captivity	285,000
Sudden deaths	7,196
Reported missing	200,000

[9] General Golovine also considers Dr. Avramov's figures as the best, but in his quotation they are somewhat different.

Casualties	*Number of men*
Died of gas	6,340
Additional losses in the Caucasian front not included in the above figures	50,000
	1,661,804
Or in round numbers	1,660,000

The total figure thus arrived at for fatal casualties is **1,660,000**.[10] The Commission considers it an underestimate, which is very plausible. Especially inaccurate seems to be the figure for deaths from diseases (130,000). If we apply to the mass of mobilized men (15.8 millions) the normal death rates of their age-groups (*see* above, p. 103), we shall infer that, if the mobilized had remained at home in normal conditions, they would have lost as result of diseases during three years about 150,000 men. It follows from this that being in the army, the mobilized had given a lesser number of deaths from diseases than they would have given at home in peace-time. If we take into account the fact that the number of mobilized must for this comparison be reduced by the killed, wounded, and taken prisoners, nevertheless, the figure of 130,000 dead from diseases seems to be too small.[11] Of course, if we would estimate the net loss *caused by the War*, we should deduct from the loss in the army the number of deaths which would have occurred among the mobilized men, if the War had not taken place, i.e., 150,000.

The number of fatal casualties thus estimated represents approximately 10.5 per cent of the number of mobilized men, 1 per cent of the total number of men of working age.

Adding to this figure of actual losses of life resulting from the War, the losses due to the change in the natural growth of the population, which were estimated in the foregoing chapter at over 6 millions, we obtain for the total loss of human lives a figure approaching 8 millions. This is about 5 per cent of the population of the Empire and equals approximately its natural growth for three years.

Such is the approximate and probably underestimated total loss

[10] Almost the same number of fatal casualities is admitted by General Golovine (1,650,000).

[11] To the same opinion about this figure Professor L. Hersch comes in his interesting study on "La Mortalité Causée par la Guerre," *Metron*, V, No. 1 [1925].

of human lives inflicted upon Russia by the War. As indicated by
the Narkomzdrav Commission, this computation obviously does not
include "those physical and moral lesions, affecting many millions,
suffered by all who participated in the War. These lesions affect, and
will for a long time continue to affect the combatants by shortening
their lives, impairing and undermining their strength, and making
them and their children more liable to diseases."

Of these physical and moral lesions an approximate estimate can
be made only in respect of the disabled men. We shall now briefly
deal with this point.

On the basis of the number of wounded and sick soldiers, as well
as on that of the approximate ratio of disabled men to the total number of men admitted to the hospitals of the All-Russian Union of
Towns (this ratio was 25 per cent for the wounded and 14 per cent
for the sick) the Narkomzdrav Commission estimates the number of
disabled at 1,400,000 men (with the reservation, however, that this
figure is probably too low).[12] The number of disabled men is thus almost equal to the number of fatal casualties.

It is interesting to quote certain figures relating to cases of disablement caused by the War, which are the result of a study undertaken by the Petrograd Committee of the All-Russian Union of
Towns.[13] The rates of disablement of sick and wounded soldiers, distributed according to age-groups, are as shown in Table 77.

TABLE 77

*Releases from Service Due to Disablement (per Thousand
Wounded or Sick of Each Age-groups).*

Age-group	Wounded	Sick
Under 20	18.6	9.6
20 to 29	25.0	13.0
30 to 39	28.4	18.8
40 and above	31.8	23.8

The percentage of disablement increases markedly with the age of
the wounded and sick soldiers. The increase is more rapid in respect
of the latter than of the wounded. The ratio of disablement is on the

[12] *Proceedings*, p. 34.
[13] *Ibid.*, p. 179. Paper of W. Novoselsky. The cases observed included
103,000 wounded and 70,700 sick soldiers.

whole greater for the wounded than for the sick, but for the older age-groups this difference is less marked.

The influence exerted by the locality of the wound may be judged by Table 78.

TABLE 78

Locus of Wounds and Rate of Disablement Thereby.

Locus of wound	Number of disabled per 100 wounded of a given category
Head (skull, face and neck)	36.5
Thorax and back	17.0
Abdomen and pelvis	18.2
Upper extremities	32.5
Lower extremities	32.9
Multiple wounds	35.4

The highest rate of disablement is produced by the wounds affecting the extremities and the head, as well as by multiple wounds, the least, by the wounds of the thorax, back, abdomen, and pelvis (the latter wounds give the highest ratio of deaths).

We give, in Table 79, the detailed figures of the distribution of the disablement of wounded soldiers, according to its cause:

TABLE 79

Causes of Disablement among the Wounded and Number of Cases for Each.

Cause of disablement	Number of cases
Cicatrice, anchylosis, contractions, false joints	5,396
Palsy, paralysis, atrophy	3,356
Amputation and mutilation of fingers	2,423
Total or partial amputation of low or upper extremities . .	1,925
Bending or shortening of the extremities	1,837
Total or partial blindness	1,126
Mutilation or defects of the tongue, palate, lips, cheeks, jaws .	517
Total or partial deafness	427
Injury to the skull	375
Other causes	1,800
Total	19,182

The cases of disablement among sick soldiers may be distributed according to their origin as shown in Table 80.

TABLE 80

Causes of Disablement among Sick Soldiers.

Cause of disablement	Number of cases
Tuberculosis	2,142
Diseases of the ear	1,444
Lunacy	891
Diseases of the ophthalmic organs	769
Hernia	700
Diseases of the viscera of the abdomen and pelvis	457
Diseases of the heart and circulatory system	436
Diseases of the respiratory system	331
Other causes	2,174
Total	9,344

Finally, in Tables 81 and 82 and connected text are the same 28,526 disabled men according to their age, family status, and profession.

TABLE 81

Age Distribution of Disabled Men.

Age-group	Percentage of total disabled men
Below 21	9.0
21 to 24	25.7
25 to 29	25.5
30 to 34	19.7
35 to 39	13.1
40 years and above	4.6
Age not specified	2.4
	100.0

The youngest and most vigorous age-group from 18 to 29 years represents 60 per cent of the total number of disabled. It does not, however, constitute more than 20 per cent of the male population.

The distribution according to the family status was as follows: 37 per cent were bachelors, 60 per cent were married, and the rest were either widowers or their family status was not specified.

The distribution according to professions exercised before the beginning of their military service was as shown in Table 82.

TABLE 82

Pre-war Occupations and Percentage of Disabled Soldiers Having Had Each Occupation.

Percentage of the total
number of disabled men

Agriculture 60.4
Manufacturing industries 17.1
Commerce 2.1
Transport 1.8
Domestic services 1.6
Liberal professions, Central, Local, Government service . . 1.0
Unskilled laborers 4.4
Not specified 11.6

————
100.0

These figures show a smaller percentage (among the disabled) of men engaged in agriculture than might have been expected.

APPENDIX I

List of Successive Orders Calling Men to the Colors.[14]

(According to the Data of the Former Ministry for War, April 1, 1917.)[15]

Year, month, and day		Classes of Men Called.	Number of men called to colors (in thousands)
1914 July	18	Total number of *peace-time army* at the date of mobilization	1,423
July	18	*Reserves*	3,115
		Territorials of the First Class.	
July	22	Transferred from the reserve force	400
		Not having previously passed through the ranks.	
July	22	Call of men not having passed through the ranks .	400
September	22	Call of men not having passed through the ranks .	300
November 12 and 20		Classes 1914–1903 (except the Caucasus and the Amur Governate General)	200

[14] *Russia in the World War*, Table 2. When considering the classes of mobilized men one should remember that formerly every successive order calling men to the colors included equally all the previously mobilized classes. In practice, however, every new order affected principally classes not previously mobilized. The only exceptions are the early orders concerning territorials of the first class.

[15] All dates in this monograph are given in accordance with the Russian calendar.

			Year, month, and day	Number of men called to colors (in thousands)

1915	January	2	Call of men not having passed through the ranks .	480
	April	1	Classes 1915–1900 (except the Caucasus and the Amur and Warsaw Governates General)	600
	August	15	Classes 1916–1898 (except the Caucasus, Amur, Maritime, Sakhalin, and Kamchatka regions) . .	800
	August	15	Classes 1916–1898 (in Asiatic Russia and Turkestan) and classes 1916–1910 (in the Caucasus)	50
	September	15	Classes 1916–1898 (territorials of the first class having not passed and having passed through the ranks and territorials of the first class according to the law of December 25, 1909 (in the Amur Governate General)	25
	October	15	Classes 1916–1906 (in the Caucasus)	30
1916	February	1	Classes 1916–1903 (in the Caucasus)	25
	March	25	Classes 1916–1897 (except the Caucasus and the Amur Governate General) . . . . }	150
	August	25	Classes 1902–1898 (in the Caucasus)	
	September	20	Classes 1919–1916–1894 (except the Caucasus) . .	150

Territorials of the Second Class.

1915	September	5	Classes 1916–1912 (except the Caucasus, the Amur and Warsaw Governates General and the province of Kholm)	900
	September	15	Classes 1916–1912 (in the Amur Governate General)	25
	October	30	Classes 1916–1910 (except the Caucasus, the Warsaw and Amur Governates General and the province of Kholm)	400
1916	February	1	Classes 1916–1908 (except the Caucasus and the Amur Governate General)	300
	March	25	Classes 1916–1906 (except the Caucasus and the Amur Governate General)	300
	August	25	Classes 1916–1903 (except the Caucasus)	360
	August	25	Classes 1916–1910 (in the Caucasus)	50
	September	20	Classes 1916–1900 (except the Caucasus)	360
	October	25	Classes 1916–1896	350
1917	January	10	Classes 1916–1906 (in the Caucasus)	30

New Classes.

1914	October	1	Class 1914	700
1915	January	25	Class 1915	700
	May	15	Class 1916	550
	August	7	Born in 1896	950
1916	May	15	Born in 1897	700
1917	February	3	Born in 1898	600
			Men of the above categories formerly declared unfit for military service of the classes 1916–1910 (holders of "white certificates")[16]	200

| | | | Total of men mobilized from July 18, 1914, to April 1, 1917 . . . . | 13,700 |
| | | | Grand total including peace-time army . . . | 15,123 |

[16] *Cf.* above, p. 13, n. 3.

APPENDIX II

Estimated Approximate Numbers of Men Called to the Colors in Fifty Provinces of European Russia.[17]

Year, month, and day			Categories (Classes Called).	Estimated number of men called to colors (in thousands)
1914	July	18	Reserves	2,490
	July	22	Territorials of the first class, transferred from the reserve force	320
	July	22	Territorials of the first class not having passed through the ranks (classes 1913–1910)	320
	September	22	Territorials of the first class not having passed through the ranks (classes 1913–1909)	240
	October	1	Class 1914	560
	November	12	Territorials of the first class	
	and	20	(classes 1914–1903)	170
			Total called during 1914	4,100
1915	January	2	Territorials of the first class (classes 1914–1902) .	385
	January	21	Class 1915	560
	April	1	Territorials of the first class (classes 1915–1900) .	550
	May	15	Class 1916	475
	August	7	Born in 1896	820
	August	15	Territorials of the first class (classes 1916–1898) .	275
	September	5	Territorials of the second class (classes 1916–1912) .	820
	October	30	Territorials of the second class (classes 1916–1910) .	365
			Total called during 1915	4,250
1916	February	1	Territorials of the second class (classes 1916–1908) .	270
	March	25	Territorials of the first class (classes 1916–1897) and of the second class (classes 1916–1906)	370
	May	15	Born in 1897	600
	August	25	Territorials of the second class (classes 1916–1903) .	325
	September	20	Territorials of the first class (classes 1919–1916–1894)	135

[17] *Russia in the World War,* Tables 2, 40 and 41; and *Proceedings* of the Narkomzdrav Commission. According to the provincial figures of the number of allowances granted to the families of mobilized men (shown in Table 40, *op. cit.*) and to the population of the former Russian Poland, we estimate that in cases where the order calling men to the colors extended over the territory of the whole Empire the share of the fifty provinces of European Russia was 80 per cent. When it did not cover the territory of former Russian Poland (such were all orders issued after the occupation of Poland by the Germans, that is, from the second half of 1915, onward (though this is not always indicated in Table 2), the share of the fifty provinces of European Russia is estimated at 86 per cent. Finally this share is estimated at 91 per cent when the order did not extend either to Russian Poland or to the Caucasus. We have no information as to the part of the peace-time army drawn from European Russia and we can only state this part proportionally to the population, which probably signifies a certain underestimate.

Year, month, and day		Estimated number of men called to colors (in thousands)
September 20	Territorials of the second class (classes 1916–1900) .	325
October 25	Territorials of the second class (classes 1916–1896) .	300
	Total called during 1916	2,325
1917 February 3	Born in 1898	515
	Total to April 1, 1917	11,190
	Holders of revised "white certificates"	160
	Total of mobilized men up to April 1, 1917 . .	11,350
	Approximate number of men mobilized after April 1, 1917	580
	Total of men mobilized during the War . . .	11,930
	Approximate number of men in the peace-time army drawn from the fifty provinces of European Russia	1,030
	Grand Total	12,960

APPENDIX III

Number of Men Mobilized in Rural Districts of Russia and the Number of Allowances Granted to Families of Men on Military Service on September 1, 1917, by Provinces and Territories.[18]

Province or territory	Number of men mobilized in rural districts according to agricultural census	Number of allowances granted		
		in rural districts	in towns and cities	in all districts
1. Archangel	41,800	94,000	6,800	100,800
2. Astrakhan	112,000	242,000	33,500	275,500
3. Bessarabia	256,300	565,700	64,900	630,600
4. Vilna	47,800	114,800	2,700	117,500
5. Vitebsk	178,600	402,500	36,800	439,300
6. Vladimir	168,300	540,500	60,200	600,700
7. Vologda	205,200	506,000	12,100	518,100
8. Volhynia	267,300	686,900	76,300	763,200
9. Voronezh	380,300	1,113,900	17,900	1,131,800
10. Vyatka	398,500	998,000	14,100	1,012,100
11. Don Territory . . .	290,800	393,900	43,800	437,700
12. Ekaterinoslav . . .	237,000	862,800	77,600	940,400
13. Kazan	277,600	803,800	38,600	842,400

18 From *Russia in the World War*, Table 40; data according to the statistics of the Ministry of the Interior and the Agricultural Census of 1917.

Province or territory	Number of men mobilized in rural districts according to agricultural census	Number of allowances granted		
		in rural districts	in towns and cities	in all districts
14. Kaluga	154,100	411,000	18,600	429,600
15. Kiev	383,900	984,500	78,700	1,063,200
16. Kostroma	190,100	519,100	28,700	547,800
17. Kursk	345,500	947,200	30,700	977,900
18. Livonia	91,700	144,400	81,200	225,600
19. Minsk	236,400	539,200	42,100	581,300
20. Mogilev	219,400	551,900	30,600	582,500
21. Moscow	166,300	430,200	304,900	735,100
22. Nizhni-Novgorod . .	190,000	596,300	26,000	622,300
23. Novgorod	183,900	413,800	16,500	430,300
24. Olonets	51,700	117,900	3,400	121,300
25. Orenburg	160,300	532,600	59,600	592,200
26. Orel	254,700	677,100	30,800	707,900
27. Penza	188,900	666,100	27,800	693,900
28. Perm	416,600	990,700	34,100	1,024,800
29. Petrograd	77,800	440,300	358,300	798,600
30. Podolia	391,000	928,100	33,900	962,000
31. Poltava	337,800	828,600	48,500	877,100
32. Pskov	164,300	385,700	18,400	404,100
33. Ryazan	255,800	640,600	20,800	661,400
34. Samara	379,900	1,399,800	71,100	1,470,900
35. Saratov	305,400	884,000	107,700	991,700
36. Simbirsk	211,700	603,900	32,200	636,100
37. Smolensk	187,800	535,400	23,400	558,800
38. Taurida	212,600	450,200	72,700	522,900
39. Tambov	387,100	1,188,500	36,100	1,224,600
40. Tver	201,700	623,400	37,700	661,100
41. Tula	189,200	523,200	22,600	545,800
42. Ufa	323,200	876,400	54,700	931,100
43. Kharkov	337,300	932,200	103,600	1,035,800
44. Kherson	438,300	848,200	230,100	1,078,300
45. Chernigov	280,200	634,600	55,400	690,000
46. Esthonia	23,500	40,400	17,400	57,800
47. Yaroslav	133,000	324,900	32,800	357,700
Total for forty-seven provinces of European Russia . . .	10,932,600	28,935,200	2,676,400	31,611,600
Caucasus	719,000	1,527,200	241,700	1,768,900
Siberia and Central Asia	1,209,800	2,916,400	274,200	3,190,600
Grand Total . .	12,861,400	33,378,800	3,192,300	36,571,100

APPENDIX IV

Pre-war Marriage Rates in European Russia, by Provinces, as Compared with the Average Rates for Two Years, 1897 and 1899.[19]

Province or territory	Average marriage rates per 1,000 population for years 1909, 1910, 1911, and 1913	Index numbers[20] of marriage rates averaged for the years 1909, 1910, 1911, and 1913 (average for '97 and '99 = 100)
1. Archangel	8.6	95.6
2. Astrakhan	10.7	109.2
3. Bessarabia	8.3	106.4
4. Vilna	6.3	81.8
5. Vitebsk	6.3	82.9
6. Vladimir	7.6	81.7
7. Vologda	8.8	102.3
8. Volhynia	7.6	80.0
9. Voronezh	7.9	75.2
10. Vyatka	9.0	93.8
11. Grodno	6.6	79.5
12. Don Territory	8.3	85.6
13. Ekaterinoslav	8.9	88.1
14. Kazan	8.8	86.3
15. Kaluga	8.3	83.8
16. Kiev	8.2	91.1
17. Kovno	5.3	77.9
18. Kostroma	8.6	93.5
19. Courland	5.9	83.1
20. Kursk	7.7	84.6
21. Livonia	7.3	94.8
22. Minsk	7.5	88.2
23. Mogilev	6.8	83.9
24. Moscow	6.6	85.7
25. Nizhni-Novgorod	7.6	80.0
26. Novgorod	7.4	92.5
27. Olonets	8.7	102.4
28. Orenburg	9.9	89.2
29. Orel	8.2	87.2
30. Penza	8.2	75.9
31. Perm	9.4	95.9
32. Petrograd	6.4	94.1
33. Podolia	8.2	90.1
34. Poltava	7.6	84.4
35. Pskov	7.6	91.5
36. Ryazan	7.1	71.0
37. Samara	9.2	86.0

[19] According to the Statistics of the Central Statistical Committee (data for 1912 omitted).

[20] The index number for a province expresses the average marriage rate for the years 1909, 1910, 1911, and 1913 as a percentage of the average marriage rate for two years, 1897 to 1899 in that same province; this is the meaning of the title parenthesis (average for 1897 and 1899 = 100).

Province or territory	Average marriage rates per 1,000 population for years 1909, 1910, 1911, and 1913	Index numbers[20] of marriage rates averaged for the years 1909, 1910, 1911, and 1913 (average for '97 and '99 = 100)
38. Saratov	7.9	78.2
39. Simbirsk	8.7	87.0
40. Smolensk	7.9	85.9
41. Taurida	8.8	104.8
42. Tambov	9.2	97.9
43. Tver	7.4	76.3
44. Tula	7.0	74.5
45. Ufa	10.6	93.8
46. Kharkov	8.7	88.9
47. Kherson	8.6	111.7
48. Chernigov	7.5	85.2
49. Esthonia	7.2	98.6
50. Yaroslav	8.1	89.0

APPENDIX V

Number of Marriages in European Russia in the Years 1913–1917;[21] Actual Numbers and Index Numbers (1913 = 100) by Provinces.

Province or territory	Total number of marriages					Index numbers (1913 = 100)[22]		
	1913	1914	1915	1916	1917	1915	1916	1917
Archangel	3,883	3,598	2,027	....	....	52.2	..	..
Astrakhan	9,579	8,421	....	....	....	..	..	..
Bessarabia	20,069	21,110	....	....	....	..	..	..
Vilna	12,500	12,065	....	....	....	..	..	..
Vitebsk	10,256	10,068	5,235	5,082	4,998	51.0	49.6	48.7
Vladimir	15,683	11,609	3,943	3,926	4,896	25.1	25.0	31.2
Vologda	15,388	12,289	5,010	....	....	32.6	..	..
Volhynia	28,599	20,300	....	....	....	..	..	..
Voronezh	31,950	23,168	10,591	13,920	....	33.1	43.6	..
Vyatka	34,827	31,300	16,814	....	....	48.3	..	..
Grodno	13,631	13,911	....	....	....	..	..	..
Don Territory	32,391	25,923	15,632	....	....	48.3	..	..
Ekaterinoslav	30,299	20,399	12,114	....	....	40.0	..	..
Kazan	24,366	24,220	12,568	....	....	51.6	..	..
Kaluga	13,089	9,840	4,814	4,719	6,290	36.7	36.1	48.1
Kiev	37,535	29,496	....	....	....	..	..	..
Kovno	9,393	9,110	....	....	....	..	..	..
Kostroma	16,116	13,655	5,705	....	....	35.4	..	..
Courland	4,531	4,612	....	....	....	..	..	..
Kursk	23,574	18,207	11,585	....	....	49.1	..	..

[21] According to the statistics of the Commission to Investigate the Effect of the War of 1914–1920 on Public Health.

[22] The index number for 1915 expresses the number of marriages in that year for any given province as a percentage of the number of marriages in 1913 in that same province; this is the meaning of the title parenthesis (1913 = 100). Index numbers for 1914 not reported although data for number of marriages is given.

Province or territory	1913	Total number of marriages 1914	1915	1916	1917	Index numbers (1913 = 100)[22] 1915	1916	1917
Livonia	11,196	9,615	....	....	....	..	..	..
Minsk	22,316	16,003	....	....	....	..	..	..
Mogilev	18,841	17,910	....	....	....	..	..	..
Moscow (province) .	13,432	10,194	4,036	4,193	....	30.0	31.2	..
Moscow (city) . . .	10,093	9,679	7,478	7,623	9,900	74.1	75.5	98.9
Nizhni-Novgorod . .	16,625	12,607	5,715	....	....	34.4	..	..
Novgorod	14,932	11,806	4,791	....	....	32.1	..	..
Olonets	4,205	3,514	....	....	....	..	..	..
Orenburg	21,093	19,890	....	....	....	..	..	..
Orel	21,321	13,984	7,417	7,963	....	34.8	37.3	..
Penza	16,441	11,166	....	....	....	..	..	..
Perm	30,440	28,408	18,543	....	....	60.9	..	..
Petrograd (province) .	7,937	6,061	....	....	....	..	..	..
Petrograd (city) . .	13,403	13,202	11,569	11,299	20,559	86.3	84.3	153.4
Podolia	30,066	30,053	....	....	....	..	..	..
Poltava	28,450	22,228	....	....	....	..	..	..
Pskov	10,549	10,275	....	....	....	..	..	..
Ryazan	17,786	16,981	....	....	....	..	..	..
Samara	34,932	30,819	16,016	15,836	....	45.8	45.3	..
Saratov	26,025	22,061	11,399	11,868	19,124	43.8	45.6	73.5
Simbirsk	18,960	14,420	....	....	....	..	..	..
Smolensk	19,472	18,873	....	....	....	..	..	..
Taurida[23]	17,194	11,015	6,393	....	....	37.2	..	..
Tambov	37,479	20,048	9,625	....	....	25.7	..	..
Tver	19,058	15,464	5,595	3,869	6,341	24.1	20.3	33.3
Tula	12,796	9,281	4,245	....	....	33.2	..	..
Ufa	31,323	27,262	....	....	....	..	..	..
Kharkov[24]	31,725	25,481	12,298	....	....	38.8	..	..
Kherson[25]	24,965	15,970	7,752	....	....	31.1	..	..
Chernigov	24,583	19,046	....	....	....	..	..	..
Esthonia	3,546	3,151	2,483	....	....	70.0	..	..
Yaroslav	10,799	9,063	3,967	3,205	4,579	36.7	29.7	42.4

APPENDIX VI

Pre-war Birth Rates in European Russia, by Provinces for 1909–1913 as Compared with the Rates for 1895–1899.[26]

Province or territory	Birth rates per 1,000 population for the years 1909–1913	Index numbers of birth rates for 1909–1913 (average rates for 1895–1899 = 100)
Archangel	45.2	107.6
Astrakhan	56.3	102.6
Bessarabia	41.9	99.3
Vilna	31.3	78.8

23 Excluding the cities of Sebastopol and Kerch.
24 The accuracy of these figures is questionable.
25 Excluding the cities of Nikolaev and Odessa.
26 According to the statistics of the Central Statistical Committee and of the Office of the Chief Medical Inspector.

Province or territory	Birth rates per 1,000 population for the years 1909–1913	Index numbers of birth rates for 1909–1913 (average rates for 1895–1899 = 100)
Vitebsk	33.3	80.0
Vladimir	42.4	80.3
Vologda	46.4	100.7
Volhynia	40.7	86.8
Voronezh	50.0	83.8
Vyatka	52.7	93.8
Grodno	34.4	81.5
Don Territory	53.2	98.7
Ekaterinoslav	50.0	84.5
Kazan	45.9	92.9
Kaluga	46.0	82.1
Kiev	38.4	79.8
Kovno	28.1	78.9
Kostroma	45.6	90.1
Courland	22.0	84.0
Kursk	45.2	85.4
Livonia	23.4	80.7
Minsk	38.6	83.9
Mogilev	37.7	80.2
Moscow	41.2	93.9
Nizhni-Novgorod	48.3	87.3
Novgorod	42.0	96.1
Olonets	46.8	98.9
Orenburg	57.4	98.0
Orel	45.7	82.9
Penza	50.9	87.8
Perm	56.5	98.8
Petrograd	31.0	93.1
Podolia	38.7	86.4
Poltava	37.6	79.0
Pskov	40.5	87.5
Ryazan	43.0	79.0
Samara	56.2	95.1
Saratov	47.7	83.5
Simbirsk	52.1	97.9
Smolensk	45.2	83.1
Taurida	45.0	88.2
Tambov	47.5	87.6
Tver	40.0	78.7
Tula	45.6	79.9
Ufa	50.7	99.4
Kharkov	44.5	80.9
Kherson	38.5	79.1
Chernigov	39.7	81.4
Esthonia	25.3	85.5
Yaroslav	37.0	83.3

APPENDIX VII

Number of Births in European Russia in the Years 1913–1917,
Inclusive, by Provinces,[27] and Index Numbers for Same.

Provinces and territories	Total number of births					Index numbers (1913 = 100)		
	1913	1914	1915	1916	1917	1915	1916	1917
Archangel	20,694	20,696	18,439	15,749	....	89.1	76.1	..
Astrakhan	50,086	52,352	43,931	....	....	87.7	..	..
Bessarabia . . .	102,397	100,871	....	....	....	..	..	..
Vilna	57,672	60,509	....	....	....	..	..	..
Vitebsk . . .	57,334	63,639	52,005	45,340	....	90.7	79.1	
Vladimir	90,305	89,028	79,192	59,541	37,793	87.7	65.9	41.9
Vologda . . .	77,732	80,204	63,389	....	....	81.5	..	..
Volhynia	145,796	142,238	100,032	....	....	68.6	..	..
Voronezh	175,310	179,175	153,298	116,108	....	87.4	66.2	..
Vyatka . . .	188,367	190,574	160,915	....	....	85.4	..	..
Grodno	60,854	62,023	....	....	....	..	..	..
Don Territory . .	172,187	174,809	154,072	104,927	....	89.5	60.9	..
Ekaterinoslav . . .	160,551	163,654	137,188	....	....	85.5	..	..
Kazan	125,067	126,363	108,493	....	....	86.8	..	..
Kaluga	68,354	69,704	61,575	42,218	30,446	90.1	61.8	44.5
Kiev	175,110	183,123	152,405	....	....	87.0	..	..
Kovno	50,344	51,346	....	....	....	..	..	..
Kostroma . . .	80,394	84,144	70,008	....	....	87.1	..	..
Courland . . .	14,629	14,341	....	....	....	..	..	..
Kursk	144,236	138,965	125,864	....	....	87.3	..	..
Livonia . . .	34,803	31,160	22,197	....	....	63.7	..	..
Minsk	109,690	110,416	89,808	....	....	81.9	..	..
Mogilev . . .	86,679	88,095	87,608	....	....	101.1	..	..
Moscow (province) .	79,333	81,710	69,324	55,901	....	87.4	70.4	..
Moscow (city) .	54,649	54,373	49,738	37,375	36,284	91.0	68.4	66.4
Nizhni-Novgorod .	94,474	96,923	80,210	56,918	34,144	84.9	60.2	36.1
Novgorod	70,780	74,673	61,757	49,022	....	87.3	69.3	..
Olonets	20,638	22,794	18,049	....	....	87.5	..	..
Orenburg	120,509	119,297	....	....	....	..	..	..
Orel	119,071	114,874	97,515	75,411	....	81.9	63.3	..
Penza	96,895	93,557	81,039	....	....	83.6	..	..
Perm	199,434	202,078	188,876	....	....	94.7	..	..
Petrograd (province)	37,354	35,638	....	....	....	..	..	..
Petrograd (city) . .	56,155	55,460	51,956	46,188	43,109	92.5	82.2	76.7
Podolia	136,054	142,692	....	....	....	..	..	..
Poltava	131,704	135,195	110,912	....	....	84.2	..	..
Pskov	56,921	57,976	48,441	40,697	....	85.1	71.5	..
Ryazan	109,780	110,140	92,004	69,039	....	83.8	62.9	..
Samara	203,545	213,734	183,292	115,876	....	90.5	56.9	..
Saratov	151,661	156,818	139,176	90,943	62,306	91.8	60.0	41.1
Simbirsk	100,861	98,843	84,276	....	....	83.6	..	..
Smolensk	96,601	95,631	....	....	....	..	..	..
Taurida[28]	87,591	85,729	69,761	....	....	79.5	..	..

[27] According to the statistics of the Commission to Investigate the Effect of the War of 1914–1920 upon Public Health.

[28] Excluding the city of Sebastopol.

Provinces and territories	Total number of births					Index numbers (1913 = 100)		
	1913	1914	1915	1916	1917	1915	1916	1917
Tambov	170,846	172,847	141,295	....	....	82.7	..	..
Tver	93,589	98,337	77,407	70,384	53,998	82.7	75.2	57.7
Tula	82,474	83,949	70,571	71,381	72,192	85.6	86.5	87.5
Ufa	147,275	147,697	121,461	....	....	82.4	..	..
Kharkov	151,958	150,710	153,117[29]	....	....	100.8	..	..
Kherson[30]	126,623	128,170	106,517	82,004	....	84.1	64.8	..
Chernigov	110,948[31]	114,546	97,141	....	....	87.4	..	..
Esthonia	11,653	11,854	10,239	....	....	87.9	..	..
Yaroslav	51,145	53,325	45,608	36,626	30,097	89.2	71.6	58.8

APPENDIX VIII

Pre-war Death Rates in European Russia, by Provinces, as Compared with the Average Death Rates for 1895–1899, by Provinces.[32]

Province and territory	Death rates per 1,000 population, averaged for 1909–1913	Death rates for 1909–1913 compared with rates averaged for 1895–1899 (1895–1899 = 100)
Archangel	27.2	107.5
Astrakhan	36.1	100.8
Bessarabia	30.3	116.5
Vilna	18.3	78.2
Vitebsk	18.9	80.4
Vladimir	28.6	71.5
Vologda	30.3	99.0
Volhynia	22.8	81.4
Voronezh	32.7	78.2
Vyatka	37.5	94.0
Grodno	20.0	76.0
Don Territory	33.0	101.9
Ekaterinoslav	25.5	87.0
Kazan	31.6	90.3
Kaluga	31.4	74.6
Kiev	24.2	80.9
Kovno	18.8	81.0
Kostroma	31.1	89.6
Courland	16.1	85.2
Kursk	27.8	76.8
Livonia	18.3	89.3
Minsk	19.2	74.4

[29] Another source (*Materyali po Estestvennomu Dvizhenyu Naselenya Ukraini*) gives the figure of 128,854 or 84.7 per cent of the number of births in 1913. This figure is more probable, though the accuracy of both is questionable.

[30] Excluding the cities of Nikolaev and Odessa.

[31] The source quoted above in note 29 gives for 1913 the figure of 114,021. If we adopt this figure the percentage of births in 1915 would be 85.2.

[32] According to the statistics of the Central Statistical Committee and the Office of the Chief Medical Inspector.

Province and territory	Death rates per 1,000 population, averaged for 1909–1913	Death rates for 1909–1913 compared with rates averaged for 1895–1899 (1895–1899 = 100)
Mogilev	19.4	76.7
Moscow	30.2	83.7
Nizhni-Novgorod	32.3	79.4
Novgorod	20.0	95.7
Olonets	34.9	105.8
Orenburg	39.0	102.9
Orel	29.8	76.0
Penza	32.8	77.9
Perm	43.1	103.1
Petrograd	24.3	89.0
Podolia	24.9	87.4
Poltava	20.6	73.3
Pskov	25.2	80.8
Ryazan	25.6	67.2
Samara	38.3	92.3
Saratov	32.3	77.1
Simbirsk	34.4	89.1
Smolensk	29.4	77.2
Taurida	24.4	94.6
Tambov	29.4	78.6
Tver	27.9	76.0
Tula	31.4	73.9
Ufa	31.5	102.9
Kharkov	25.7	77.2
Kherson	23.0	85.8
Chernigov	22.8	73.8
Esthonia	18.4	93.4
Yaroslav	26.8	79.3

APPENDIX IX

Number of Deaths in European Russia in the Years 1913–1917 and Index Number Changes in the Number of Deaths in 1915, 1916, and 1917 as Compared with 1913.[33]

Provinces and territories	Total number of deaths					Index numbers (1913 = 100)		
	1913	1914	1915	1916	1917	1915	1916	1917
Archangel . . .	12,272	13,587	12,709	12,694	....	103.6	103.4	..
Astrakhan . . .	30,059	29,166	33,060	....	....	110.1	..	..
Bessarabia . . .	77,745	79,202	....	....	....	..	..	..
Vilna	33,490	34,087	....	....	....	..	..	..
Vitebsk	34,425	34,049	42,016	38,073	....	122.1	110.6	..
Vladimir	60,397	53,331	52,841	48,132	41,490	87.5	79.7	68.7
Vologda	52,557	49,964	45,126	....	....	85.9	..	..
Volhynia	84,511	90,733	74,702	....	....	88.4	..	..
Voronezh	109,194	110,219	102,033	87,704	....	93.4	80.3	..

[33] According to the statistics of the Commission to Investigate the Effect of the War of 1914–1920 upon Public Health.

Provinces and territories	Total number of deaths					Index numbers (1913 = 100)		
	1913	1914	1915	1916	1917	1915	1916	1917
Vyatka	136,613	142,545	149,781	....	....	109.6	..	..
Grodno	36,942	35,541	....	....	....	..	..	..
Don Territory . .	99,138	102,833	101,041	89,192	....	101.9	90.0	..
Ekaterinoslav . .	78,283	76,676	89,582	....	....	114.4	..	..
Kazan	85,265	86,173	84,471	....	....	99.1	..	..
Kaluga	46,090	48,265	44,333	36,782	34,136	96.2	79.6	74.1
Kiev	104,327	107,838	116,408	....	....	111.6	..	..
Kovno	30,733	31,414	....	....	....	..	..	..
Kostroma . . .	54,758	50,241	47,501	....	....	86.8	..	..
Courland	11,848	11,957	....	....	....	..	..	..
Kursk	87,667	81,912	81,346	....	....	92.8	..	..
Livonia	27,110	25,155	25,256	....	....	93.3	..	..
Minsk	55,376	60,057	69,862	....	....	126.2	..	..
Mogilev	44,621	46,781	46,164	....	....	103.4	..	..
Moscow (province) .	57,392	54,159	50,067	45,451	....	87.2	79.2	..
Moscow (city) . .	41,940	42,198	52,710	49,714	44,542	125.7	118.5	106.2
Nizhni-Novgorod .	66,366	60,172	57,175	44,672	36,168	86.2	67.3	54.5
Novgorod . . .	48,320	43,554	43,517	42,109	....	90.1	87.1	..
Olonets	16,927	14,625	13,788	....	....	81.5	..	..
Orenburg	81,318	68,502	....	....	....	..	..	..
Orel	73,443	74,196	74,155	....	....	101.1	..	..
Penza	64,251	57,353	61,725	....	....	96.1	..	..
Perm	153,457	149,547	163,115	....	....	106.3	..	..
Petrograd (province)	26,517	25,149	....	....	....	..	..	..
Petrograd (city) .	45,446	47,597	52,866	55,980	61,000	116.3	123.2	134.2
Podolia	87,272	82,123	....	....	....	..	..	..
Poltava	72,148	70,064	74,190	....	....	102.8	..	..
Pskov	35,044	35,971	34,657	32,893	....	99.0	93.9	..
Ryazan	61,011	61,877	61,328	53,449	....	100.5	87.6	..
Samara	117,661	124,676	159,291	....	....	135.3	..	..
Saratov	93,825	95,470	108,505	....	....	115.6	..	..
Simbirsk	64,187	60,247	62,248	....	....	96.9	..	..
Smolensk	59,938	61,180	....	....	....	..	..	..
Taurida[34] . . .	45,828	46,327	44,084	....	....	96.0	..	..
Tambov	105,183	106,199	101,655	....	....	96.7	..	..
Tver	66,673	61,633	59,190	64,968	54,399	88.8	97.4	81.6
Tula	61,754	57,711	48,114	52,095	56,077	77.8	84.3	90.8
Ufa	92,785	84,641	90,546	....	....	97.6	..	..
Kharkov	85,419	80,364	82,072[35]	....	....	96.1	..	..
Kherson[36] . . .	72,117	68,866	64,764	65,978	....	89.8	91.5	..
Chernigov . . .	61,706[37]	65,334	69,130	....	....	112.0	..	..
Esthonia	9,089	9,212	8,780	....	..:.	96.6	..	..
Yaroslav	38,094	34,493	31,018	32,417	36,754	81.2	85.1	96.5

[34] Excluding the city of Sebastopol.

[35] Another source (*Materyali po Estestvennomu Dvizhenyu Naselenya Ukraini*) gives the figure of 91,571 or 105.9 per cent of the number of deaths in 1913. This figure is more probable, though the accuracy of both is questionable.

[36] Excluding the cities of Nikolaev and Odessa. Our figures are from the source quoted above in note 35 because the figures of the *Proceedings* of the Narkomzdrav Commission for this province contain obvious misprints.

[37] The source quoted above in note 35 gives for 1913 the figures 63,274. If we adopt this figure, the percentage of deaths in 1915 would be 109.2.

II

SOCIAL COST OF THE WAR

By BARON ALEXANDER F. MEYENDORFF

INTRODUCTION

NUMEROUS attempts to estimate the pecuniary costs of the World War have been made.[1] They have been related to the annual national incomes, and in some cases the War was costing more in a single year than the estimated income of the whole people. It has been held that only in the case of the United States there remained appreciable resources which could defray future costs.[2] Professor Edwin R. A. Seligman, who expressed this opinion in 1918, already then noticed the immense difficulties of drawing up a tolerably correct balance sheet. The diminution of the "social patrimony" and the diversion of current social output from productive to unproductive channels are not altogether susceptible of being put into dollars and cents.

The case of the Russian Empire will serve as an illustration of these difficulties. The closer one studies the Russian economic situation during the War, the more one notices the gradual separation of national economy from the State economy, and again, within the former, a fragmentation, both vertical—into geographical regions, and horizontal—into layers or classes.

It is obvious that a distinction must be made between the war zone and the non-invaded part of the Empire. Likewise peasant farming, only loosely dependent upon the market, almost self-contained and capable of producing the necessaries of life, with the aid of a local exchange of goods, was less exposed to direct losses than would be, in case of a new war, the industrialized agriculture which now the Soviet government is so eager to build up with the aid of American tractors.

The problem of industrial mobilization, the conversion of industries to war production, the diversion of the energies required, to use H. G. Wells's expression, "the fighting with science, the fighting with economy, the fighting with machines and thought against destruction and division," the war-time regulation of trade and industry,

---

[1] Ernest L. Bogart, *Direct and Indirect Costs of the Great World War* [New York: Carnegie Endowment for International Peace, 1919]; *Readings in the Economics of War*, ed. J. Maurice Clark, Walton H. Hamilton, and Harold G. Moulton [Chicago, 1918].

[2] Edwin R. A. Seligman, "What Do We Mean by War Costs?" in *Readings in the Economics of War*, p. 541.

had more than anywhere else their limitations in Russia. To greater or lesser degree the more advanced belligerent countries succeeded in approximating the ideal of a general mobilization of labor and economic resources, and in making all human and material resources effectively available for the prosecution of the War. England's machinery for industrial control was different from the German, French, or American, all of them had their own difficulties to overcome, more often than not prevalent habits and traditions of individual freedom and independence. These could finally be overcome and under modern conditions of transportation and large-scale machine production it has been possible for the nations, in a degree never attained before, to throw their entire productive energy into the struggle.

In the course of the War the diversity in Russia's structure became less plastic and subservient to hierarchical control; the peasant masses became less manageable, less disposed to accept an economic and political solidarity forced upon them from above. Moreover, modern conditions of transportation and large-scale machine production were inadequate and out of keeping with the rest.

When, in crisis, the proper perspective was obscured, it could be said[3] that Russia had "neglected" her economic organization. The mobilization took from the factories those who were essentially needed for the conduct of the War. The only ports left—Archangel, Vladivostok, later Murmansk—were inadequately equipped for the indispensable imports. The railway system broke down by the end of the first year, and railway repair shops were converted into munition factories. All output being diverted for the needs of the army, the open market was short of everything. Herds of cattle brought together in the rear of the army were slaughtered where meat was needed for the soldiers; hides were thrown aside to rot, and leather became scarce. The removal of numerous Germans from business concerns in Russia led to the employment of a personnel unaccustomed to their task. Non-bureaucratic organizations, like the Union of Towns, and the Union of Zemstvos, though in favor of State control, were hampered in their activities by the central government.

All these observations refer to an aspect of Russian conditions

---

[3] Samuel H. Harper, "How Russia Neglected Economic Organization," in *Readings in the Economics of War,* p. 202.

which, as later developments have shown, could not be altogether altered. No doubt a number of factors were not inherent in the basic conditions. But it was naïve to expect that the Russian genius for self-defense and self-assertion would manifest itself in a way that would amaze the world and would prove creative enough to organize and coördinate the activities of more than half a continent with a single end in view.

After the fall of the Empire in March, 1917, the Provisional Government, headed in succession by Prince Lvov and Alexander Kerensky, tried in vain to make the people understand that the government is not a thing apart that carries on the war. The appeal to the democratic masses for coöperation sounded hollow to many people. Good resolutions could not bring 15 millions of peasant households to throw all their energy into the fight with the external enemy. War lords, whether emperor or Provisional Government, could not break the temper of the people, the temper of their bureaucracy, nor even secure the loyalty of all sections of the educated classes to help the realization of the nation's whole strength.

CHAPTER I

THE NON-ECONOMIC CONSEQUENCES OF THE WAR

The Conscription Law.

UNDER the Russian Conscription Law of 1874 the duty of military service was, in principle,[1] equally shared by all sections and classes of the population throughout the Empire. Some primitive tribes in the more remote parts, some denominations, such as the Mennonites, were exempted or were freed from carrying arms. Finland, after the abolition of its special law, was practically exempted. Nevertheless one is justified in saying that Russia's unity was firmly expressed in the legal provisions referring to its military organization. There was a certain unity in Russia's educational, financial, and judicial system, although this uniformity was not absolute. Local divergencies did, however, not impair the country's unity, either in the eyes of the foreigner or of the native. The predominance of the Russian language was a powerful corollary of that unity, impersonated by the Tsar.

Yet this unity, when it came to be tested, proved fallacious, even from the military point of view. The well-meant provisions of the conscription laws did not, in the opinion of General Golovine, reflect in a sufficiently stringent and systematic way the basic ideas of national defense—equality and universality of obligation primarily for the young able-bodied men. Under the law the youth was not always among the first to be called up, as he ought to have been. The Cossack population was enrolled on a different basis, and the educated classes were not utilized as they might have been. Thus there was ample ground for complaint and dissatisfaction, and the system, though well grounded in its modern principle of the armed citizen, was still imperfect as a fighting agency, and as a school of citizenship. The educated classes and the school authorities were apathetic toward the idea of the defense of the country by armed force. In spite of all this, the figures of those killed, wounded, incapacitated,

---

[1] General Golovine, *The Russian Army in the World War* [Yale University Press, 1931], in the series of the "Economic and Social History of the World War."

and made prisoners of war seem to indicate that the defects of conscription under the Russian law did not really destroy the fighting power of the nation. We therefore pass on to those immediate consequences of the War, which contributed more directly to an internal disruption of the nation's collective energies. Owing to the configuration of the Empire, the social and racial conditions were, as will be seen later, regarded by the different components in a different way. Russia herein did not labor under an evil unknown to other nations subjected to the test of war, but it certainly exhibited the symptoms in a peculiar way, harboring rancor, and exploding under the pretext of inefficient military and political leadership.

The "German Yoke."

When the War broke out an influential section of Russia's public opinion was under the delusion that it was a short cut toward the economic emancipation of the country from the German yoke in a sense very different from the one implied in the western European journalistic terminology. As the Russian Government formulated it in October, 1914, when initiating the policy of the liquidation of the estates belonging to enemy nationals:[2] "the anti-German and anti-Austrian feeling, which is deeply rooted in various classes of the community,[3] and which came into existence at the outbreak of the War, is now steadily growing under the influence of reports concerning the cruelty displayed by the enemy and its complete contempt for the rights of the civilian population. . . . The War creates especially favorable conditions for the definite and final solution of the aforesaid problem." As Professor Nolde remarks, after citing this passage, "the governing principle was: 'Freedom from the German yoke!' a watchword which became soon very popular. . . . The War was simply a convenient moment for achieving certain aims of domestic policy."

[2] Baron Boris E. Nolde, *Russia in the Economic War* [Yale University Press, 1929], pp. 12, 104, in this series of the "Economic and Social History of the World War."

[3] Sir Bernard Pares wrote in *The Edinburgh Review* of July, 1916: "No wonder that this was for Russia a religious war. The war of itself by the simple force of facts, brought within reach of fulfilment all these hopes . . . all the dearest instincts came like a wonder . . . by beginning the war Germany at one blow wrecked her work of internal domination of Russia."

The "long delayed problem" of getting rid of the enemy land-owners was rapidly taken up by public opinion, especially by the conservative faction. And at once the problem was so amplified that it covered also the rights of settlers of German origin. These farmers who had been either invited or welcomed by the rulers of the eighteenth and the beginning of the nineteenth centuries, and who in some measure were responsible for the development of the wheat-exporting areas of south Russia, nevertheless were found to be ill adapted to the national conditions. Their prosperity seemed offensive to the Russian peasantry, their perseverance in German racial and religious conceptions was resented by the overstrung nationalistic aspirations of the epoch. Baron Nolde remarks[4] that the measures intended at first for the liquidation of German landed property only were developed into a policy of a more drastic character against "land ownership and land tenure by certain categories of immigrants from Austria, Hungary, Germany, and Turkey who are subjects of the Russian Crown." This policy was intended as an expropriation in favor of the Russian peasants, at least in the frontier zone affected by the laws of February 2, 1915. Thus this secondary problem "began to be identified with the problem of agrarian policy—the transfer to peasants of Russian lineage of lands whose quality and great extent (some 8 millions of acres) caused them to be coveted by the Russian wish for a compulsory redistribution of the land."[5] The furor raised by this comparatively minor matter, taken up vigorously by some of the influential English journals[6] as sign of patriotic feelings gaining strength and momentum, ended "in an extension of the policy of expropriation to all landed property, irrespective of the nationality of the owner, by means of the revolutionary seizure of the land by the peasants."[7]

What the War helped to reveal as a factor of primary importance in the sphere of distribution of property was not the only symptom of an ensuing process of dislocation.

[4] Nolde, *op. cit.*, p. 104.   [5] *Ibid.*, p. 114.

[6] The London *Times,* Russian Supplement, January and September, 1915; *The Edinburgh Review,* July, 1916.

[7] Nolde, *op. cit.*, p. 115.

National and Religious Problems.

There were the multifarious interracial and interdenominational problems which in the course of the War, far from remaining stationary, accumulated a kinetic power. At first a sort of truce or "union sacrée" of all the peoples of Russia produced the impression of a complete unity and solidarity.[8] All apprehensions regarding Russia's composite character, so often with great force voiced by students of Russian affairs,[9] seemed relegated to the realm of theory. Russia was not Austria-Hungary. Its unity was well grounded both in economic interests and radiant hopes. Had not the Polish section of its population just received the assurances of the commander in chief, the Grand Duke Nicholas, that its desires would find satisfaction? However vague, the announcement promoted by a fraction of the Cabinet was a half-hearted admission that warfare in the purely Polish provinces was no small test of their loyalty, the more so as even the greatest of optimists knew the meaning of Polish aspirations. Here real statesmanship was required to find a *modus vivendi.* The slogan "Slavs versus Teutons," as one might guess, would prove to have only a preliminary significance, pending the realization of greater Polish hopes.

Anti-German feeling was as readily fostered in the Baltic provinces among the Esthonians and the Letts, as pro-German tendencies were to be checked in Finland, and among the Baltic nobility. The Letts, after the first year of the War, obtained the privilege of separate Lettish military units. Scores of Baltic Germans were deported, more often than not, on the ground of fantastic denunciations. The presence of a number of them in court circles and prominent positions strengthened the rumors—now discarded by historians—of powerful pro-German influences associated with the commanding personality of the Empress.

The millions of Mohammedan subjects were to be kept loyal to Russian rule while they were to take an active part in a fight against the Ottoman Empire. Still more acute was the Jewish problem. Had not the Jews for several decades marshaled all European influences, financial and revolutionary, against Russian autocracy as the arch-

[8] On August, 1914, this unity was voiced by the Fourth State Duma in session.

[9] Otto Hoetzsch, *Russland* [1912].

enemy of their emancipation? Were they not, although more thor-
oughly assimilated than the other national minorities, justified in
connecting with the eventual defeat of Russia in the War the fall of
a *régime* which they hated?

The Trans-Caucasian area, so important not least for its oil fields
for military operations, was afflicted with internecine disputes between the Armenians, Tartars, and the Georgians, not to speak of
minor elements of the checkered population controlled by an un-
popular and often unsympathetic Russian bureaucracy.

Last, but not least, the great international influences, Roman
Catholicism and socialism, were to be conciliated unless they were to
cause disruption in a body insufficiently integrated.[10]

Curiously enough socialism in Russia underwent, during the War,
a process of disintegration as it did in other belligerent countries.
Large majorities broke away from the international program and
made a truce with their respective governments for the period of the
War. Friction could not be completely eliminated. The War itself
created modes of control over political activities which, like "Dora"
in Great Britain, were indigestible to radicals and even liberals. No
doubt the socialists who "accepted" the War were often disappointed
when expected to resign, in favor of a "reactionary" government,
their hold over the industrial workers and over the intellectuals. In
fact their loyal coöperation did not last long, and perhaps we shall
find that the attitude of the leaders was dictated by the passing
moods of the rank and file, a phase which did not outlive the second
year of the War and the disheartening period of reverses.

The Roman Catholic attitude toward the Russian Government
cannot be described in a few sentences. It must, however, be said that
from the truce in the beginning of the War a curve can be drawn as
running up to the pitch of overt contempt and hostility. The crucial
moment in the relationship between Tsardom and the Greek-Ortho-
dox clergy on the one hand, and the Roman Catholic church, on the
other, came during the Russian occupation of Galicia. Very much
against the desire of the Governor General of the occupied provinces,
the leading Russian bishop undertook a campaign for the reunion of

---

[10] Even Arthur Henderson proclaimed in a manifesto to the British people
issued on August 1, 1914, on behalf of the British Section of the International Socialist Bureau: "The success of Russia at the present day would be
a curse to the world." *See* G. D. H. Cole, *Labour in War Time* [1915].

the Catholic uniates with the Orthodox church. The removal of deportation into the interior of Russia of the uniate bishop Sheptizki was one of the measures which the civil authorities unfortunately did not oppose. We must refrain, however, from the detailed examination of the moral and religious effects of the War, and concentrate upon the war cost and losses.

The Breaking up of the Empire.

In the following pages there will be found an attempt to trace the spirit in which the sacrifice in men and wealth was borne by the various classes of the population and by the inhabitants of the various geographical areas affected by events to a very unequal degree. This might be helpful to the understanding of the after effects of the War, among which the dismemberment of the Russian Empire (succeeding the fall of the monarchy) is as significant as is the advent of a socialist oligarchy to dictatorial power.

During the War the material basis of Russia's economic unity and coherence was impaired by the loss of several industrial areas and the restriction of her natural resources, as they fell under the enemy's control. The following table shows the extent of this territorial loss and its economic implications.

TABLE 1

Loss of Territory and Population.[11]

Transferred to:	Area square kilometers	Percentage of the total area of European Russia	Population Number (in thousands)	Percentage
Poland	246,000	4.5	19,100	14.4
Finland	390,000	7.2	3,500	2.7
Esthonia	43,000	0.8	1,000	0.8
Latvia	65,000	1.2	1,850	1.2
Lithuania	52,000	0.9	3,000	2.3
Rumania (Bessarabia) .	46,000	0.8	2,600	1.9
Total	842,000	15.4	31,050	23.3

[11] These figures refer only to European Russia. Cf. *Rossya v Mirovoi Voine (Russia in the World War)*, published by the Central Statistical Office, Moscow [1925], Table 71.

From the economic point of view the losses of territory and population (estimated by other authorities at 817,000 square kilometers and 27 to 28 millions of inhabitants) represented the loss of about 14,000 miles of navigable rivers, 4,000 miles of railways (or 10 per cent of the whole system), one-third of all industrial enterprises employing one-sixth of all industrial workers and producing goods to the value of one-fifth of the total annual production.

Foreign investments in this area amounted to 10 per cent of the total.[12]

Russian Poland, Finland, and the Baltic provinces were responsible for the production of 70 per cent of Russian paper, 74 per cent of jewellery, 71 per cent of knitted goods, 33 per cent of woolens, and 57 per cent of ready-made garments.

These statistics need to be carefully analyzed in drawing any inferences in social history. The four or more millions[13] who, in Russia, were driven from their homes, on the exposed outskirts, into the interior of the country where everything, even the language, was alien to them, had a very different story to tell from that of the people remaining in their homes. Neither do the lives or property lost by the former figure at all among the war costs in an adequate way. The

[12] Grinevetsky, *Post-war Perspectives of Russian Industry,* quoted in Yugov, *Economic Trends in Soviet Russia,* tr. by Eden and Cedar Paul [London, 1930], Chapter 11, also L. J. Lewery, *Foreign Capital Investment in Russian Industry and Commerce* [Washington: Department of Commerce, 1923].

[13] "The action of the local officials and sometimes even direct orders of the army authorities undoubtedly played a part in the size of the movement. Some of the army commanders had no hesitation in ordering wholesale destruction on the theory that the advancing enemy must find nothing but a desert. Moreover army authorities felt a strong distrust of certain groups of the population, and one time expelled all persons of Jewish faith from a zone twenty miles wide adjoining the front. However, even such measures cannot fully explain the wholesale character of the movement" (T. I. Polner, Prince V. A. Obolensky, and S. P. Turin, *Russian Local Government and the Union of Zemstvos* [Yale University Press, 1930], p. 160, in this series of the "Economic and Social History of the World War"). *See* also Paul P. Gronsky, "The Central Government," and Nicholas J. Astrov, "The Municipal Government and the All-Russian Union of Towns," in the volume, *The War and the Russian Government* [Yale University Press, 1929], pp. 30–36, 175, 192, 231–241, in this series of the "Economic and Social History of the World War."

sacrificed areas of Russia largely inhabited by national minorities
(in 1914 already 18 millions) were in a position similar to that of
Belgium. If numbers and size account for anything, they would re-
quire a close examination. A synthetic view of the effects of the War
upon the Russian people eliminates almost completely the quasi-
Belgian chapter on the largest front of the Great War between the
Baltic Sea and the Black Sea. For the sake of comparison one must
remember that the losses of Turkey in her war against Greece will
not reflect what her Greek subjects in Asia Minor suffered. We have
to emphasize the fact that a number of the most heavily devastated
areas find no place in official records. Therefore a summary such as
the one submitted here is bound to be both incomplete and unreal.
If, for example, an estimate of those who lost their lives in the War
can be ascertained for the whole of Russia, with discrepancies of
computation amounting to hundreds of thousands, it is almost impossible to derive relative losses[14] of the various regions. The privileged condition of the Finnish population, which was almost entirely
spared, has its antithesis in those regions where the civilian was almost as exposed to danger as the combatant. It would not be just to
contrast the areas directly affected by the War with those indirectly
affected. The losses of the former imply primarily economic ruin
whether under the enemy or under their own national forces. The
losses of the latter are primarily personal, while at the same time
economic gains may be excessive. This feature, however, is a mere
contingency of comparatively small importance in the case of a perfectly homogeneous country. In the Great War Russia appeared as
such only nominally; in reality, the western border of the Empire
neither racially nor linguistically was identical with the rest. Since
the War on the Russian front had to be fought on the territories inhabited by national minorities, it became inevitable that they should
suffer particularly heavy losses; and since the War was not merely a
war for their defense from invasion, it happened that they were
sacrificed when national considerations made such a sacrifice im-
perative.

[14] To mention but one instance: "After the battle of July, 1915, a great
wave of refugees from Armenia—some 250,000—flooded the Caucasus.
Thousands of them, exhausted, died of hunger and disease, and from them
spread a violent epidemic of typhus." These were natives of an enemy state.
Astrov, *op. cit.*, p. 266.

One would be hardly justified in discarding this fact as irrelevant in the estimate of the social and political consequences of the War. In the course of this study it will not be possible to record separately the losses in blood and wealth suffered by the border regions. The destruction attending military operations in modern warfare has been represented by the countries in question with some justifiable claim to accuracy. We might quote the statements made on account of Latvia, Lithuania, Poland, and Georgia by their respective governments when asserting their independence. It is perfectly obvious that none of the provinces of the interior of Russia were affected by the War in the same way and in the same degree. The point one has to keep in mind is that the aggregate of losses in man power, money, and goods, when divided or specified according to various zones or regions of the Empire forming historical, economic, and national entities, each ready to break away, if sacrificed, is full of internal contradictions. It is possible that the special studies of every one of these regions would present widely differing features of losses and gains; only such special studies would be representative of the actual social effects of the War, or at any rate be more representative than the imperial averages.

An instance of such complications was the Russo-Polish conflict. The parties could never agree whether the Empire or the subjugated Poles were the losers from a purely economic standpoint, and some Russians have gone so far as to state that Poland was deriving profit from the Russian garrisons kept on her territory. Similar squabbles were perennial with regard to Finland.

CHAPTER II

THE PEASANTS

War and Agriculture.

NUMEROUS observers were so impressed by the ever growing hostility of the peasants toward the prerevolutionary distribution of land that they considered it pure folly that the Imperial Government and the ruling classes did not surrender in order to secure a more effective support in the War, and to gain to their side the majority of the nation. Gradually a curious situation developed. National losses were being identified with those of the peasants. Since the losses in man power were in the main those of the peasants, the latter appeared to be the victims of the War, as far as absolute numbers were concerned. On the other hand, statistics established a larger proportion of casualties among the officers than among the men. Polish and Latvian writers, not without reason, claim greater sacrifices as having been made by their nationals than by the Russians.

Whatever the truth may be, the relevant fact consists in the disintegrating action of the Great War, and in the strong impetus it gave to the forces working for the breaking up of the Empire. The soundness of the imperial structure was put to tests which it could not survive, failing military success. The latter would probably have consolidated unity, both territorial and social.

The general effects of the War upon large estates and peasant farming are well known.

A sharp reduction of the area of cultivation on large estates was observed as early as the second year of the War and has continued ever since. . . . There can however be no question that it was mainly owing to its downfall [of the landed gentry] that Russia ceased to be "the granary of Europe."

The effect of the War upon peasant farming was very different. When the War began it had not yet finally lost its primitive form of production for consumption on the farm, and was not run on modern lines as a business enterprise or irrevocably connected with the market —and this fact proved to be its salvation at that trying moment. It not only remained unshaken but went on developing further. The area under cultivation by the peasants considerably increased in the second year of the War [by 18.5 in European Russia]. A certain reduction in it during the next two years was of no great importance for peasant farming as such, although it had an unfavorable effect on the country as a whole.[1]

The different elements of the problem, such as withdrawal of labor, prohibition, requisition of draft animals and cattle, lack of machinery and fertilizers, the changes in the state of the market and in consumption, the prices and the accumulation of money in the country and the profits of the producing areas, must be taken into account.

The mobilization of men which absorbed up to 40 per cent of the able-bodied male population, true not at once but by stages, together with the requisition of horses and the decrease of live stock did affect agricultural production. A number of factors, however, mitigated the effects of the War upon the supply of agricultural labor and capital. (1) Not all peasants who were mobilized had been exclusively occupied with work on the land. What is still more important, agricultural work often failed to absorb the whole labor power of the peasant family, and part of their energy was wasted, to the extent of 50 per cent and, according to some, to the extent of 80 per cent. All observers of peasant life during the War testify that the output of labor by the nonmobilized men, women, and adolescents, was much greater than usual, and the peasants could make better use of their available labor resources. (2) Compulsory temperance had a very favorable effect upon the amount of work done, especially in the first months after the prohibition had been introduced. (3) The landed gentry were far worse off for labor, the peasants, engrossed in their own work, less eager than before to hire themselves out as laborers. Yet the prisoners of war—in 1917, up to 430,000—and the refugees—their number uncertain—made good in part the loss of about 800,000 workers absorbed by the army. (4) Though the provinces which used to hire over a million of workers yearly suffered from the shortage of hands, and the provinces near the front were badly hit, the general conclusion as to the comparatively slight effect

---

[1] Alexis N. Antsiferov, Alexander D. Bilimovich, Michael O. Batshev, and Dimitry N. Ivansov, "Rural Economy," in the volume *Russian Agriculture during the War* [Yale University Press, 1930], p. 295, in this series of the "Economic and Social History of the World War."

of the mobilization upon the agricultural life of the country remains unaffected.

Nearly everything which has been said about the withdrawal of labor may be repeated with regard to the requisition of horses and oxen.[2]

The very substantial decrease in agricultural machinery and fertilizers had an unfavorable effect on farming. Yet "except in the southern and southeastern provinces . . . [the writer forgets Poland and the Baltic provinces where the use of agricultural machinery was fairly widespread] the peasantry may hardly be said to have suffered from lack of machinery."[3]

The Market.

The change in the state of the market, new sources of revenue (compensation for horses and cattle, not to mention the Government and zemstvo allowances to the dependents of mobilized men) increased the income and reduced the expenditure of the family farmer, that is, the major part of the peasantry. The fact that the peasants had really accumulated more cash than they could profitably use is proved by the immense increase in deposits in the cooperative banks and a decrease in the number of loans made by the latter.[4] At the same time the increased ratio of farming for home use indicated that the peasants were not satisfied with providing pre-war rations for a smaller number of consumers. This, however, was no inducement for intensive production for the market, since the supply of the more important manufactured articles was greatly reduced, and liquor was no longer obtainable. Therefore "the War cannot be said to have brought about a crisis severe enough to shatter the foundations of Russian farming,"[5] or at least peasant farming. This applies, in the opinion of Professor Antsiferov, in particular to the black-soil region, "which presented a more favorable picture than

[2] *Ibid.,* pp. 116–126.   [3] *Ibid.,* p. 130.

[4] For a detailed treatment, *see* Alexis N. Antsiferov, "Credit and Agricultural Coöperation," and Eugene M. Kayden, "Consumers' Coöperation," in the volume *The Coöperative Movement in Russia during the War* [Yale University Press, 1929], pp. 17–18, 307, 343, in this series of the "Economic and Social History of the World War."

[5] Antsiferov and others, *Rural Economy,* p. 140.

other parts of the Empire."[6] These conclusions are not, as the writer himself admits, free from a certain hypothetical character. In our opinion, the main difficulty resides in the embarrassing diversity of conditions not only in the regions with surplus or the deficient agricultural production, but, in the main, in the degree of the direct action of the War upon the various parts of the country.

The question is a controversial one. Mr. Kayden writes:

In the rural communities the shortage of labor was an acute problem since the beginning of the War. The effect of this labor drainage after two years of War reflected in the rise of labor costs of almost 300 per cent above the level. In 1916 the peasant women shouldered the burden of cultivating the fields. In twenty-seven provinces there were 13,200,-000 women workers to 8,400,000 men. . . . In 1917 the labor of the women did not suffice. The cooperative organizations came to the relief of the needy peasant households. In many districts they saved the fields from remaining untilled by timely aid with seeds, fertilizers, implements and credit. . . .[7]

The war-time consumption both in the army and among the peasants increased in quantity and improved in quality. The population of the provinces occupied by the enemy amounted by the end of 1914 to 18 millions and only about one-fifth, possibly one-third had moved to the interior. The number of consumers accordingly decreased.[8]

The gross cereal harvest during the War, exclusive of the provinces of Kovno, Courland, Vilna, Grodno, Volhynia, and Podolia which were nonproducing and the Kuban territory which represented usually an important item, were nearly equal to peace-time harvests, at least for the principal crops. The year 1915 was by 10.2 per cent above the average.[9] The Russian Empire had an adequate supply of cereals throughout the period of the War. The potato crop after the occupation by the enemy of the northwestern prov-

[6] Antsiferov and others, *Rural Economy,* p. 139.

[7] Kayden, *op. cit.,* p. 19. The census of 1917 gives the following data for the adult workers employed on 12,127,348 farms covering a larger area: Male—15,603,804, female—16,340,007.

[8] Antsiferov and others, *Rural Economy,* pp. 185–186.

[9] S. S. Demosthenov, "Food Prices and the Market in Foodstuffs," in the volume *Food Supply in Russia during the World War* [Yale University Press, 1930], p. 309, in this series of the "Economic and Social History of the World War."

inces and Poland declined as of 4.2 million deciatines under potatoes, 1.7 millions represented the pre-war share of those provinces. "In any case the decline does not imply that the inhabitants of the interior were less well supplied with potatoes in 1915 than previously."[10]

Earnings.

From a different point of view M. Demosthenov analyzes the changes brought about in the war-time earnings of the rural population. He writes:

Here, we are fortunate in having at our disposal more reliable and comprehensive data than we have in respect of the urban population. The monetary earnings and resources of the peasantry increased during the War to an extraordinary extent. To begin with there was a radical transformation in the very budget of the rural classes, as a result of the liquor prohibition. This in itself would have been sufficient to increase the cash resources of the peasants even if its aggregate cash income had remained stationary, by about 600 million rubles a year. Another factor was that the peasants were paid large sums for their horses, vehicles, drivers, etc. According to a calculation of M. Prokopovich, this item alone yielded them approximately the following sums: in 1914–1915, 310 million rubles; in 1915–1918, 180 millions; and in 1916–1917, 90 millions. Lastly the allowance paid to families of mobilized men amounted, approximately, to 340 million rubles in 1914–1915; 585 millions in 1915–1916; and 386 millions in 1916–1917. These families continued, of course, to work their farms, so the special allowances formed a handsome addition to the money earnings of the peasantry during the War.[11]

As prohibition reduced the normal expenditure of the peasant household by approximately one-third, the new revenues accruing to the peasants from autumn 1914 to autumn 1917 must have almost doubled, or, according to the other estimate, more than trebled the annual income per peasant household numbering some 15.7 millions in European Russia outside the war zone. The growth of cash resources induced the peasants, on the one hand, to buy more sugar, higher grades of flour, textiles and other articles; on the other hand, it strengthened their position as sellers of goods, and led to an increased consumption of their own products since it lessened the necessity of selling those products at the expense of their own needs.

[10] *Ibid.*, pp. 310–311.   [11] *Ibid.*, p. 342.

Thus it appears that the purchasing power of the peasants was increased during the War. Yet they had been held to belong to the most destitute peoples of Europe. It is therefore not easy to view the outbreak of 1917 as a general peasant rising. In fact, the peasantry had already ceased to be a homogeneous mass.

The Harvest.

During three years of the War (1917 being omitted, since no figures are available) the average of the yield was nearly equal to the peace-time harvest, in spite of the scarcity of labor.[12] As to the consumption, it became heavier and more varied on account of: (a) the requirements of the army "raised to city standards," and (b) the requirements of different sections of the population (especially the workers and no less the rural population), disposing of the increased available cash. The demand of the foreign consumer was almost entirely eliminated.

It seems therefore correct to assume that those provinces which were predominantly self-contained and those peasant farmers who were able to revert or to maintain a *régime* of natural economy, proved to a considerable degree immune to the economic burdens of the War, as long as their assets were protected against invasion and requisition.

It is no less probable that, under natural economy, the individual household did manage to cover most of its requirements more easily than the townspeople.

In the regions invaded by the enemy or under the complete control of the defensive forces, industrial plant was destroyed or removed, raw materials, private and public property were commandeered, and the population was removed into the interior. Outside those regions mobilization of men and the requisitioning of farm animals was the chief burden.

In Trans-Caucasia the area under cereals had been 2,800,000 deciatines in 1914, in 1916 it amounted to only 880,000 deciatines. Cis-Caucasia had 7,000,000 deciatines in 1914, 5,600,000 in 1916. In Siberia it was apparently the shortage of labor which caused the reduction from 6,400,000 deciatines to 5,000,000 deciatines. In the black-soil zone the area of cultivated land surpassed the figure of

[12] Demosthenov, *op. cit.,* Chapter V.

1914 and in the less fertile zone it remained stationary. This rough estimate reflects the comparative immunity of the territories outside the theater of war.

Peasant Farming.

The situation may be better understood in the light of observations made in other belligerent countries. In France no less than 45 per cent of the population belonged to the agricultural class. It was held that owing to the War 40 per cent of the agricultural area had been lost to cultivation, and that the fertility of the most important crop-producing sections had declined by from 20 to 30 per cent. In Austria, as in other belligerent countries, food was controlled and rationed. However, the "kit-bag" trade in Vienna in flour, potatoes, eggs, milk, butter, etc., points to the advantage enjoyed by the producing farms.

When Germany and Austria succeeded in occupying all the western part of Russia and the Ukraine, a grain producing region *par excellence*, the question whether they would obtain large food supply depended upon their ability to organize the country for the furtherance of their own purposes. It is in handling this problem that they drove the peasant masses for a time into the fold of communism.

Undoubtedly the forces which reduce food production in time of War (diversion of labor, depreciation of machinery, bad cultivation, selling of seed, depletion of herds, risk and uncertainty) have not affected the Russian peasant farmer outside the war zone to the degree of devastation. Far from it. The War was the great disturbance which led the peasants to realize their power.

Standard of Living.

The measurement of the changes in the cost of living is, according to Professor Bowley,[13] strictly limited to the case when habits of living and commodities purchased are not dissimilar, and is almost futile as between, say India and England, or as between 1814 and 1914. In comparing dissimilar standards he thinks it preferable to give accurate descriptions and not to attempt numerical measurements.

[13] A. L. Bowley, "The Measurement of Changes in the Cost of Living," in the *Journal of the Royal Statistical Society*, 1919 and 1930.

The simplest way to obtain a fairly accurate description of the standards prevailing among the majority of the Russian population outside the war zone is to eliminate, for the sake of comparative description, from the agricultural budget of an English family, the items which are not likely to appear as commodities to be purchased by the consumer, either as being beyond their standard of living, or because they are produced at home. As regards the foodstuffs for the self-contained farmstead, only two of the seventeen principal items usually figuring in the budget of an agricultural worker in England,[14] namely, tea and sugar, would represent a purchasable element in the cost of living. In the English farm workers' itemized expenditure, besides foodstuffs, are mentioned: rent, cleaning material, insurance, fuel, light, and the cost of boots, clothing, household linen, and household utensils; for a family of five and one-half persons they are estimated at 10s. 7d.[15] Undoubtedly the structure of the Russian peasant's budget was different in this respect, owing to a certain amount of goods produced at home. At the same time his position as an owner[16] of his farmstead implied some expenditure on buildings and implements. The tabulation of peasant budgets has been frequently attempted by Russian statisticians, and the difference between these budgets and those referred to before is obvious. There is no need to enter into a detailed analysis, for the present situation in Soviet Russia serves well to illustrate the greater independence of the Russian family farm from the market, both in respect of the fluctuating prices and in regard to services and goods.

[14] Agricultural budget: 1, bread; 2, flour; 3, beef and mutton; 4, pork and sausages; 5, bacon; 6, lard; 7, new milk; 8, skimmed milk; 9, cheese; 10, butter; 11, margarine; 12, potatoes; 13, rice and oatmeal; 14, tea; 15, coffee, cocoa; 16, sugar; 17, syrup, jam, other food.

[15] "The Cost of Living of Farm Workers in England," in *The International Review of Agricultural Economics* [Rome, 1925], pp. 697–704.

[16] It cannot be repeated often enough for a proper understanding of Russian rural conditions that both leases of agricultural land and hired agricultural labor were less important and different from the hire of land and labor in other agricultural countries than is often imagined. The lease of extra-allotment land after 1905 was insignificant—and where it existed the payment of the rent, whether in kind, services or money, was hardly enforcible during the War, and less so after 1917. As to farmhands during the War, their small number was still further reduced by mobilization. Antsiferov and others, *Rural Economy*, pp. 35–37.

The farmer is often in a position to produce substitutes[17] for the commodities not to be found on the market or too expensive and is able to keep body and soul together, while eventually the urban population may become completely destitute. Payments to both the State and to private landowners were of no importance at the time when the War began. More important were the local taxes. Hence the peasant farmer, holding a middle-sized farm in the non-invaded part of Russia, was relatively free from the economic losses attending the War, and so were in a different degree all peasant farmers when compared with other classes of the population. In a way the self-contained farmer can realize a degree of economic independence from the incidence of national economy not to be dreamt of by any other class. And this may well account for the irresistible move toward the end of the War throughout the European continent in

[17] The following table may serve to illustrate the variation in the peasant-grown food supply as a result of the breaking-up of the national market in the province of Moscow (within the boundaries of 1924) as compiled by the Statistical Department of that province. There is very little information available on this important matter. The table shows how wheat, millet, and buckwheat, usually imported into the region from other parts of the country, made their appearance, and how flax cultivation was to make good the deficiency in textiles. It furthermore shows the revival of an almost all-round natural economy in a division of the country which more than many others was removed from that stage of rural economy. (The year 1920 illustrates the effect of the then applied methods of war communism.)

	1914	1916	1917	1920
		(in thousands of deciatines)		
Total area sown .	451.2	439.1	468.9	357.8
Rye	208.4	192.9	196.9	185.2
Wheat	0.06	1.4	0.4	0.6
Oats	117.1	99.8	114.9	66.1
Barley . . .	2.9	2.6	2.3	0.5
Potatoes . . .	57.4	57.8	55.3	33.2
Millet	0.0	2.4	0.9	14.1
Buckwheat . .	9.3	13.4	14.0	12.2
Flax	20.4	57.8	55.3	33.2
Grass	26.2	37.2	51.4	17.3

This table speaks volumes. It is regrettable that no comparable data are available for other regions. *Ezhegodnik* (*Year-book*) for the Moscow Province [Moscow, 1925]. The millet crops proved poor and millet was dropped. Oats, the main marketable crop required by the city of Moscow, fetched high prices. The farm animals still had fodder.

the direction of that type of peasant rural property. It is precisely this attitude of the detached and semidetached peasant which has elicited an ill-concealed contempt for the individualistic peasant from such writers as Maxim Gorky and from communist doctrinaires, for he leaves the community without resources, as soon as he has difficulties in obtaining the goods he needs. The economic policy centers around the urgent need to incorporate the whole of the peasant population in the all-absorbing national economy of the country at war. All imaginable devices are applied, from propaganda to force, in order to induce the peasant farmer to part with his surplus. This topic filled the governing bodies of the war period with anxiety. Toward the end of the War rural Europe was profoundly disturbed. In Russia the moral force seemed on the side of the peasant. Everything derogatory to the organizing State, and to the large landowners, was eagerly listened to. The irresistible pressure of the peasant masses toward an extension of their holdings was believed by many to lead to higher returns. The large landowner was frequently proclaimed the culprit of bad cultivation.[18] Chernov, the Minister of Agriculture in the Provisional Government, made in his "Instruction" of July 16, 1917, a desperate effort to divert the peasant movement into the channels of production for the nation, and failed.

The Peasants and the Nation.

Thus one comes to one of the most important social consequences of the War, the Russian peasant's secession from the economic fabric of the nation. This breaking away from the national solidarity proved the more unfortunate as the interdependence between the producing and consuming areas remained as inevitable as before. We have here a secession much more real and fatal than the one which is alleged to have taken place in 494 B.C. in Rome, and to have been brought to an end by the eloquence of Menenius Agrippa and his fable about the revolt of the stomach. The Roman secession brought about the popular institution of the tribunate. The secession of the Russian peasant is a more complex affair.

The attitude of the peasants toward the war sufferers was sympathetic. In the Moscow province instances were noted of peasants bringing to the hospitals cartloads of cabbages and other vege-

[18] Antsiferov, and others, *Rural Economy,* Chapter II.

tables, as their contribution to the welfare of the wounded. In other places they subscribed sums of money for a hospital to be maintained in their name (Orel) and a number of other instances have been observed.[19] There was a tendency in Russian economic literature and literature in general to idealize the peasant.[20] This may have been one of the reasons why, in the speculations on the effects of the War, the displacement effected in the life of the peasantry was left entirely out of consideration. The remark of M. Demosthenov[21] that the War did not cause anything like a revolution in the national food supply, but rather in the demand and distribution of foodstuffs,[22] is a well-founded but not a generally accepted proposition. He finds it impossible to express the consumption demand of the population in definite figures,[23] but gives ample evidence that the higher wages, higher prices, and extra revenues, together with the dislocation of the market, brought about an improvement in the economic position of large sections of the peasantry. The War and the Revolution offered unexpected opportunities for satisfying the long-suppressed desires of the peasants. Two months before the abdication of the Emperor, on November 29, 1916, a grain levy for "needs connected with national defense" was proclaimed. In the wording of the levy order no mention is made of the civil population. "It takes into account," writes M. Demosthenov, "the already manifest hostility of the peasantry, towards the urban elements of the population," and urges the peasants to make sacrifices for the sake of the army. On March 2 of the following year the coming power in the State, the Soviet of Soldiers' and Workmen's Deputies, gave orders to the local supply authorities to requisition, while continuing the levy, commercial grain supplies from dealers, banks, and landowners with an acreage of not less than fifty deciatines (135 acres). On March 25 the amount of grain left to the farmers for seed, food, and fodder was being fixed.

All this plainly meant that the farmer was not disposed to part with his grain. The importance of this attitude from the national point of view cannot be overestimated.

Those who are inclined to reduce every significant fact to its eco-

---

[19] Polner and others, *op. cit.*, pp. 110–113.

[20] Antsiferov and others, *Rural Economy*, pp. 36–37.

[21] Demosthenov, *op. cit.*, pp. 341.

[22] *Ibid.*, p. 328.   [23] *Ibid.*, p. 336.

nomic essentials will no doubt be justified in referring to the open protest of the peasants during the War against the fixing of the prices of grain, when the price of other articles which they needed remained uncontrolled. It is of common knowledge that since 1916 and 1917 this remains the key problem. The seizure and the redistribution of the land did nothing toward its solution.

Prince Lvov's View.

Before closing this chapter two statements will help to describe the complexity of the situation.

One statement belongs to a man who was both at the head of the Union of Zemstvos and later on the head of the Provisional Government. The other is a contemporary statement issued by the Minister of Food Supply in July, 1917. These two statements will help us to form an opinion on the problem of agriculture and the War. Prince Lvov writes:

At the outbreak of the Great War the zemstvos had gained in strength and experience. Driven by a common feeling of patriotism, they sent their representative to a conference in Moscow and organized the All-Russian Union of Zemstvos for the Relief of War Sufferers. The Union was joined by 42 provincial zemstvos, and by the Cossack territories of the Don, Kuban and Terek. Siberia, which was still waiting for the introduction of the zemstvo institutions, nevertheless kept in touch with the Union through her municipal organizations. In this way the whole of Russia, irrespective of the fact whether certain portions of it did or did not enjoy the benefits of local government, joined hands in helping the army. The direct participation of the masses in the work stimulated patriotic feelings and brought home the realization of the national importance of the War.[24]

The concluding words refer to a sunny aspect. But there were forebodings of a different, and even sinister kind.

The Other Side of the Picture.

In July, 1917, the Minister of Food Supply wrote:

In many places, the inhabitants are resorting to violent, unlawful acts which prevent the farmers from attending to their harvests. Peas-

[24] Introduction by Prince George E. Lvov to Polner and others, *op. cit.*, p. 9.

ants are preventing the harvesting of the grain crops with the aid of
agricultural machinery; they are withdrawing from State and private
land prisoners of war, and regular as well as temporary laborers; they
force proprietors and farmers to pay to the prisoners of war higher
wages than those fixed by the Government; they compel both laborers
and owners to raise wages already agreed to; they compel owners and
farmers to pay farm labor in grain instead of money; they forcibly
seize supplies of grain and forage, meadows, live stock and equipment;
they obstruct the harvesting of grain and hay, the threshing, the preparation of fields for winter sowing, etc. The local food supply and committees not only fail to stop at their source these unlawful outbreaks,
which bring general disorganization, but they themselves are issuing
orders and passing resolutions that furnish the population with excuses
for indulging in these illegal and subversive acts. The exhortations to
save the fatherland and the Revolution remained mere words and led to
no result.

The enthusiasm of the first year of the War was waning. "At the
same time," writes M. Polner[25] still more emphatically, "the entire
structure of peasant farming was beginning to show alarming symptoms of deterioration."

Many of the zemstvos kept a close watch on the economic development in the rural districts, the Moscow zemstvo showing exceptional
zeal and foresight in this direction. By repeated statistical inquiries
obtained through its numerous correspondents, the Moscow district
zemstvo boards were in a position throughout the War to watch the
life of the peasantry and to issue, from time to time, valuable reports.
Similar work was accomplished by many other zemstvos, and gradually a picture of alarming deterioration of rural Russia began to un-
fold. It was evident that the calamity was spreading rapidly. It was
affecting an ever increasing number of peasant households and demanded imperatively a drastic remedy. On the surface, the situation
appeared to be fairly normal. In fact, as far as the condition of the
individual peasant was concerned, there seemed to be even something
like an improvement. We know that money was flowing freely into
the villages. The peasants now consumed more of their home produce
and were increasingly averse to selling grain. Of course, this was
more common in the producing regions, but there was evidence of it
also in consuming regions for instance, in the province of Moscow.

[25] Polner, *op. cit.,* p. 149.

However, along with these manifestations of outward prosperity, sinister symptoms of serious trouble became apparent. For one thing, the equipment of the peasantry was deteriorated. Again, there was the drain upon the labor supply as each successive mobilization took more men from the fields. The consequence was that those who still remained were compelled to work to the point of exhaustion. Another difficulty was that in the consuming provinces there was often considerable delay in the delivery of the seed provided by the zemstvos. Live stock was, moreover, growing scarce with the resulting shortage of manure, and mineral fertilizers, ordinarily imported from abroad, could no longer be obtained. It was, finally, impossible to obtain a sufficiency of agricultural implements, not only expensive machinery, but even the most common tools. There were neither scythes nor sickles, and there was no way of obtaining steel parts for plows and harrows, iron for wagon tires, and nails and leather, so that not even ordinary repairs could be properly executed. In these circumstances it was useless to lease additional land from the large estates the peasant being unable to take care even of his own land.

Under these conditions the area cultivated by the peasants was shrinking and gradually coming down to the level of their bare requirements. The peasants were sowing chiefly rye, partially neglecting their spring crops. With increasing frequency one now finds in the zemstvo reports appeals for help, not only for the wives of the soldiers, but for farms undermined by the War generally.

On the estates of the landlords conditions were even worse. Rents declined, much land ordinarily leased out to the peasants now lay fallow, labor was almost unobtainable, and wages mounted so high as to leave no assurance that the cost of producing grain could ever be covered. The area under cultivation shrank perceptibly. The reports describing these conditions found their way in the newspaper, often in an exaggerated form, and, coupled with the declining consignments of food to the cities, seriously alarmed the public.

The Two Main Phases.

The official material consisting of reports from local authorities gives ample evidence of the two main phases, before and after July, 1917. The communist commentator is right in stating that at first the peasants were resorting to quasi-legal methods of ousting the large landowners, issuing through their village assemblies and local land committees orders and prohibitions interfering with and making often impossible the management of the estates. In these maneuvers they were not frankly opposed by the Social-Revolutionary element strongly represented in the Provisional Government under Kerensky. Early in July, 1917, the Provisional Government suppressed with unexpected success and speed a Bolshevik rising of a section of the Petrograd garrison. Subsequently it showed more vigor in the countryside, where by that time, communism was eager to spread distrust in the Government's serious concern with the peasant problem. Hence the peasant movement was gradually diverted into methods of unorganized civil war. The Bolshevik reading is that the Social Revolutionaries had forfeited the peasants' confidence and the peasants thus were brought to back Lenin's plans. But neither the Provisional Government, nor the Communist State, can tolerate open defiance of law and order and the breaking of peace. In encouraging such[26] acts among the peasant masses and among the industrial workers the Bolshevik party was inviting the Government, however weak, to take some kind of action. This action consisted of half measures, but even a semblance of resistance to the temper of the mob at that time was sufficient to stir the masses to greater violence. This is what actually took place.

[26] *Krestyanskoe Dvizhenie v 1917 Godu* (*The Peasant Movement in 1917*) in *Arkhiv Oktyabrskoy Revolyutsii* [Moscow, 1926]. The argument of the communist commentator evades the main fact which disproves his allegations. The Bolshevik Government in issuing the Decree on the Land applied, contrary to its own program, a Social Revolutionary scheme. The principle was adopted by the Constituent Assembly of which the Social Revolutionaries were the majority. Subsequently the peasant became under Communist Law a tenant at will under the State. The State pretends to rationalize agriculture and disregards the interests of a would be bourgeois. *See* also, S. Dubrousky, *Die Bauernbewegung der Russischen Revolution* [Berlin, 1929].

CHAPTER III

INDUSTRIAL LABOR

Labor and Modern War.

MODERN war is almost wholly a matter of industrial technique. We have seen that the Russian Government found it comparatively easy to have a conscript peasant army, but met with insuperable difficulties to force the peasants to supply the State with foodstuffs. The peasant families parted with their sons, but restricted cultivation and increased consumption. In his economic activities the peasant managed longest to remain strictly independent. By those who know the French nation, it has been alleged that if it had not been for the invasion, the attitude of the French peasant would have been a similar one.

The highly industrialized countries and more particularly Great Britain had to organize their man power with due regard to the existing and acknowledged labor organizations. J. Keir Hardie and Arthur Henderson on August 1, 1914, had invited in a manifesto the British people to "stand together for peace. . . . Down with War. . . . Up with the peaceful rule of the people. . . . The success of Russia at the present day would be a curse to the world." Six days later we find Henderson's name in conjunction with W. C. Anderson's signature under a declaration pointing out the measures to be taken to mitigate the destitution "which will inevitably overtake our working people while the War lasts." Then comes the recognition that the War must be fought. Soon after the War is declared a "laborer's war." The government in response strives in England, France, Germany, and later in the United States to restrict war profits and to enforce a minimum wage, and to prevent the breakdown of protective labor regulations. In Great Britain the trade unions, at the request of the Government, gave up for the duration of the War all their rules and customs interfering with maximum production. They laid aside all resistance to the admission to the trades of nonunionists, boys and even women, all opposition to piecework payments. They even accepted the position of being forbidden to leave their employment under a heavy penalty. All this at a time when it was generally assumed that the War would mean distress and unemployment. Whereas it soon appeared that the wage-earning population of the United Kingdom found itself, as a whole, better off financially than during the years of prosperity which preceded the War.[1]

Industrial unrest during the War was not avoided altogether. The want of sufficient housing, liquor restrictions, industrial fatigue, and a feeling that there was inequality of sacrifice, caused dissatisfaction. However, most far-reaching changes in legislation and administration, all to the advantage of labor, were obtained from British statesmanship by the pressure of the organized but loyal labor movement.

Nature of the Labor Problem.

In comparison with the English developments the labor problem in Russia during the War appears from a distance crude and simple. The war-time labor policy of the Russian Government in its claim for loyalty, so spontaneously and surprisingly apparent among the Petrograd and Moscow workers in August, 1914, later resorted to administrative pressure, and took the fullest coöperation of labor as a matter of course. Industrial strife came to be regarded as something akin to high treason. After the middle of 1916 it became evident to government circles that important sections, especially the skilled workers, were being organized, and that their voluntary coöperation was needed. But by that time organized labor was prepared to coöperate, even outside its strictly occupational sphere— not with the Government, but against it.

Within the modern large-scale industry, claims for social justice were voiced through the revolutionary machinery for over twenty years before the War. Of uncorrected evils there were many. Distrust of the modern type of factory worker was common among the nonrevolutionary section of the public and, of course, even more so among government circles. The workers came to form also a sort of denationalized minority contrasting strongly in outlook with the Russian people at large. The following incidents will perhaps serve as an illustration of the developments:

[1] Sidney Webb (Lord Passfield), "British Labor Under War Pressure," in *North American Review,* CCV, 874–884.

George Thomas Marye, American Ambassador in Russia,[2] noted on April 20, 1915:

The Emperor who is travelling in southern Russia went recently to Biejitza (province of Orel) and visited there the extensive Bryansk works. . . . All the people at the works and in the working men's town, something like forty thousand in number, turned out to meet the Emperor. A delegation of workmen made up of foremen, each one of whom had been at the works no less than twenty years, offered the Emperor bread and salt. One of the men, addressing the Emperor, said: "Great Ruler (tsar), we are glad that thou hast come to see our work which we are doing with joy for thee and for the country while our children and our brethren and their children are away fighting on the fields of battle." In making this little speech the spokesman used the familiar "thee" and "thou" which is the language of affection as well as of familiarity in the Russian. The Emperor gave him a watch and went afterward to the town where the workmen live and visited several of the workmen's houses. He conversed with their families and gave watches to their wives. His visit to the works and to the town lasted four hours. The warmth of the Emperor's reception at the industrial plant shows that the working men employed in the towns are as devoted to him as the peasantry in the country.

During the months of March, April, and May of the following year the Bryansk works were involved in extensive strikes. The work was resumed after an increase of from 5 to 20 per cent in the wages, but the report of the Ministry of Commerce and Industry adds that 4,250 workmen left the works and never returned.[3]

Again about a year later the American Ambassador referred in his diary to the apprehension of disturbances among the workers when the Duma was adjourned on September 17, 1915. He added:

But there have been none, though the military chief in Petrograd deemed it expedient to issue a notice that workmen of military age and fit for military service employed in factories turning out munitions of War, who would absent themselves from their places of employment, or refuse to work, or interfere with the work of others, would be brought

[2] George Thomas Marye, *Nearing the End in Imperial Russia* [Philadelphia, 1929], p. 143.
[3] *Rabochee Dvizhenie v Godi Voini* (*Labor Movement During the War*) [Moscow, 1926], p. 163.

before a military court, and pending execution of judgment, sent to the front to remain until the close of the War.

In the reports of the Ministry of Commerce and Industry based on the information provided by the factory inspectors, the passage referring to the same month of 1915 reads as follows:

In Petrograd political strikes occurred in 33 enterprises employing 62,221 workers. The adjournment of the Duma and the arrest of workmen in some of the works of Petrograd were given as reasons for these strikes. The strikes . . . lasted from ½ to 2½ days; the participants belonged mostly to the metallurgical industry.[4]

Among the larger works which were involved, the Putilov Works, shipbuilding yards and three munition factories, were mentioned. In Moscow 22,000 men went out on strike.

Maurice Paleologue[5] made a note of the movement in his diary. His informant described it as "a rehearsal" for a greater move.

The predominantly agricultural character of Russia did undergo considerable changes during the War. The agricultural community lost gradually one of its important components, the large-scale producer. As the War approached its end Russia became a country exclusively of peasant farms. Of industry, the reverse may be said to be true. It developed on lines somewhat similar to those which have been observed in the highly industrialized countries. Government orders, government regulations, and control of the market together with financial measures were intended to foster large-scale production and thus to weaken the effects of the industrial blockade.

This situation contains in a nutshell the essence of the labor problem during the War. The position of the worker in industry depended upon the extent to which the country was able to supply with man power the army, the fields, and the factories. *A priori*, very little trouble was expected to arise from a lack of the suitable human material in a country of 175 millions. However, as the War went on the exhaustion of human reserves was greatly felt. The surplus agricultural population was unwilling to seek employment in industry unless some palpable advantages were offered, such as exemption from conscription, wages high enough to meet the daily increasing cost of

[4] *Ibid.*, p. 95.

[5] Maurice Paleologue, *An Ambassador's Memoirs,* tr. by F. A. Holt [1925], III, 74.

living, and so on. Moreover, they demanded that the advantages should not prove revocable[6] and inadequate as the pressure of war conditions was growing worse. This being so, industries had to fall back upon juvenile and female labor. A mass exodus of the town workers back to the villages set in after the February revolution when the life in the cities became intolerable owing to the lack of food and fuel.

It would be of the greatest help for a proper understanding of the position of labor if reliable figures were available on the proportion of industrial workers who still maintained a connection with land. One thing is certain, that since 1905, a great change amounting to something like an industrial revolution was rapidly leading to the concentration of industries, and to the increase in the number of the industrial proletariat. Russia, in 1913, had a greater number of enterprises employing over 1,000 workers than Germany. She was on the way to develop an industrial proletariat urban in character and imbued to a surprising degree with socialist ideas. In 1913 the number of workmen on strike was larger than in any other country. So it had been during the years of revolutionary unrest—1905 and 1906. The first six months of 1914 foreshadowed a similar intensity of labor disputes. Although the causes of these disputes were predominantly registered as "economic causes," no doubt can be entertained as to their having been the outcome of "political education" and socialist organizing influences.[7]

This was coinciding with the growth of the internal market. After 1906 and, in particular, after 1909, the demand for manufactured goods indicated that a new situation was developing in the towns and in the country. The capital invested in metallurgy, mining, chemical industries, and development of urban life (piping, electricity) doubled and trebled between 1911 and 1913. The returns of the largest iron and steel trust (Prodamet) indicates that the government orders were no longer responsible for the largest portion of the demand, and foreign capital ceased to play the leading part it had at the time of the preponderance of government orders. When by 1907 the latter became scarce and uncertain, as an after effect of the

[6] General Golovine, from the military point of view, deplores the permanent character of the exemptions.

[7] The strike involving inacceptable demands has, since 1897, been considered by the extreme elements as the best tactics.

disastrous Russo-Japanese war, the business circles could think of no
other remedy than a fixed program of large government orders.
Such at least was the view expressed by the mine owners' conference
of the south, and it was then the only hope of many. However, the
staple iron industries which reflect the fluctuations in a nation's production forces took, after 1909, an upward flight full of significance.
The *per capita* consumption of iron indicated that the equipment of
the nation was changing. The nation's economic development took a
course increasingly independent of government orders and State
credit, because of the stratification of the peasantry owing to the
Stolypin Acts.[8] A businesslike lower middle class was in formation,
a fact to which the astonishing growth of the coöperative movement
bears testimony. At the same time, this "spontaneous movement from
below was part of the widespread and industrial agrarian discontent," writes Mr. Kayden.[9] "In the course of six years—between
1908 and 1914—the number of loan and saving associations increased almost three-fold, and that of credit associations, five times.
. . . This was an outgrowth of the changing position and requirements of Russian agriculture," writes Professor Antsiferov.[10] True,
these organizations were dependent upon a system of government
credit grants on favorable terms implying government supervision.
The membership of over 8 millions in 1914, January 1, was chiefly
composed of those peasant groups which were engaged in farming on
their own account. Administrative interference was dictated mainly
by the fear of a possible spread of radicalism in the steadily growing
membership of the coöperatives. At the same time the control and
audit of the books of the coöperative institutions met with difficulties
and hostility and was inadequate. Their cultural activities were extensive but, as the second national Coöperative Congress of 1912
showed, the "co-operative forces" were not only averse to submit-
ting readily to government control, they were also against a closer
coördination of their work with the zemstvos. In fact, the coöperative movement, though in the country dependent on government sub-

---

[8] Alexander D. Bilimovich, "The Land Settlement in Russia and the
War," in the volume *Russian Agriculture during the War* [Yale University
Press, 1930], in this series of the "Economic and Social History of the
World War," Chapter III.

[9] Kayden, *op. cit.*, p. 20.

[10] Antsiferov and others, *Rural Economy*, pp. 248–249.

sidies and on the peasants' landed interest, was, politically speaking, subsidiary to the urban labor movement controlled by the same socialist intellectual leadership, at least at the period of its initial growth before and during the War.[11] The socialist cravings among the more advanced section of the urban workers and among the leading circles of the petty bourgeois and peasant organizations was getting more important as their numbers increased. The coöperative movement and the labor movement, but more particularly the latter, have been closely watched from both official and revolutionary quarters. In confronting the two statements we are likely to obtain a clearer view of the effect of war conditions upon the industrial workers than if we limit ourselves to controversial statistical data.

Two Views of Labor Disturbances.

The State Police Department in a report addressed to the Minister of the Interior gives a brief description of the labor movement in the capital during the month of November, 1915. Mention is made of the strong feeling among the workers in favor of the building up of coöperatives independently of any subsidies from the employers and the exclusion of the employers from the administration of the industrial workers insurance acts. The cost of living, the importation of "yellow labor," exemptions for workers from military service, grievances against the municipal authorities on account of prices, housing and transportation, subscriptions and donations in favor of political prisoners, and, lastly, the revival of trade-unions activities, are mentioned among the main objects commanding the attention of the workers.[12]

As spokesmen of the labor movement, the socialist members of the State Duma intervened on various occasions. Their interpellations were supported by the Constitutional Democratic party as, for instance, after the events at Kostroma and Ivanovo-Voznesensk, of July 5 and August 10, 1915. In both cases the police and military forces had fired upon workers. The casualties in Kostroma were four killed and nine wounded, in Ivanovo-Voznesensk, between twenty and thirty. As described by the interpellants, the strikers at Kos-

---

[11] M. L. Kheisin, *Istorya Koopeartsii v Rossii* (*History of the Co-operatives in Russia*) [Leningrad, 1926], p. 4.

[12] *Rabochee Dvizhenie v Godi Voini*, p. 220.

troma demanded the release of their comrades, who, according to rumor, were being ill-treated. Such was the story as told in the Duma.[13] We may now turn to the official source referring to the same events. In that important industrial area of Ivanovo-Voznesensk after a succession of strikes for higher wages which had been ineffective, a general strike was proclaimed involving 25,182, mostly textile workers. "The cause of the strike was to protest against the War," continues the report, "and the stoppage of work was brought about by small groups through the use of intimidation and violence. The mass of the workers were against the strike." The interpellation briefly states that many thousand unarmed workmen were marching toward the town hall, and were met without any warning by infantry fire. In response to the events at Ivanovo-Voznesensk workers at Petrograd, over three hundred miles away, went on strike. Another instance will serve to illustrate the ease with which labor troubles could arise. In the shipyards of Kherson, over 600 men stopped working because of one man having been arrested by the police.[14]

The above-mentioned instances seem to indicate the existence of some political influences eager to involve the industrial workers in a definite pacifist and revolutionary movement. This was to be accomplished by directing economic grievances into a political channel, and by using for this purpose the mishandling of the increasingly difficult situation by the authorities, which the reverses on the front threw into sharp relief.

On December 30, 1915, the Emperor was informed by the Minister of the Interior, Khvostov, that

owing to an increasing agitation of the Social-Revolutionaries and Social-Democrats, directed towards the spreading, under the influence of German intrigues, among the workers of Petrograd, of false rumors as to our military reverses, revolutionary feelings are running so high that labor has decided to commemorate the anniversary of January 9, 1905[15] not only by the usual one day's stoppage, but by a demonstration in favour of political liberties and immediate peace.[16]

The more detailed report of the local police authority, dated January 8, 1916, mentions that while the Social-Democrat Menshe-

---

[13] *Ibid.*, pp. 70, 89, 211, 214.   [14] *Ibid.*, pp. 90–91.
[15] Usually referred to as the "bloody Sunday."
[16] *Rabochee Dvizhenie v Godi Voini*, pp. 232–233.

viks were witholding their participation in the arrangements for January 9, and the Social Revolutionaries refrained from dictating any special program for the demonstration, leaving it to the participants to act according to circumstances, the Bolsheviks regarded January 9 as the first day in a second revolution, recommended armed resistance, and felt sure of the support of some of the regiments of the Petrograd garrison. Accordingly, Colonel Globachev reported on December 31, his department proceeded to the arrest of the Petrograd Bolshevik Committee together with a "former pupil of the Social-Democratic School of Gorky on Capri" as well as of the Social-Revolutionary Activists. The colonel regarded these arrests as having undermined the confidence of the workers informed of the *coup,* but anticipated the probability of some resistance to police orders and the looting of shops by the mob. The report on the events of the following day contained some significant indications of isolated attempts to develop the stoppages in numerous works into a political manifestation. Thus the hold of the extremists appeared as yet insignificant, and only in Petrograd did the number of strikers on January 9 reach the large figure, 45,000, whereas in Moscow only 850 persons stopped work. Nevertheless, as noted before, the workers of Petrograd and Moscow exhibited a considerable interest in politics when, in September, 1915, 62,221 in Petrograd and 22,092 in Moscow stopped work because of the prorogation of the State Duma. There were also cases, in 1915, indicating anti-German feeling. Thus here and there strikes were declared because of some German or Austrian engineer or foreman who was still employed. The Putilov Works may serve as an instance of the transformation of anti-alien feeling in 1914 into an overt revolutionary movement in March, 1916, under the direction of the Bolshevik organization. The importance of these munition works induced the Government to draft a bill for their militarization, whereas their temporary closure and the arrest of the Bolshevik ringleaders induced the State Duma to discuss the case in a private session. Having been informed by the Minister for War, Polivanov, "that our enemies are stabbing us in the back," it passed a resolution supported by a large majority amounting to an appeal to both the employers and the employees to fulfil their duty as citizens.

The Mobilization of Industry.

The unofficial movement[17] for the mobilization of industry found its expression at a congress of the representatives of industry and commerce in May, 1915, which decided to set up a network of war industries committees with a Central War Industries Committee in Petrograd. Toward the end of 1915 twenty-eight provincial committees were formed. The composition of the committees included delegates from labor. The object of the committees was to rationalize the industries. The inclusion of labor "was a great victory for the democratic sections of public opinion." All the factories employing more than five hundred workers were to take part in the elections of labor representatives. M. Zagorsky continues:

The elections of the voters produced great excitement among the workmen. The more intellectual of them were divided during the War into two sections. One section represented the defeatist idea, which was prevalent among the extreme wing of the Social-Democratic Party. . . . The contrary view was held by the sections of the Social-Democrats, known as Mensheviks, by the Social-Revolutionaries and the great majority of the working class. Their point of view was known as "defensism" (*oboronchestvo*). They considered that Russia's defeat would bring nothing but harm to the whole country including the working classes.

They also thought that, however adverse the political conditions might be, it would serve as a means of voicing their demands to take part in the elections of the voters, whereas the Bolsheviks considered it a mere mockery. In Petrograd, on September 27, 1915, 176 voters met to elect 10 delegates to the Central Committee. The meeting, however, by a small majority passed a resolution in favor of boycotting the committees. New elections were appointed and ultimately 10 representatives were elected. The same situation occurred in Moscow. "In May 1916," writes M. Zagorsky, "there were labor representatives in twenty districts and ninety-eight local committees, one hundred and seven workmen in all." Labor formed 3.4 per cent of the total membership of the committees. "The group of labor delegates in the Central Committee became a center of labor representa-

---

[17] S. O. Zagorsky, *State Control of Industry in Russia during the War* [Yale University Press, 1928], pp. 82 *sqq.,* in this series of the "Economic and Social History of the World War."

tion for all Russia." The same writer enumerates among the reasons for the strained relations between the Committee and the official bureaucratic authorities and a number of influential firms the allegation of its political activities and mentions the efforts made for its dissolution.[18] It must be emphasized that the funds administered by the committees were obtained from the Government, and amounted to 50 per cent of the total expenditure for munitions.

It is only since 1926 that the more precise substantiation of those allegations has been published by the Soviet Government. During the War the workers were the "object of every kind of restriction and administrative repression," revolutionary elements were sent to the front, and the working classes were deprived of the possibility of organized defense of their interests. The war industries committees offered a loophole for this defense and for a revolutionary action, on a larger scale and under the cover of official activities and powers, supported by government funds. Remaining true to their party allegiance, most of the labor delegates to the committees kept to their own ways.

A special report on the revolutionary activities of the labor representatives was drawn up by the State Police Department in March, 1916.[19] It refers first of all

to the breaking up of the patriotic attitude of the working classes of the capital in the autumn of 1915 owing to the rise in the cost of living, military reverses and the indefinite prolongation of the War, circumstances which were favorable to the activities of the opposition parties in their efforts to discredit the Government and to seize the power, to which must be added the latest session of the State Duma which bore the stamp of an antigovernment character.

The report contains documentary evidence of an unexceptionable character, substantiating the accusation directed against the parties of the Left. Only a few passages are relevant to the labor problem during the War. The report with reference to the Zimmerwald Conference convened by Lenin, distinguishes three currents of which only the Plekhanov group considered a defeat of Russia and a German victory as undesirable, whereas the "Leninites," or overt defeatists, and the "Liquidators," or secret defeatists, were each pur-

[18] Zagorsky, *op. cit.,* p. 104.
[19] *Rabochee Dvizhenie v Godi Voini,* pp. 269–292.

suing their objects, the former of transforming the War into a class war, the latter of an immediate peace without "annexations and contributions," leading to the fall of Tsardom.

The institution or recognition, on August 27, 1915, by the Imperial Government of the Central War Industries Committee was, according to the memorandum, used by the secret defeatists in more than one way as a "legal opportunity" for attaining their goal.

The instructions given to the labor delegates contained the following paragraphs:

The Russian irresponsible Government by entering the War, at the same time was fighting and is fighting against its own people—thereby bringing the country to the verge of ruin. But we also maintain that a share in the responsibility belongs to the State Duma and to the parties forming its majority, since they for a whole year have supported the military dictatorship and have been hiding the truth lest the people should realize it. And when it became impossible to keep silence any longer, they failed to find the courage to seek support among the people for a determined struggle against a regime which is leading the country towards its ruin. Therefore we consider it to be the immediate task of the working classes and of the whole democracy . . . to fight for the summoning of a Constituent Assembly.

Then follows an enumeration of reforms including the introduction of the eight-hour day, and an amnesty. The Government is accused of using the War as a pretext for depriving the workers of the few rights of organization which they previously possessed. Hence the participation in the central and local war industries committees must be regarded as a means only to developing a joint action of the working classes throughout the country. On December 3, 1915, a declaration was read on behalf of the workers at the session of the Central Committee stating that under the existing political conditions they could not be responsible for the defense of the country. At a subsequent meeting of the Committee, the delegates of the workers are alleged in the report, to have declared bluntly:

It is quite clear to us, that the representatives of the industries have established the Central Committee for three objects: for the defense of the country, for taking the power in their hands, and for filling their pockets. The interests of labor are perfectly immaterial to them. Therefore we, the representatives of labor, will assume the care of the organization of the workers and of the safeguarding of their interests.

Having obtained funds from the Treasury for the organization of their clerical staff and for traveling expenses, the workers' delegates in the main centers such as Moscow, Kiev, Kharkov, organized their activities and urged among other objects the summoning of an All-Russian Workers' Congress. The labor group in the Samara War Industries Committee was faithful to the movement when it claimed, as an immediate necessity, the expropriation of all private lands.

The chairman of the Central War Industries Committee, M. Konovalov, by showing great leniency, was evidently hoping to attain the best possible results for the Committee's main purposes. It has been even alleged that the extravagant claims of the workers' delegates were inspired by the State Police with the object of undermining the prestige of the unofficial organizations. The reckless policy of the last Minister of the Interior, the half-witted Protopopov, served to countenance such rumors.

A summing up of the characteristic features of the labor conditions prevailing at that time is found in the interpellation on the strike movement submitted to the Duma in June, 1916, over the signatures of Khaustov, Chenkeli, Tulyakov and twenty-seven other members of that Assembly. If biased, it nevertheless deserves quoting, along with the above-mentioned report coming from the official sources. Moreover, it brings out the economic hardships of which industrial workers had a particularly heavy share.

M. Zagorsky[20] refers to the facts which are substantiated by the interpellators. He writes:

Ever since the outbreak of the War strikes had been prohibited by the Government. Most of the factories engaged on war work were under martial law. The workmen were either released from conscription to work at the factories, or were skilled workmen returned from the front and were considered as soldiers. The Government had an effective means of preventing strikes by sending the refractory elements off to the trenches . . . when the Government decided not to tolerate strikes, any attempt to organize one was put down with all the severity of which the Russian military authorities were capable. . . . Demands for higher wages were constantly reiterated in the course of 1916. But the working classes had no possibility of pressing their claims by strikes. These claims were satisfied in a few cases, either owing to the intervention of labor groups or war industries committees, or at the instance of the

[20] Zagorsky, op. cit., pp. 210–211.

military authorities, who were anxious to maintain production. . . .
Thus when the Revolution broke out, a mass of inflammable material
had accumulated.

The interpellation presented to the Duma in June, 1916, also
mentions that the real value of wages remained low, that the working
hours had been lengthened, that the working class, consisting to a
great part of women and children, was physically in a state of exhaustion. The main argument, however, is based upon the excessive
frequency and extension of the strike movement in all the main works
in Petrograd during the first six months of 1916, and its gradual
spreading into other important industrial centers. Here one of the
danger points in the Russian industrial system revealed itself.

Strikes.

In the majority of the strikes the causes or objects were economic.
In spite of this the authorities were incapable of coping with the
movement. Military measures were obviously insufficient and inap-
propriate and the movement continued to grow.

A warning must be given as to the statistics of strikes; though
quite elaborate, they do not always cover the fifty-six enterprises
which were under the management of some of the military depart-
ments and which employed about 211,000 workmen. Nor do they include railway employees whose number was considerable. Another
point to be kept in mind is the preponderance in Russia of the war
industries in the broadest sense of the word, though we think the following statement somewhat overprecise.[21]

Seventy-one per cent of the total production was taken up by the
army (44.6 per cent), by the Government (10.8 per cent), and by
public institutions (15.5 per cent), leaving for the open market only
29.1 per cent. The enterprises directly controlled by the military
authorities, numbering 56, employed 211,868 workers. Thus a total
of about 2,000,000 workers were being either exclusively or partly
engaged in war work and nearly all in large enterprises.[22] This shows
both the relative weakness of Russia's industrial development, and
the excessive danger from the industries being involved in trade
disputes.

[21] *Rossya v Mirovoi Voine*, p. 7.   [22] *Ibid.*

An official source[23] which covers all industrial and mining activities—probably with the exception of the 56 establishments referred to above—gives the following composition of the working classes, on January 1, 1917, in 12,492 establishments.

TABLE 2

Composition of the Working Class.

Aged 12–15		Aged 15–17		Adults over 17		Totals	
Boys	*Girls*	*Boys*	*Girls*	*Males*	*Females*	*Males*	*Females*
28,873	21,083	141,849	101,017	1,083,906	717,134	1,254,628	839,234
Total *49,956*		*242,866*		*1,801,040*		*2,093,862*	

This small fraction of Russia's population exercised a considerable influence upon the course of events.

In the light of the official figures it appears that the strike movement had by no means been broken.

The workers' strength is gaining, the labor ranks grow more numerous and united, and their blows are more determined. The way in which they commemorated the victims of January 9, 1905, illustrates well that growth of the labor movement. In 1915 only 2,039 workers were on strike in six concerns; on January 9, 1916, 53,489 workers, in 38 enterprises; on January 9, 1917, in Petrograd alone, 137,536 workers in 114 factories.[24]

In Petrograd province on January 1, 1917, the number of workers was 277,876, which shows the importance of that purely political strike.

The power of the working classes is best illustrated by the proportion of strikes resulting in favor of labor.

TABLE 3

Strikes in 1916.[25]

The economic strikes:

Number of strikes	1,049
Number of strikers	650,662

[23] *Recueil de Statistique pour la periode de 1913–1917 (Statistichesky Sbornik za 1913–1917 gg.)* [Moscow, 1923], Tables III and IV, pp. 38 and 39.

[24] *Rabochee Dvizhenie v Godi Voini*, p. 5.

[25] Data of the Central Statistical Department.

The claims of the strikers referring to:
    (a) *Wage increases:*
        Number of strikes   877
        Number of strikers 512,340
    (b) *Hours of labor:*
        Number of strikes   19
        Number of strikers   2,573
    (c) *Other working arrangements:*
        Number of strikes   153
        Number of strikers 135,549
Number of days lost in economic strikes 3,976,215
Results of economic strikes:
    (a) *In favor of labor:*
        Number of strikes   275
        Number of strikers 153,230
    (b) *Compromised:*
        Number of strikes   403
        Number of strikers 283,977
    (c) *In favor of employers:*
        Number of strikes   349
        Number of strikers 200,584
The political and non-economic strikes:
        Number of strikes   242
        Number of strikers 310,290
        Number of days lost 673,101

The above figures show the importance of the strike movement.

During the War almost every strike, whether economic or non-economic, had a political significance, and every attempt to interfere with the process of production meant a blow to the resources of the State. Therefore Lenin and Zinoviev, in their pamphlet, *Socialism and the War*, were to a considerable extent right in rejoicing that so few of the strikes during the War in Russia had a patriotic cause. Of the 1,410, writes M. Fleer, a Bolshevik writer, only 15 strikes could be tabulated as patriotic.

The deplorable happenings in Kostroma and Ivanovo-Voznesensk in June and August, 1915, confirmed the old militant revolutionary tactics laid down by Martov in the nineties,[26] that there is no better means of propaganda than extravagant demands provoking police or military action against strikers.[27]

[26] Y. Martov, *Zapiski Sotsial-Demokrata (Reminiscences of a Social-Democrat)*, Vol. I [1922].

[27] The signatories of the interpellation presented to the Duma, on June

A description of the organized and unorganized strike movements and their comparison would show how the war situation enabled the socialists of all description to accelerate the formation of the class conscious workers. All socialists needed him. The Bolsheviks alone proved able to control him. More often than not the Russian worker became class conscious before he became efficient, hence dislocation followed in the wake of social and political changes.

The Cost of Living.

The question of the cost of living naturally was one of great concern to both the Government and the public. Where even official statistics are subject to an admitted variation of 20 per cent and more and the others lack even this partial authority, it is well to accept all numerical data with due reserve.

There can be, however, no doubt that the food situation in the urban industrial centers was extremely serious, and was getting increasingly worse throughout the War. The initial confusion, in the spring of 1915, was followed by a period of animation and revival. The subsequent period (autumn 1915—autumn 1916) of organized control raising industrial production to its highest level brought no relief to the urban population including industrial workers. This situation was fraught with danger. The discontent among the workers as revealed by the character of the strike movement became an explosive force, in spite of the fact that a part of labor, for example, in the textile industry, was not a proletariat in the European sense. They were half-workmen, half-peasants. Their ties with the land were not severed. The textile workmen of the Moscow district took every opportunity of returning to their villages to work on their fields. . . . In the mining industry of the Donets Basin the supply of labor was also seasonal. In spring the men left to work in their fields and did not return till autumn. "Wretched housing con-

14, 1916, mentioned in the text, enumerates a great number of important factories where in their opinion the workers struck spontaneously. "The outstanding features of all these workers' disturbances is their elemental character: the participation of the masses, the colossal swing of the movement. There are strikes in all types of works; in the textile industry; in establishments where men work, and where women are employed, in State factories and in private works, and irrespective of their working for the national defense or for the market." *Rabochee Dvizhenie v Godi Voini*, p. 298.

ditions in the Donets and Ural region, and in the petroleum fields of
Baku made men unwilling to remain there long, and this was the case
in many other places. Of course the productivity of labor was low,
and notwithstanding low wages, costly."[28]

It appears from the available data that the average real wage, between 1913 and 1917, was increasing.[29] It seems, however, that even
the police reports and the reports of the factory inspectors offer a
better insight into the situation, from the point of view of labor. A
few excerpts will help to sketch the change of conditions under the
influence of the War.

Not until February, 1915, was the discrepancy between wages and
prices for the necessaries of life given in official reports as the cause
of strikes.

The monthly report for April, 1915, started with the remark that
most of the economic strikes (97 of 103) had for their object higher
wages, due to the rise in retail prices causing unrest among the industrial workers. In many cases the employers had averted trouble
by raising the rates of wages in time, but 34,110 workers went out on
strike. In the province of Vladimir over 5,000 men struck. In most
cases the strikes were successful for the workers. The average duration of the strikes in the provinces affected by the movement was of
7.41 days which was considered rather long.[30] In May of the same
year, the general character of the strike movement remained the same.
It was not only the prices of the necessaries but their shortage which
brought about the strike movement. In the town of Shuya, where
26,000 stopped work peacefully and started an inquiry in every
shop, in order to ascertain whether there was indeed a shortage of
supplies in the town, the municipality aided by the local employers
was able to cope temporarily with the shortage. In Ivanovo-Voznesensk all the workers stopped working on May 26 for the same reason. The mayor of the town eased the situation by taking extraordinary measures. On May 28, the Governor of the province informed
the public that fixed prices were to be lowered, and work was resumed. It will be noticed that strikes in these two important industrial centers had been started on the same day. In June the town of

[28] Zagorsky, *op. cit.,* p. 19.
[29] *Ibid.,* Appendix XXV, and *cf.* with *Recueil Statistique,* Table III. The
figures do not quite coincide, as regards the nominal wages.
[30] *Rabochee Dvizhenie v Godi Voini,* p. 59.

Shuya experienced the recurrence of the strike movement which involved some 23,000 workers. The Governor of the province, M. Creighton, suggested that the rise in prices was due to profiteering, an accusation which was supported by an investigation of the municipal council.

The close ties between some of the workers and their villages is illustrated by the fact that they went on strike in June as a protest against the refusal to grant them leave of absence for the period of work in the fields.

In October, 1915, a strike in the tobacco factories originated in excessive retail prices. Boots which had been obtainable at five rubles went up to thirteen, and so had firewood become dearer while winter was nearing. In some cases there were complaints against the excessive rents for lodgings. The year 1915 ended without indicating that the conditions had become intolerable, but even a perfunctory perusal of the reports compiled by the Ministry of Commerce and Industry in the usual official and jejune manner leaves the impression that labor was no longer an inert mass.

In 1916 the workers revealed the determination to oppose the conscription of strikers and the arrest of their leaders. Only a minor part of the economic strikes, usually less than one quarter, were settled in favor of the employers. The inadequate supply of foodstuffs, their shortage on the market, the diminutive rations, all simultaneously indicated that the economic causes of the strikes could no longer be eliminated by the employers. Strikes ceased to be labor disputes in the strict sense of the term. Every stoppage was likely to arouse the conflict between the partisans of peace and the partisans of war. There was never any serious doubt as to the Government's position in this conflict. Here, then, arose a concatenation of interests which, in an unfriendly way, was revealed by a group of Duma deputies in their interpellation of June 14, 1916. The association of the Moscow employers, representing 818 factories with 381,000 operatives, was alleged to have suggested to the Moscow Special Commissioner of the Special Council for Defense and the Chairman of the Factory Board,[31] the issue of a joint circular letter addressed to all factories of the Moscow region, dated January 12, 1916, and worded as follows:

[31] *See* for the powers of the Special Council for Defense, its composition, etc. Zagorsky, *op. cit.*, p. 98.

In communicating herewith the list of 67 former workers of the General Electric Company noted as especially troublesome, you are requested not to employ any one of the said workers, pending a special order, since prior to the strike the workers were informed that the names of strikers would be circulated among the owners of factories of Moscow and the Moscow region, in order to prevent the employment of these men.

This measure, advocated in the interests of the defense of the country, was described by the signatories of the interpellation as "a means of enslavement devised by the employers." Here we have an instance of how the "conscious and systematic action of certain public bodies and of the Government" which resulted in a decided increase in output,[32] was interpreted in 1916 by those, who, later, like Kerensky—one of the signatories—were to initiate the subsequent phases of State intervention and of State control. After the March revolution of 1917, the labor question, and in particular the supply of labor, became the object of comprehensive regulation. Under the Provisional Government's program labor conscription was to be introduced.[33] A number of organs were established and, after many vicissitudes, were shaped into some sort of system. However, the dislocation of economic life in town and country together with the indifference, if not hostility, to the watchword, "All for the War," rendered all efforts futile.[34]

At present very few writers assert that the country's productive forces were exhausted before 1917, or that the rise of prices was already abnormal. The economic events alone, therefore, offer no sufficient explanation of the development that followed.

It has been said about Germany, that the breaking up of the prewar social structure was not the inevitable consequence of the economic ruin of the majority of the people—ruin has been often, before, the result of war. "The collapse of old structure," writes Professor Lederer, "was caused by the irrevocable will of all classes which make up the great number—the peasant and the working classes—to be regarded no longer as mere material, as hands, swords, and rifles."[35]

[32] *Ibid.,* p. 20.   [33] *Ibid.,* p. 178.
[34] *Ibid.,* pp. 179 *sqq.*
[35] Emil Lederer, *Deutschlands Wiederaufbau und weltwirtschaftliche Eingliederung durch Sozialisierung* [1920], p. 27.

The Russian peasant and labor movement of 1917 seem to indicate that Professor Lederer's observation would not be far from true with regard to Russia.

Labor Conditions under the Provisional Government.

The labor movement during the last year of the War, no less than the peasant movement, was primarily a protest against unequal distribution of wealth. It was not mere anarchy, when the peasants proceeded to seize large estates or when the workers introduced the eight-hour day without meeting practically any resistance on the part of the Provisional Government and its democratic following. The passive attitude of the latter was to some degree, at any rate, due to what a German writer has called an intellectual and spiritual phenomenon (*eine geistige Veraenderung*).

This statement applies to the general background of the labor movement until 1917, and more particularly to the critical events of the revolution, in February, which led to the abdication of the Emperor Nicholas II, and to the October revolution, which brought the Bolsheviks into power. A close examination of the strike statistics for the year 1916 demonstrates the predominant rôle of the metal workers, on the one hand, and of Petrograd, on the other. The all-important strikes in January, 1917, in the enterprises engaged in war work involved 232,025 workers in 267 establishments over the whole of Russia. Petrograd and Moscow were at the head of the movement.[36] In February, 1917, when almost the whole of Petrograd and Moscow stopped working, the leading rôle of the capitals is still more evident. About 200,000 went on strike in Petrograd, and 161,000 in Moscow. The figures for the rest of the Empire did not exceed 71,000 as far as the enterprises subject to the factory inspectors are concerned. Only in March did the participation of the provinces become somewhat more important.

Only under the Provisional Government did organized trade-unionism enter the field. Those who wanted to divert the labor masses into the channels of social revolution were feverishly active in organizing the widely diffused discontent, and were especially successful among the comparatively best paid metal workers. Clearly

[36] *Rabochee Dvizhenie v 1917 Godu (Labor Movement in 1917* [Moscow-Leningrad, 1926], pp. 21–22.

the tripartite division advocated by Lenin's revolutionary strategy
—into leaders, vanguard and masses—was materializing.

The Provisional Government, on the whole, confident in, and true
to democratic liberties, became almost immediately embarrassed by
their application. The food problem was complicated by the rising
tide of peasant disturbances. The dislocation of the army went hand
in hand with the dislocation in the workshops and the upheaval in the
villages.

A few words on the successive stages of the process that went on
among industrial workers will suffice to show the trend of development. The second half of February, 1917, up to the abdication of the
Emperor on March 2, was a period of violent labor disturbances.
The workers of Petrograd, supported by the rebellious troops of the
Petrograd garrison, constituted the driving force which overthrew
the monarchy. But they were not satisfied with a political revolution
and clamored for palpable result of their victory.

The second phase centering around the eight-hour day began.
The Executive Committee of the Workers' Soviet, created at the beginning of the revolution, soon appeared to be too conservative for
the taste of the masses who simply proclaimed and enforced the eight-
hour day. The employers demanded subsidies from the Provisional
Government, and, in Petrograd, agreed to the introduction of the
eight-hour day without any reduction of wages, to the organization
of factory committees elected by the workers, and to the creation of
conciliation boards. Shortly after similar concessions, at least on
paper, were made throughout the country, to which collective bar-
gaining was soon added as a logical result of active trade-unionism.
The conciliation boards at first were concerned with the question of
wages for the period of the general or partial cessation of work.[37]
The victorious working classes were now in a position to dictate conditions, and the Provisional Government was forced to use the printing press and to issue paper money without, however, succeeding to
satisfy the ever growing demands of labor.

The third phase of the labor movement centered around attempts
to reconcile the troops at the front with the demands for shorter
hours and higher wages. These would naturally appear to the men in
the trenches as unpardonable amenities. Labor, however, succeeded

[37] *Ibid.,* pp. 39–64.

in winning the sympathy of the soldiers: overtime work, it was argued, would secure a high level of production. The trade unions were now controlled by revolutionaries of experience and soldiers at the front and in the rear were backing them. When two Moscow papers announced that the garrison of Tsarskoye Selo, numbering 75,000 bayonets, was against the eight-hour day, the information proved incorrect. On April 23, 1917, the Provisional Government passed a law on the powers of the factory committees. These committees, however, assumed much wider powers than was intended. A resolution moved by the Bolshevik Zinoviev at a conference of the committees proclaimed measures amounting to the socialization of all means of production and the cessation of the imperialistic war.[38] The membership of the unions in the second half of 1917 increased to 1,326,000. Headed by the metal and textile workers, they succeeded in increasing wages by as much as 500 and 600 per cent. The conference of June, 1917, shows the trade unions occupying a commanding position. The Bolsheviks were still in a minority but they could be well satisfied with the resolutions of that conference which proclaimed the centralized control of trade-union policy and its support to the proletarian struggle for power.[39] At the same time, in the summer of 1917, the Provisional Government was making attempts to keep workers' organizations within the limits of law and reason.[40] However futile, these efforts were denounced as counter-revolutionary intimidation. The employers' unsuccessful refusal to pay wages for the hours spent by the workers in the numerous committees which had sprung up everywhere was branded as another feature of the "betrayal of the revolution." The minimum wages fixed by the workers' organizations were actually enforced and retrospective effect was given to the rates, sometimes for a whole year. The Ministry of Labor supported conciliation along such lines,[41] without being able to placate the resolute enemies of the continuation of the War who were ably using the labor movement for their purposes. In July the Provisional Government, consisting since July 2 of Socialists only, obtained from the Central Executive Committee of the Soviets a promise of support in its endeavor to clear Petrograd of armed mobs. The Provisional Government, headed by Kerensky, felt strong

[38] *Rabochee Dvizhenie v 1917 Godu*, pp. 79, 80.
[39] *Ibid.*, p. 89.   [40] *Ibid.*, p. 72.
[41] *Ibid.*, pp. 60–64.

enough to suspend the publication of the Bolshevik paper, *Prayda*, to issue orders for the reëstablishment of discipline on the front,[42] and to arrange the prosecution of some Bolshevik leaders. The re-election of the local soviets proved, however, that Bolshevik propaganda was gaining ground. Local authorities were almost everywhere compelled to abdicate their powers in favor of self-appointed revolutionary bodies.

The employers in a number of cases, owing to alleged or actual shortage of fuel and raw materials, resorted to lockouts. The Supreme Economic Committee,[43] in September,[44] submitted to the Provisional Government a bill for the prevention of lockouts and labor disputes. The leading workers' organizations were for the elimination of the employers, or at least for the fixation of their profits, which were to be controlled by the workers. The employers, on the other hand, adopted counter-resolutions, as futile as the circular letters issued by the Minister of Labor, Skobelev,[45] on August 23 and 28, 1917, in which he attempted to enforce the Act of April 23 on the factory committees. In some individual cases the employers sought a solution by private agreements.

Conclusion.

Three chronological, three logical, and three structural stages characterize the gradual concatenation of the revolutionary machinery. The almost complete liquidation of the old State machinery begun with the abdication of the Emperor in March, 1917, continued under the Provisional Government as the former administrative and military personnel were being replaced. It culminated in the dissolution of the law courts under the Bolsheviks in November, 1917, followed by the closing of the Constituent Assembly. Here we have the continuous dislocation made necessary by the propagation of the idea condemning all old forms of political organization. This idea first conceived by a few—Lenin and his followers—became rampant among the industrial workers and at last among the transport workers—who had been part of the old machinery. It found the army and the peasants ready, the one being out for peace, the others

[42] *Ibid.*, p. 146.   [43] Zagorsky, *op. cit.*, p. 189.
[44] *Rabochee Dvizhenie v 1917 Godu*, p. 159.
[45] *Ibid.*, p. 114.

for more land, and it culminated in the fall of the Provisional Government. This process would have led to nothing but anarchy, if it had not been for the consolidation of the urban proletariat. The old State had practically neither power nor prestige left. The self-appointed Petrograd Soviet rested upon the threefold organization of labor: in the factories, within the occupations (trade unions), and, covering both, in the soviets. It controlled the constant extension of the powers of the subordinate organizations, absorbed gradually the sphere reserved to the old authorities, and exercised its newly acquired powers supported by both the soldiers and the peasants whose sympathies were won by the peace and land policies of the Bolsheviks. The doctrine of the latter was in harmony with the trend of events; therefore the Bolsheviks were successful in building up the revolutionary machinery, of which organized labor became the mainstay in spite of its numerical weakness.

CHAPTER IV

THE EFFECTS OF THE WAR UPON INVESTMENTS

Trend of Foreign Investments.

IF it had not been for the political pressure of the State during the War, with its borrowing, vast expenditure, and, until 1917, its power of guaranteeing handsome profits to private investors, a great deal of the capital invested in Russia would have migrated abroad. The confidence of the public that property rights would be respected, although rapidly vanishing with regard to landed property, was almost unshaken with regard to industry and commerce. There were no indications that agriculture should have attracted investors during the War, apart from the coöperative movement. The long term credit for such investment provided by the State Land Banks was discontinued with the outbreak of the War. The peasant farmer produced largely for his own consumption, and the capitalistic farmer reduced production because he had not enough capital to meet the demands of labor, and could find no credit. Economists merely hoped that under the stimulus of rising prices of agricultural produce the farmer would continue to produce for the market, notwithstanding the gradual destruction of value of his fixed capital, which could not be replaced.

The pouring of enormous sums into industry appears to be the most telling evidence of the fragmentation of the economic fabric of Russia. During the War the reports of the joint-stock companies registering new issues reached a total of 1,256 millions of rubles, of which no less than 920 millions were invested in buildings, machinery and plant. G. Strumilin,[1] estimates the increase of the productive capacity of industry between 1913 and 1918 at 40 per cent. It is unfortunate that all such estimates suffer from grave defects and must be used with considerable caution. The volume of employment (including State-owned factories and mines) is more reliable.[2] Some idea of the position of industry may be gathered from the following table:

[1] *Planovoye Khozaystvo (Planned Economics)* [1925] No. 4, quoted by Yougoff, *Economic Trends in Soviet Russia* [London, 1930].
[2] *Planovoye Khozaystvo*, 1925, No. 6.

TABLE 4

Volume of Production and Number of Workers Employed.

	Gross production in thousands of gold rubles	Index	Workers employed Number	Index
1913	5,621,000	100	2,518,000	100
1916	6,831,000	121	2,926,000	113
1917	4,344,000	77	3,024,000	116
1920–21	961,000	17	1,480,000	57

Assuming that these figures are correct, the volume of production for the year 1916 corresponds to the highwater-mark of capital investment.[3] P. Ohl,[4] in his study of financial capital in Russia, accepts on the best authorities 2,242,974,600 gold rubles as the total of foreign investment within the Empire for the year 1914, representing approximately one-third of all capital invested in Russian industry. Mr. Keynes believes that the foreign share in the total investment reached one-half.[5] One thing, however, seems fairly certain: the share of foreigners during the decade before the War was diminishing. During the War the financing of Russian industry depended upon foreign and domestic Government loans.

Government Orders.

During the War the Government, through gigantic orders placed in the country and advances for the development of war industries, caused the upward trend of business. Large profits resulted and were reinvested in war loans and industry. This was especially the case with regard to the metal, chemical, and leather industries.[6] "The demands of the War stood apart from the general economic life of the nation." The industries with little or no war work were, naturally, in a less favorable condition.[7] All the same, the gradual depreciation of

[3] The recession of production is usually asserted. *See* Kheisin, *op. cit.,* p. 220; Zagorsky, *op. cit.,* p. 53.

[4] *Finansovy Kapital v Rossii (Financial Capital in Russia),* 1922, p. 89. Also Lewery, *Foreign Capital Investments in Russian Industries and Commerce,* Department of Commerce, Miscellaneous Series, No. 124 [Washington, 1923].

[5] *Manchester Guardian,* Commercial Supplement, 1922.

[6] Zagorsky, *op. cit.,* p. 62.

[7] *Ibid.,* p. 67, a table covering 1,597 enterprises indicating the value of

the currency was a handicap for the investor, who, in October, 1917, was left with less than one-sixth of his nominal income. The repudiation of all previous liabilities and the cancellation of all interest-bearing bonds, shares and securities, public as well as private, by the Bolshevik Government proved that capital investment in Russia had been a miscalculation. This measure anticipated the utter depreciation of the currency and sanctioned it. Moreover the nationalization[8] of all kinds of property which amounted to confiscation, left the former owners of capital without any holdings, often even without the title deeds to their former property.

The Attitude of Lenin.

This "expropriation of the expropriators," to use Lenin's phrase, was one of the outstanding economic and social effects of a process in which the War was no doubt an important component. It is still usual to emphasize the connection between the Tsarist *régime*, the War, the democratic revolution, and the proletarian revolution, as a succession from cause to effect. The link between the first and the second stage in the process of events is still a question *sub judice*. The filiation—war, revolution—seems fairly well established. Lenin in a letter dated March 17, 1917, to Madame Kollontai,[9] calls the events of the previous fortnight "the first of the revolutions bred by the War." The day before, he pointed out that the Provisional Government "was a mere stage of transition." He concludes:

The workers have been fighting in bloody battles for a week, yet Miliukov, plus Guchkov, plus Kerensky are in power! The same "old European pattern." . . . After the great rebellion of 1905, the "glorious" revolution of 1917. . . . We, of course, retain our opposition to the defense of the fatherland, to the imperialist slaughter directed by Shingarev, plus Kerensky and Co. . . . Not a shadow of confidence to Kerensky, Gvozdev, Chenkeli, Cheidze and Co.

their production. The group working for army supply shows markedly higher production as against the groups of enterprises which worked only partly for the army or not at all.

[8] A. G. Hoichbarg, *A Year in Soviet Russia. Brief Account of the Legislative Work of 1917–1918* [London, 1920].

[9] Lenin, *Collected Works*, tr. by J. Kunitz and M. Olgin, ed. by Trachtenberg [London, 1929], Vol. XX, Book I.

There is no need to press the subject any farther since it is perfectly clear that the disturbance in the economic structure of the country was caused by the War. This disturbance set in at the weakest point—the transport system, and again in the transport system the labor problem was of minor importance. It was the insufficient equipment which was not adequate to war requirements. And even the equipment as it existed was not fully utilized. It will suffice to remember the thousands of railroad cars used for weeks as dwellings for war refugees;[10] or the loads of machinery from the invaded zone carried sometimes far away from its destination into the interior of the country. Or again, the goods, and food supplies massed near the stations and awaiting shipment. Though it is impossible to find out what the actual conditions were, there are indications at least as regards the coal mines of the Donets Basin that the output, though declining, was far ahead of the available shipping facilities.

Causes of Industrial Difficulties.

Among the causes which have affected industrial activities during the War six aspects of the economic situation are usually mentioned. (1) The isolation of Russia from the world market which, before the War supplied it with the raw materials, fuel, coal, petroleum, iron, and other articles she needed. (2) The dislocation of transport. (3) The shortage of labor and its diminished efficiency. (4) The increase of the cost of production owing to the rise in prices of raw materials and fuel. (5) The transformation of the currency system into one consisting exclusively of inconvertible paper money. (6) The rise in the cost of living in the urban and industrial districts.

Every one of these aspects was observed in most of the belligerent countries, to a lesser or greater extent, but more especially in Germany, where, however, the distribution system continued to work in the main satisfactorily.

The Position of Investors.

The Revolution had introduced new dangers for the various profit-making elements in the business community. Both commercial and industrial capital paid lip service to the new order established

---

[10] A. Polivanov, *Memuary (Memoirs)* [Moscow, 1924], p. 7, writes: "In 1915 the refugees were occupying no less than 115,000 cars."

with the advent to power of the Provisional Government, but there could hardly be much doubt as to its impotence to bridle the desires of the peasants and workers.

The previous Government had practised a system of liberal advances, for instance, to mine-owners who had insufficient capital. But this practise was severely attacked by the workmen, who considered that it placed the owners in too favorable a position, and left them without inducement to increase their output. This led to a stricter control of the system of loans. But the control of loans involved also the control over the system of the working of the subsidized colliery.[11]

The revolutionary parties insisted from the outset on the transfer of all key industries into the hands of the Government. The Government was directly influenced by the "abnormal"[12] relations between employer and employed, which hampered the efficient working of industry, but which after the Revolution were to be regarded as the normal relations. Commercial interests were threatened even before the Revolution by the control of prices for grain, textiles, leather, and other goods of mass consumption. After the Revolution the Government was, naturally, more directly influenced by public opinion whose support it had to seek; both the control of the market and of distribution had to be more rigorous, and business became a dangerous gamble. Yet the Provisional Government, as mentioned already, could not escape the suspicion of being pro-capitalist, even after the non-socialist ministers had retired.

The Last Stage.

The action of capital during the period between March and October, 1917, was fluctuating between resistance and retreat. The latter became more prominent in those transactions which transferred the holdings of Russian concerns into the hands of foreigners.[13] Their legal position would, at that time when the Provisional Government was dependent on foreign credits, so people thought, strengthen the hand of the Government, and enable foreign investors to make

[11] Zagorsky, *op. cit.*, p. 213.   [12] *Ibid.*, p. 217.
[13] Professor Lujo Brentano, *Russland der kranke Mann* [Munich, 1918], enumerates the British and American firms which entered the field. We have not been able to check his information. He alleges that the total covered an area exceeding in size the whole of non-Russian Europe.

profits where Russians could not succeed. Russia was being sold out, as the opponents of private enterprises put it. Municipal enterprises found themselves in no better conditions, nor did State enterprises. And the draft contract passed by the municipality of Petrograd in order to insure essential municipal services with the admission of foreign control, would probably not have been an isolated instance, if events had not ousted altogether all capital, foreign as well as Russian.

A leaflet of unknown origin under the heading: "What is Russia

TABLE 5

Foreign Capital Investments in Russian Industries and Commerce.[14]

Nationality	Within the Empire 1914 In thousands gold rubles	Percentages	Remainder within the U.S.S.R. boundaries[15] In thousands gold rubles	Percentages
French	731,747.4	32.6	648,089.7	32.6
British	507,479.8	22.6	500,564.4	24.8
German[16]	441,593.3	19.7	317,475.7	15.8
Belgian	321,602.1	14.3	311,812.4	15.4
American	117,750.0	5.2	117,750.0	5.9
Dutch[17]	36,456.7	1.6	35,456.7	1.8
Swiss	33,479.1	1.5	31,666.7	1.6
Swedish	23,772.3	1.1	16,646.7	0.8
Danish	14,727.7	0.7	14,537.7	0.7
Austrian	7,550.0	0.4	5,900.0	0.3
Italian	2,506.2	0.1	2,106.2	0.1
Norwegian	2,300.0	0.1	2,300.0	0.1
Finnish	2,000.0	0.1	2,000.0	0.1
Total[18]	2,242,974.6	100.0	2,007,306.2	100.0

[14] Dr. W. Mautner, *Der Kampf um und gegen das russische Erdöl* [Vienna, 1929]; A. Yugoff, *Economic Trends in Soviet Russia* [London, 1930], p. 25.

[15] That is, exclusive of the territory now separated as the Baltic States, Russian Poland, and Bessarabia.

[16] Germany has renounced its claim for pre-war investments under the terms of the Rapallo Treaty of April 16, 1922.

[17] The Royal Dutch Shell has been added to the English total. P. Apostol et A. Michelson, *La Lutte pour le Petrole et la Russie* [Paris, 1922].

[18] P. Ohl, *op. cit.*, p. 89, approximately one-third of all capital invested in Russian industry.

sacrificing from day to day for the War?" voiced the views which Professor Lujo Brentano expressed in the *Frankfurter Zeitung*, and maintained that Russia was being reduced to the status of Persia. The Swedish *Aftonbladet*, of June 10, 1917, advanced the opinion that Russia was carrying on the War with foreign money.

If figures could be adduced, they would probably show a process similar to the one which took place in Germany, and which Professor Brentano might have described in similar terms, if writing a few years later. Domestic capital and savings during the first years of the War were placed at the disposal of the State Savings Banks, co-operatives, and industries, to a degree, which, for Russia, was surprisingly large and indicated rapid accumulation. All of it was lost owing to the depreciation of the ruble, and the last resort was to invite foreign investment. In Russia preference was given to allied enterprise, whereas Germany, after the War, readily enough suffered the influx of ex-enemy funds.

All those who share the view that capital and labor are merely enemy forces could be content with the results of the War. Capital was defeated in Russia and so were the forces which assisted its formation—the so-called educated classes and the legal order based on property rights.

INDEX

Agrarian policy, 162.
Agriculture, effect of the war, 169, 175; machinery, 171.
All-Russian Union of Zemstvos for the Relief of War Sufferers, 180.
All-Russian Workers Conference, 196.

Birth control, 81, 87, 88, 97.
Births: Russia's high rate, 77; territorial changes, 78, 89; number, provinces and cities, *1913* war years, 79; variation of index numbers *1917,* 80; influence of withdrawal of mobilized men, 81, 84, 86; index of decline, 83, 86, 88; age-groups of fathers, 84; comparison of rural and urban rate, 94; Kiev, 95; Petrograd, 96; Moscow, 96; illegitimate, 97; stillborn, 98; effect of decrease on death rate, 105; index *1914–1916* and *1913,* 108; estimated decrease during the war, 128; pre-war rates, 149; number and index *1913–1917,* 151.

Casualties, 8, 111, 133, 135, 169; fatal, 137; missing, 136; disease, 136; release from service, 139; wounds, 140; sick, 141; age distribution, 141.
Cattle, 158.
Census, *1897,* 16; agricultural, *1916* and *1917,* 5, 17, 21, 22, 34, 36; prisoners of war, 37.
Central Statistical Committee, 3, 4, 8, 13, 16, 25.
Central War Industries Committee, 193.
Cereals, 172, 174; area sown, 177.
Chief Medical Inspector, of the Ministry of the Interior, marriages, 3; mobilization, 16; births, 77.
Civil prisoners, 33–37.
Clergy, source of statistical material, 3.
Commission for Investigating the Effect of the War upon Public Health, *see* Narkomzdrav Commission.
Committee of the Grand Duchess Tatiana for the Aid of the Victims of the War, 6, 32.
Communism and the peasant, 178.
Conscription, 8; evasion of, 30; Law of *1874,* 160; dissatisfaction, 160; *see also* Exemptions.

Coöperative movement, 189.
Cost of living, 200.
Currency, depreciation, 211.

Deaths, geographic distribution, 30, 112; war refugees, 32; pre-war rate, 99, 152; *1913* and war years, 100, 101, 117, 120, 153; age-groups, 103; infant, 106, 121, 125; decline, *1915–1917,* 110; urban, 119–120; tuberculosis, 121; Moscow, 122, 123; accidental and violent, 122; mobilized men, 129.
Defence of the Realm Act, Great Britain, 164.
Demobilization due to disablement, 139.
Disabled, *see* Casualties.
Divorced persons, remarriage, 75.

Earnings, peasantry, 173.
Eight-hour day, 205.
Emperor, abdication of, 179, 204, 205.
Enemy aliens, 33; landowners, 162.
Epidemics, 115, 124.
Estates, effect of the war, 169, 182.
Exemptions from military service, 31, 160; factory hands, 71.

Factory committees, 206.
Finland, 9, 163; exemption from military service, 167.
Foreign investment, 166, 209, 212, 214.

Galicia, Russian occupation, 164.
German employees in Russia, 158; landowners, 162; deportation in Baltic provinces, 163.
"German yoke," 161.
Gorky, Maxim, 178.
Government orders to war industries, 210.
Grain levy, 179.
Great Britain, war organization of man power, 184.

Harvest, 174; effect of migration, 37; cereal, 172; potatoes, 172; difficulties, *1917,* 181.
Hospitals, disabled men, 139; prisoners of war, 39; aid by peasants, 178.

Industrial mobilization, 157, 158, 193.

LIST OF THE VOLUMES OF THE RUSSIAN SERIES

RUSSIAN PUBLIC FINANCE DURING THE WAR

Revenue and Expenditure by Alexander M. Michelson.
Introduction by Count V. N. Kokovzov.
Credit Operations by Paul N. Apostol.
Monetary Policy by Michael W. Bernatzky.
1928. 501 *pages.*   *Price $5.00.*

RUSSIA IN THE ECONOMIC WAR by Baron Boris E. Nolde.

1928. 248 *pages.*   *Price $2.50.*

STATE CONTROL OF INDUSTRY IN RUSSIA DURING THE WAR by S. O. Zagorsky.

1928. 371 *pages.*   *Price $4.00.*

THE WAR AND THE RUSSIAN GOVERNMENT

The Central Government by Paul P. Gronsky.
The Municipal Government and the All-Russian Union of Towns by Nicholas J. Astrov.
1929. 347 *pages.*   *Price $3.50.*

RUSSIAN SCHOOLS AND UNIVERSITIES IN THE WORLD WAR

Introduction by Count N. Ignatiev.
Primary and Secondary Schools by Dimitry M. Odinetz.
Universities and Higher Technical Schools by Paul J. Novgorotsev.
1929. 265 *pages.*   *Price $2.75.*

THE COÖPERATIVE MOVEMENT IN RUSSIA DURING THE WAR

Consumers' Coöperation by Eugene M. Kayden.
Credit and Agricultural Coöperation by Alexis N. Antsiferov.
1929. 436 *pages.*   *Price $4.00.*

RUSSIAN AGRICULTURE DURING THE WAR

Rural Economy by Alexis N. Antsiferov, in collaboration with Alexander D. Bilimovich, Michael O. Batshev and Dimitry N. Ivantsov.
The Land Settlement by Alexander D. Bilimovich.
1930. 413 *pages.*   *Price $4.00.*

FOOD SUPPLY IN RUSSIA DURING THE WORLD WAR under the general direction of P. B. Struve.

Organization and Policy by K. I. Zaitsev, and N. V. Dolinsky.
Food Prices and the Market in Foodstuffs by S. S. Demosthenov.
1930. 497 *pages.*   *Price $4.50.*

RUSSIAN LOCAL GOVERNMENT DURING THE WAR AND THE UNION OF ZEMSTVOS by Tikhon J. Polner in collaboration with Prince Vladimir A. Obolensky and Sergius P. Turin. *Introduction* by Prince George E. Lvov.

1930. 335 *pages.*   *Price $3.25.*

THE END OF THE RUSSIAN EMPIRE by Michael T. Florinsky.

1931. 290 *pages.*   *Price $3.00.*

THE RUSSIAN ARMY IN THE WORLD WAR by Nicholas N. Golovine.

1931. 300 *pages.*   *Price $3.25.*

THE COST OF THE WAR TO RUSSIA

The Vital Statistics of European Russia During the World War, 1914–1917 by Stanislas Kohn.
Social Cost of the War by Baron Alexander F. Meyendorff.
1932. 236 *pages.*   *Price $3.25.*

PUBLISHED FOR THE CARNEGIE ENDOWMENT FOR INTERNATIONAL PEACE
DIVISION OF ECONOMICS AND HISTORY
BY YALE UNIVERSITY PRESS · NEW HAVEN · CONNECTICUT